Leslie, David W.

Wise moves in

hard times

DATE DUE

SEP 8 '9			
OCT 14 '9			
SEP 27 '99			

Wise Moves in Hard Times

David W. Leslie

E. K. Fretwell Jr.

Wise Moves in Hard Times

Creating and Managing Resilient Colleges and Universities

Jossey-Bass Publishers • San Francisco

Library of Congress Cataloging-in-Publication Data

Leslie, David W.
    Wise moves in hard times : creating and managing resilient colleges and universities / David W. Leslie, E. K. Fretwell Jr.— 1st ed.
        p.   cm.—(The Jossey-Bass higher and adult education series.)
    ISBN 0-7879-0196-2
    1. Education, Higher—United States—Administration. 2. Education, Higher—United States—Aims and objectives. 3. Stress management—United States. 4. Educational change— United States. I. Fretwell, E. K. date. II. Title. III. Series.
LB2341.L43   1996
378.1'00973—dc20   95-40653

FIRST EDITION
HB Printing   10 9 8 7 6 5 4 3 2 1

The Jossey-Bass

Higher and Adult Education Series

Contents

Preface

Higher education is "under attack." Higher education is in a "state of emergency." Higher education is facing a "crisis." Readers of this book probably recognize these words from the steady assault of media stories—and might well feel that such terms sum up, harshly but realistically, the daily experience of presidents, board members, faculty leaders, and others who care about the health and well-being of colleges and universities.

We undertook this study to find out how colleges and universities have been affected by hard times, how academic professionals have risen to the challenges they have faced, and what these professionals' responses mean to the public and its support for beleaguered institutions of higher education.

We found enormous pride and great resilience among those who were laboring mightily to sustain institutions they care about deeply. Our book is about the lessons these people have learned from hard times, and it is about the wisdom they shared with us about how to improve, how to become stronger, how to make tough decisions, and—above all else—about how to do what society needs colleges and universities to do: to contribute to the economic, political, and cultural life of a great democracy and to give undergraduate students an opportunity to learn, grow, and develop.

Among the lessons learned by the many people who shared their experiences with us are the following:

- The roots of fiscal stress are deep and complex.
- At each institution we looked at, many factors interacted in

unique ways to create stress; money was only one of those factors.

- Pressure for change affects *all* aspects of the institution: its mission, its organization, and its programs.

- Institutions can analyze themselves, make hard decisions, change in enlightened and valid ways, and build qualities of resilience into themselves.

- It is important, perhaps above all else, to regain the public's trust—and to complete unfinished business on the agenda of change.

- There is work to be done on many fronts, because the pace of change is faster than ever before and institutions must learn to adapt continuously.

The Message

With all due modesty, we think this book should be read carefully— by trustees, presidents, vice presidents, deans, department leaders, faculty, and leaders in the broader community—for ideas about how higher education can better serve the public on whom it depends for support. Faculty should also read the book, because they have the highest stake in the long-term health of their colleges and universities. They will have to lead from the inside as colleges and universities find more efficient ways to operate and more effective ways to educate undergraduates. Higher education has enjoyed the public trust for centuries; it is now challenged to earn that trust anew in ways it has not faced before.

At the conclusion of our study, we have come to believe that the present crisis has both deeper and broader implications for the future than the repeated periods of stress facing colleges and universities since about 1970. It is a common refrain among those with whom we have consulted to suggest that things are not going to be the same this time, or ever again.

Our data suggest strongly that the present crisis is not merely one of resources, although it is certainly that. Perhaps more important, it is also a crisis of confidence and a crisis of values. It has become crystal clear that the public values higher education and wants it to be universally available—but the public also wants higher education to be responsive and responsible to the real needs of real people. It has also become apparent that the value systems of many colleges and universities have become too narrowly focused on faculty interests in research or in intellectual trends that the public does not understand.

So this book became something more than we originally intended. We imagined that we might be able to find some common steps that would restore fiscal stability and help to frame strategies that institutions could use to assure their long-term health. In fact, we do have some ideas about these issues and have reported them in as much detail as we are able.

But we also want readers to understand in the clearest possible terms that the enterprise of higher education as a whole needs an awakening to its role in serving society. Funding is going to become even more difficult in the future for many institutions. Public policy will place more pressure on colleges and universities to meet the demands of the marketplace. The institutions that thrive are going to be the ones that *respond* in focused ways—to the demand for efficient and effective undergraduate education, to the demand for graduates who are prepared to work and produce, to society's social and economic problems with practical and realistic solutions, to the need to educate good citizens who will understand and take responsibility for the civic community.

No amount of money guarantees that a college or university will act as a leading corporate citizen in a turbulent and confused society. But no institution of higher education that fails to be a leader in helping society through its most troubled eras will deserve or get that society's support.

Overview of the Book

We have divided the book into two parts. Part One, "Hard Times," describes the study itself in detail (in Chapter One) and reports on our principal findings. In Chapter Two, we look first at the sources of fiscal stress—particularly at how the broader trends in public policy and support have contributed to the current sense of crisis. We also raise our concern that it is difficult to track the many converging trends that we saw and to associate these trends directly with causes of stress in individual institutions; often it is something that can be understood only after the fact. In many colleges and universities this has meant that readiness to act comes too late. For some of our site institutions, internal divisions and defensiveness blocked proactive responses to the gathering crisis, and the problems simply multiplied until the pressure could no longer be resisted.

In Chapter Three, we look at the many simultaneously developing problems that led our site institutions into a state of stress. These "strands" acted jointly to some extent and independently to some extent. But we observed that it mattered a great deal whether an institution's leaders recognized the strands as part of an overriding pattern or simply treated them separately as individual symptoms of different problems. Fiscal stress opened many of those we interviewed to questions about their work, their institutions, and the larger purpose for which they were "in business." While it galvanized them into real searches for solutions, it also led to fatigue and low morale.

Part Two, "Searching for Solutions," reports on those searches. We concentrated on three major ways in which institutions are changing themselves as they adapt to stress. Chapter Four explores the changes in mission and organization. At most institutions, there was broad recognition that missions had become too loose, that too many different programs were being offered, and that scarce resources were being spread too thin across too many activities. But it was also proving difficult—sometimes in the face of faculty opposition, and sometimes in the face of opposition from external constituencies—to reach a working consensus about a firmer and more focused sense of mission. This is an important first step in dealing with stress, though, and both resistance to change and the risks associated with change have to be confronted openly.

These two tasks are proving difficult for the decision-making process that is rooted in academic culture. In Chapter Five we look at how this process tends to screen out some options and to favor others—independent of whether they may be valid solutions and whether the status quo is really sustainable. For the most part, we found that the power to decide was widely dispersed, and that this dispersion actually narrowed the range of choices on which agreement could be reached. Conflict among interest groups—rather than rational planning—seemed to drive decisions in many cases.

Presidents especially felt exasperated by the inability of constituencies to make hard choices and to commit to real change. At the same time, crises pushed the presidents to take responsibility and decide. We concluded that neither centralization nor decentralization of decision making was working well, but we found a promising pattern at some institutions that we labeled *simultaneous tracking*. This pattern involved working on the separate dimensions of fiscal crisis simultaneously—but within the framework of an agreed-upon general strategy. This approach avoided the excesses of top-down control, which does not readily gain the cooperation of faculty, and the anarchic indecisiveness of radical democratization, which seldom results in worthwhile change.

Chapter Six draws on particular cases in which major changes in teaching and learning have transformed several of our case-study institutions. We were impressed by the degree to which undergraduate instruction is at the core of higher education's responsibility to society and that fiscal health at the vast majority of colleges and universities depends directly on whether the public thinks it is getting good value for its tuition (and tax) dollars. New ideas about undergraduate education at our site institutions concentrated on what kind of value to add and on how to do it in an effective and accountable way. We believe that the most competitive institutions in the future will be the ones that develop just such programs. But there are substantial challenges, especially in changing the way faculty are prepared to teach and in how they are rewarded.

In Part Three, "Wise Moves," we change our focus to report on the practices that we believe are helping our site institutions to take control of their futures and become more resilient. Chapter Seven explores how institutions can analyze their current situations. Since we found that stress resulted from different sources and was manifested in different ways among the institutions, we concluded that no one set of benchmarks would be useful to all of them. Instead, we focus on an array of signposts that would help institutions recognize trends and spot areas of concern. We look at how to analyze

- Markets
- The competition
- Trends in public policy
- Financial patterns
- Management patterns
- The educational vitality of programs
- The interaction of all of these factors

Generating good information is the essential first step in starting to change.

Triage was a major issue at most of our institutions. It was managed successfully in some cases and not so successfully in others. When an institution is overextended—much as a lifeboat or a medical staff gets overburdened—hard decisions about how to use scarce resources have to be made. In Chapter Eight we adopt the medical community's definition of triage and use it to illustrate how to monitor the situation, how to establish priorities in using scarce resources, how to make tough decisions, and how to deal with the human dimensions of trauma and change. Using the triage idea, we conclude that institutions facing stress should engage in continuous adaptation, rather than one-shot strategizing.

Since not all institutions faced problems of equal intensity or with identical causes, we think that they will have to pick their way through the many alternatives for change in an intelligent way. In Chapter Nine we explain how we concluded that enlightened change involves a balance between strategic planning and continuous learning from experiments. We learned that there is great risk in adopting mindless, across-the-board budget cuts. We also found risks in adopting the "command and control" approach that is implied by the strategic-planning metaphor, but we saw an equal degree of risk in rampant incrementalism—or in uncontrolled opportunism. We suggest adopting a mix of strategy and opportunism to adapt successfully.

What are the qualities of colleges and universities that have stronger prospects for the future? In Chapter Ten we group these qualities under the general concept of "resilience." The resilient institution, we believe, has a clear sense of its mission, its educational philosophy, and its commitment to add value to students and society. Resilient institutions need not be wealthy as measured in traditional economic terms, but they succeed because their faculty, staff, students, and friends are committed to them. Resilience for most institutions derives principally from a commitment to quality in undergraduate education. People will pay for quality, and institutions that provide it will do well in both good times and bad. But "quality" means big changes in the way many institutions now conduct their undergraduate programs.

The public now expects service, quality, and accountability from its institutions of higher education, and it will not defer to tradition and expertise as it might once have been willing to do. The public also has learned to drive a hard bargain for what it wants. Thus, we think the current hard times are in substantial part a result of "market discipline"—a painful application of public demands for results. No longer is higher education isolated and protected from public scrutiny; to the contrary, it is besieged with demands for accountability. So to regain the public trust and to restore the health of colleges and universities that are now encountering serious stress, there is great pressure to redefine "quality" in terms of student learning.

Responsibility for change has to be more widely shared than it now is on many campuses. Faculty, for example, have effective control of curricula and of their own incentives through peer review; they will have to become much more committed to quality teaching at the undergraduate level if their own futures are to be secure. But commitment is also needed from outside the academic community. Business leaders, community leaders, and policy makers can all play a substantial role by participating in positive change.

No amount of superficial change, though, will be adequate if colleges and universities do not recommit to their moral base—namely, to teach well and to help students learn well.

We conclude the book with Chapter Eleven, which provides an overview of what we call "unfinished business." Our site institutions were at different stages in their search for appropriate missions, for an appropriate balance of action and consultation in decision making, for broader and deeper public support, and for more-coherent and more-effective ways to deliver undergraduate education. Because much of these institutions' work is indeed unfinished, we feel strongly that restoring the health of higher education has only begun. The condition of the economy, the changing expectations and characteristics of our students, the dramatic shifts in federal and state support for higher education, and the internal resistance to change all show signs of intensifying. The process of change will require more persistence, wisdom, and effort than we originally anticipated; it must also continue indefinitely into the future as the environment becomes more—not less—challenging and unpredictable.

This book is our effort to help leaders of colleges and universities (and their friends in business, government, the professions, and the community) to understand what institutions of higher education are facing and how they are coping. If we can stimulate productive discussions among those who are in a position to help, we will have accomplished our goal.

Acknowledgments

We are grateful to many people who have helped—some by working closely with us at one stage or another, others by their thoughtful analyses and observations on which we have relied for perspective. We take full responsibility for the content of this book, but we wish to recognize others for their support, counsel, and wisdom.

The project was supported by Teachers Insurance and Annuity Association/College Retirement Equities Fund (TIAA/CREF), and we undertook it at the suggestion of Peggy Heim, senior research officer at TIAA/CREF, who retired during the course of the project. We acknowledge the continued support and interest of Francis King, her successor.

We consulted widely during the early stages of the project, especially during our effort to identify the site institutions to which we would make visits. Our consultants were promised anonymity and were absolved of any responsibility for the choices we made, but we wish to thank them for their interest, support, and helpful suggestions.

We are deeply grateful to the busy presidents of all our site institutions; they took large amounts of time to talk with us and to help arrange our visits, and their candor and insights were little short of profound. So often, college and university presidents are the targets of anger, of conflict, of "free" advice—and of the books that are written about higher education. The presidents themselves are perhaps not often enough asked about their own views, and here we wish to acknowledge how important their views were to the completion of this project.

So, too, we thank those helpful staff to whom we delegated responsibility for collecting documentation and reports—as well as coordinating our sometimes complex interview schedules. Our site visits were uniformly fruitful, informative, and well organized. Many hands made this possible.

Closer to home, we wish to make special mention of the close reading of the manuscript by Ana Bernardini, a graduate student at Florida State University, and of several early chapter drafts by Dale Lick, a faculty member at Florida State. Their helpful and incisive comments challenged us to think more deeply about a number of key points. Other graduate students at Florida State have assisted logistically and in other ways. Mary Jo Ott, of Florida State, and Elaine Deese, of the University of North Carolina at Charlotte, have provided us with administrative support and assistance through months of extensive travel, with elaborate arrangements for communication back and forth, and with help in navigating our respective university bureaucracies.

Finally, our thanks to our spouses, Jan Leslie and Dorrie Fretwell, who let us work on this book together. Our collaboration matured into something more than a mere coauthorship—it became a floating seminar about higher education in the broadest sense, and it engaged our joint interests in a wide array of topics. We shared our homes with one another, and our spouses patiently listened to our debates and discussions in each other's kitchens, and indulged our need for unfettered time to put the manuscript together.

In the end, this book belongs to those who talked so freely with us about their institutions and their experiences, and who obviously care so deeply about the future of their institutions. We reported what we learned from them; we have organized what they told us and have tried to give it meaning. Our hope is that both the message and the interpretations will help a besieged academic community focus on solutions.

Tallahassee, Florida   David W. Leslie
Charlotte, North Carolina   E. K. Fretwell Jr.
December 1995

The Authors

David W. Leslie is professor of higher education at Florida State University. He holds a B.A. degree (1964) in psychology from Drew University, an M.Ed. degree (1965) in school psychology from Boston University, and an Ed.D. degree (1971) in higher education from Pennsylvania State University. He has served on the faculties of the University of Virginia and the University of Illinois (where he also served as executive assistant to the president), and he was department head in educational administration at both Illinois State and Florida State Universities. He has served as president of the Association for the Study of Higher Education, as an associate editor of *The Review of Higher Education*, and as a resident scholar with the Florida Department of Education. His most recent book was *The Invisible Faculty: Improving the Status of Part-Timers in Higher Education*, coauthored with Judith Gappa and published by Jossey-Bass.

E. K. Fretwell Jr. is chancellor emeritus of the University of North Carolina at Charlotte. He holds a B.A. degree (1944) in English from Wesleyan University, an M.A.T. degree (1948) in English from Harvard University, and a Ph.D. degree (1953) in higher education administration from Columbia University. He was an associate professor at Teachers College, Columbia University, and served on the summer faculty of the University of California at Berkeley. In addition to the Chancellorship at the University of North Carolina at Charlotte (1979–89), he served as president of the State University of New York College at Buffalo (1967–78), and as interim president of the University of Massachusetts system

(1991–92). He served on the Carnegie Council on Policy Studies in Higher Education and as elected head of the Carnegie Foundation for the Advancement of Teaching, the American Association of State Colleges and Universities, and the American Council on Education. He has also chaired the Council on Postsecondary Accreditation and the Middle States Association of Colleges and Schools. Dr. Fretwell's most recent publication is *Interim Presidents: Guidelines for University and College Governing Boards*, published by the Association of Governing Boards.

Part One

_____

Hard Times

Chapter One

Common Lessons
from Hard Times

"How do we get out of the mess we are in?" has been the working title for this book. "The mess" originally referred to the stressed financial conditions that most colleges and universities were experiencing between 1989 and 1995. The phrase has taken on new meaning as we have tried to understand what got us into the present period of adversity, how colleges and universities are responding to it, and what the prospects are for recovery. "The mess," more than we anticipated, now appears to be a complex array of *internal* and *external* conditions that demand a clear and immediate plan of attack.

This book is about how higher education got into the current state of widespread fiscal stress, but it is also about what we learned from thirteen diverse institutions about changing and getting out of "the mess." We will cover three main themes:

- The sources and impact of fiscal stress on colleges and universities
- Their search for solutions to fiscal challenges
- Understanding how to respond with resilience and reestablish the long-term robustness of higher education

Although we began our study by analyzing the fiscal condition of our case-study institutions, we soon realized that what appeared to be "fiscal" on the surface really was but a symptom of several problems that interacted with one another to produce stress:

- The impact of new demands by the public on higher education
- Rapidly shifting policies at federal and state levels
- Demographic and market changes
- How clear the missions of colleges and universities are and how they go about marketing themselves
- How colleges and universities are organized and make decisions
- How colleges and universities meet the needs of their students (and other constituencies) with effective programs of teaching, research, and service
- How colleges and universities work in conditions of stress

In this chapter we explain why we undertook our study and how we conducted it. We also examine the context in which the current period of stress arose, explain why both external and internal conditions are at the root of the most significant problems, review previous research on the relationship between fiscal health and quality, and briefly summarize the solutions we are recommending.

Our Study

We undertook this study because by 1993 it had become clear that a deep economic recession and fundamental changes in state and federal support were having a serious impact on higher education. Fears were broadly expressed that the two historic commitments of American colleges and universities—to provide universal access to postsecondary education and to maintain world-class leadership in the advancement of knowledge—might not be sustainable.

We wanted to know if these fears were valid. After all, we recognized that higher education had been through a "new depression" (Cheit, 1971), energy crises, and assorted other economic reversals over the past twenty or more years. Was this just the latest in a long string of problems to which creative and imaginative leaders would adapt—more or less successfully—as they had before? Or was it something deeper, and perhaps more permanent in its impact? If deeper change was beginning, what kinds of institutions would emerge as the more resilient and robust? What were those institutions doing to make their own futures more secure? How would these changes affect the kind of education the institutions offered? And what would these changes mean to students and to the public?

We felt that broad statistical summaries—the macroeconomics—of fiscal stress told only a small part of the story. So we set out purposefully to study how thirteen diverse colleges and universities in all regions of the country were changing themselves in response to "hard times." Although we felt that financial condition was the starting point, we selected institutions that had demonstrated their resilience by making real efforts to change, facing up to their fiscal challenges with creative and promising solutions. Our case-study institutions (to which we refer throughout the book as *site institutions*) were selected because they had begun to think and act their way through—but not in all cases out of—fiscal stress.

We selected our site institutions following wide consultation with panels of leaders in the study of higher education, as well as with numerous experienced observers of the national scene. We sought institutions that had faced real fiscal problems and had undertaken serious efforts to change consciously in at least some of the following ways:

- Reviewing and reforming a mission statement
- Developing a strategic plan
- Evaluating and redirecting programs
- Developing new programs
- Involving faculty in solving the problems
- Restructuring finances

- Seeking new sources of funds
- Exercising symbolic leadership to orient people toward change
- Redefining markets and constituencies and adopting new communication strategies
- Downsizing or "right-sizing" in keeping with new goals
- Making more effective use of technology for off-site learning, "telecourses," and other alternative methods of education
- Improving the quality and diversity of new students

We obviously could have selected from hundreds of other colleges and universities, but the thirteen we chose formed a diverse and—we think—very representative sample.

Altogether, twelve presidents from thirteen institutions agreed to participate. (Mayville State and Valley City State universities in North Dakota share a president and several administrative officers.) Only two institutions declined to participate, largely because their chief executive officers felt that they could not afford the time and effort involved in providing us with data and arranging interviews.

California was not represented by the institutions in our study. Although we made our sampling decisions before its release, the California Higher Education Policy Center's report *A State of Emergency? Higher Education in California* (Breneman, 1995) documented the severe impact of economic and policy problems affecting colleges and universities in the state. The report recommended that the governor declare a state of emergency "of indefinite duration" for California's higher education (p. 10). It argued that the economic condition of the state and the responses of the legislature, governor, and leaders of the educational system were such that "California is not going to be able to meet its obligations to the next generation of students through state support" (p. 5). The problems detailed in the report were so deep and so firmly rooted in a political economy that had gone terribly sour for higher education—and appeared to be as yet unaddressed in a systematic way—that California was, in our opinion, an unrepresentative outlier in the broader population of American higher education.

The site institutions ranged in size and complexity from Pennsylvania State, a major Research I university with more than 37,000 students, to Tusculum College, a small, independent liberal arts college with fewer than 500 resident undergraduate students at the time of our visit. The institutions included a major urban community college district (Maricopa County in Phoenix) and rural comprehensive institutions (Mayville and Valley City State universities in North Dakota). And they spanned the continent, from the University of Massachusetts at Boston to Southern Oregon State College. One of our institutions was a historically black college (University of Maryland—Eastern Shore), another had identified fifty ethnic groups among its students (Bloomfield College), and yet another enrolled a primarily Hispanic student body (University of Texas at El Paso). Two universities (Syracuse and Trenton State) had undertaken imaginative, student-centered reforms, while one (Virginia Commonwealth) had undertaken a major strategic restructuring effort. (See Table 1.1 for a list of site institutions and their characteristics.)

In the letter we sent to potential site institutions seeking their cooperation, we identified the data we would need and the people we wanted to interview:

- Institution's history, especially in the last five years
- Current (1993–94) catalog and 1988–89 catalog
- President's annual report for each year since fiscal year (FY) 1987
- Executive summary of most recent regional (and/or professional) accreditation reports
- Strategic plan(s) completed with the last five years
- Audited annual financial reports from each year since FY 1987

Table 1.1.   Characteristics of Site Institutions.

Institution	Location	Carnegie Classification	Enrollment	Control
Bloomfield College	Bloomfield, NJ	Baccalaureate II	2,036	Presbyterian Church, USA
Mayville State University	Mayville, ND	Baccalaureate II	716	State
Valley City State University	Valley City, ND	Baccalaureate II	1,052	State
Maricopa County Community College District	Phoenix, AZ	Associate	94,643	State/local
Pennsylvania State University	University Park, PA	Research I	37,658	State related
Southern Oregon State College	Ashland, OR	Master's I	4,515	State
Syracuse University	Syracuse, NY	Research II	19,354	Independent
Trenton State College	Trenton, NJ	Master's I	5,167	State
Tusculum College	Greeneville, TN	Master's II	1,144	Presbyterian Church, USA
University of Massachusetts at Boston	Boston, MA	Master's I	13,316	State
University of Maryland—Eastern Shore	Princess Anne, MD	Master's II	2,637	State
University of Texas at El Paso	El Paso, TX	Master's II	16,999	State
Virginia Commonwealth University	Richmond, VA	Research I	21,854	State

Source: Higher Education Directory, 1995.

- Budget proposals, including management analyses of capital, operating, and program needs for each year from FY 1988 to FY 1994
- Reports by external consultants or internal committees that are strategically important in reshaping programs and finances
- State master plans, budget requests, legislative reports, or documents outlining special initiatives that would help establish a context for what is happening on campus (public institutions only)

Prior to our campus visits, we reviewed documents about the financial status, programs, and strategic plans for each institution. During our site visits between December 1993 and January 1995, we conducted searching and extensive interviews with as many people as we could accommodate in our schedule. Our goal was to get as complete a picture as possible of how these institutions were changing and of what these changes would mean to their futures, both individually and collectively.

We conducted three site visits together to ensure that our separate but simultaneously recorded field notes corresponded on main points as well as detail. Assured that we both were following the same protocol and that our observations were trustworthy, we then divided responsibility and conducted solo visits to the remaining ten institutions. We recorded our notes contemporaneously with the interviews, both during and after the site visits.

Our interviews were loosely structured around three questions about each institution:

- What was the basic state of the institution's fiscal health during 1989 through 1993?
- What did you do to change the situation?
- What have you learned from your efforts?

Within this broad outline, we tailored our interviews to the specific data we had gathered about each institution. We requested one-hour interviews to be scheduled in advance with the following people:

President (of whom an exit interview was also requested)

Board chair and/or other leaders

Chief academic officer

Chief financial officer and/or chief budget officer

Director of planning

Chair and leading members of the strategic planning committee

Community leaders

Deans of major academic units

Selected department chairs

Faculty governance leaders (includes faculty senate officers, executive committee members, and union representatives, if applicable)

Student government leaders

We knew in advance about the major reductions in state appropriations at the University of Massachusetts, and about some of the actions the Boston campus had taken in response. We knew that Tusculum had adopted a particularly innovative focus for its curriculum, and that Syracuse was reorienting itself to being a student-centered research university. We also knew about particularly interesting efforts to restructure Virginia Commonwealth and about strategic planning exercises at several other institutions.

We aggregated our interview data in two ways. First we developed composite summaries of each institution's current condition. Then we compared the summaries to identify common experiences, to contrast the differences among institutions, and to converge on the generalizations that underlie this report. By developing a composite picture of sorts, we felt we could identify issues and trends that affected them all. But we also wanted to recognize ways in which they differed.

Since each institution was in a relatively fluid state of change at the time of our visits, we found it desirable to update our observations with a follow-up interview. In early summer 1995 we conducted telephone interviews with the CEOs or their designees to confirm the current situation on each campus.

The interviews confirmed that the reforms we have described are continuing. Most institutions are concentrating on making undergraduate education more effective. They are increasingly specifying outcomes and devising measures with which to assess their performance. In several cases, internal savings have been allocated to new graduate programs. The public institutions in particular have recognized the need to regain public support and they are working assertively to do so. Increased campus autonomy (from state system control) has helped colleges in states such as Oregon and New Jersey. Institutions in Virginia and Texas have benefited from incentives to initiate change. All appear to be seeking funding for specific projects as well as for general institutional support, and several have experienced further changes—some favorable, some not—in the external environment.

While we have made every effort to present a fair and complete picture of what we learned, we offer the following qualifications:

- The institutions themselves were at *varying stages in adapting to their problems*. While some had made dramatic progress, others were still facing major unresolved issues.
- We found great variability in each institution's *internal readiness for change*. In a few cases, we saw evidence of a real communal effort to seek and implement changes; in others, it was clear that the several constituencies had yet to come to agreement on at least some of the major issues.

- A degree of *random chance* played a role in events at all the institutions. Factors such as an election result, the unexpected inheritance of an estate, or a board member's change of heart all added a small element of serendipity to the course of events. Some institutions were lucky while others were not, and there was little they could do about some of these unanticipated events.

While we looked for commonalities in the experience of this purposely diverse set of institutions, we nevertheless came away with the strong feeling that good solutions are local solutions. Each institution could offer some good lessons to many others facing similar problems, but the experience of each was also unique. We have tried to take the common lessons from them, but we also can assure our readers that they will have to rely on their own experience and wisdom to adapt and change in their own institutions.

Things Will Not Be the Same

Shortly after we began our study, we came to understand that higher education was being reshaped in fundamental ways by the fiscal crisis of the early 1990s—that it would never be the same again. Two basic trends tell the story. On one hand, there has been an unprecedented flattening out—in some cases even an absolute decline—in state appropriations for higher education in many states over the last few years. This alone suggests a system facing serious decline. On the other hand—with regional and sector variations—recent projections of higher education enrollment all show increases, not decreases ("Fact File," 1994).

These trends put institutions in many states in the position of educating more students with substantially less money. Their leaders have to make major strategic choices about their institutions' missions, about the breadth and quality of their programs, about the maintenance and improvement of their infrastructures, about their ability to provide effective access to minorities and the handicapped, about their commitment to an overwhelmingly tenured (and increasingly expensive) faculty and traditional ways of doing business, and about how they can manage change in a time of decreasing resources.

In short, after two decades of what turned out to be *marginal change*, we face the possibility of real *structural change* in the economic foundations of higher education. Most of those we interviewed shared this alarming perception, but we also came to understand that legislators and the public have very high expectations of colleges and universities. They want results—real learning, efficient operations, commitment to economic development, and public accountability—and they want it immediately.

So while we will attempt to explain the impact of fiscal stress on colleges and universities and to outline ways in which we think they can change to meet these new demands, we will also conclude with an urgent message: higher education can expect public support—and therefore a return to better fiscal condition—only if it produces results and earns the public trust.

A Brief History of Financial Stress

American colleges and universities have always faced fiscal problems. In his history of American higher education, Frederick Rudolph pointed out that Harvard and other colonial colleges could not have survived without the appropriation of public funds for their operations. In the nineteenth century, colleges survived only by accepting donations, by receiving state support, by pursuing endowments from the new class of wealthy industrialists, by providing students with discounted or free tuition, and by "underpayment and exploitation" of their faculty (Rudolph, 1962, pp. 177–200). A great many failed—more than seven hundred before 1860 (p. 219).

More recently, Earl Cheit's *The New Depression in Higher*

Education (1971) marked the beginning of a period of stress that began in the late 1960s and was based largely on what were then perceived as revenue shortfalls. Almost a decade later, *The Three "R's" of the Eighties: Reduction, Reallocation, and Retrenchment,* by Kenneth Mortimer and Michael Tierney (1979), pointed out that "colleges have been adjusting to the cost-income squeeze since the early 1970s" (p. 53). Carol Frances's *Successful Responses to Financial Difficulty* (1982) began with a chapter on "responses to fiscal stress" during a time when economic growth began to outstrip income. Oil embargoes, inflation, shifting enrollment patterns, the tenuring-in of faculty, and a variety of other so-called crises have produced an extended period of financial stress for higher education dating back more than two decades.

The current period of stress has different causes and probably will have more lasting effects than these earlier "crises."

The Relationship Between Fiscal Health and Quality

Bowen's (1980) seminal work and that of both earlier and more recent students of higher education finance (such as Brinkman, 1992, and Cheit, 1971) have all concluded that *variability* is the rule. It is extremely difficult to generalize about costs, and it is extremely difficult to generalize about fiscal health. Waggaman (1991, p. 2) notes that, "although financial problems may appear similar among many institutions, the solutions are often shaped by local history and culture." (We are reminded of the Carnegie Council's 1980 report, *Three Thousand Futures,* which concluded that American institutions of higher education are marked by their distinctiveness and individualism.)

In fact, accounting methods currently in common use have made it extremely difficult to develop objective comparisons of fiscal health. Recent looks at "wealth" (Bradburd and Mann, 1993) and accounting theory (Winston, 1992) have yielded startlingly revised means of assessing institutional financial condition. Bradburd and Mann (1993, p. 476) suggest, for example, that wealth should be calculated on the basis of all "resources that allow an institution to set its level of tuition and fees below the operating cost of educating a student." They propose that calculating wealth on the basis of all income flows provides a more realistic examination of financial status because so few institutions have endowments of any real consequence. "Fewer than 13 percent of all institutions have an endowment capable of sustainably financing 5 percent or more of their annual E&G expenditures. Thus, the vast majority of institutions are very dependent upon public appropriations, gifts and grants, and tuition and fees" (pp. 477–478). This method shows considerably greater variability in "total wealth" for both public and private sectors than traditional methods. Dividing the universe of all institutions into "deciles," their method shows that the "wealthiest 10 percent . . . have a level of wealth per student that is more than 12 times greater than that of the poorest 10 percent of schools! (. . . $167,937 per student versus $13,440 per student)" (p. 481).

Using this method, the strengths and vulnerabilities of both sectors become much clearer. The public sector, for example, is highly dependent upon the flow of appropriated funds, while the private sector is similarly dependent on endowment income and tuition. The public institutions depend directly on healthy state economies and the goodwill of politicians; the private institutions depend directly on the flow of students and on income from gifts, grants, and endowments. Economic, demographic, and policy conditions that affect any of these variables have direct and substantial impact on the health or vulnerability of institutions.

Although the extreme variability in wealth among institutions means that it is very difficult to generalize about solutions to any single institution's fiscal distress, research has indicated that certain practices are fundamental to fiscal viability. Beginning in the early 1970s, a number of important studies focused on institutions in fiscal distress. Cheit's study (1971) was among the earliest and most disciplined, but others have followed and have largely been consistent in recommending that each institution develop a sense of its own mission and position in the market *before* making irreversible fiscal decisions. In other words, they largely confirm that *costs follow income, income follows strategy,* and *strategy follows mission.* Conversely, short-term economizing is not the key to fiscal health, but it could well damage the institution's ability to achieve its mission. The major lesson of this line of research is that no amount of micromanagement on the cost side will save institutions that cannot develop a consensus about their mission, strategy, core values, and educational philosophy. (See Gilmore and To, 1992, p. 44, for evidence that micromanagement may in fact increase costs in some situations.)

Most of the studies that have looked directly at cases of institutional adaptation to fiscal stress agree with the proposition stated by Chaffee, that "effective turn-around strategy needs to be unique to an institution" (1984, p. 233). Finkelstein, Farrar, and Pfnister (1984) also found that change was "unique" and "organization specific."

The research we have reviewed rather clearly suggests that being distinctive in a market in which there is diversity among institutions is healthy. Conversely, when institutions become more and more alike, when the market provides "buyers" with little to choose from, failure of the weaker among the "conforming" institutions is more likely.

There is considerable evidence that institutions that have tried to become *less* distinctive and *more* conforming while nevertheless broadening the base of their enrollment have courted decline. The most recent study, that of Gilmore and To (1992), found that "underproductive" institutions (as measured by student retention and graduation rates) "were trying to do too much without adequate resources. . . . Admitting less well prepared students, maintaining a diverse clientele, and emphasizing both teaching and research may be more than they can afford" (pp. 45–46).

Earlier, Anderson had examined strategies undertaken by private colleges facing stress during the decade between 1965 and 1975. He found them scrambling to recruit from a broader range of students, giving more financial aid, and starting up new programs. He concluded that they risked their long-term futures in the process because they were entering a different marketplace, one principally occupied by low-tuition public institutions with whom they could not expect to compete well. Chaffee's (1984) findings were similar: institutions that tried to expand their markets and increase the flow of resources *only* through program changes and more aggressive recruiting failed to thrive as well as other institutions that tried to reaffirm their core values and internal consensus on matters of mission and philosophy.

Perhaps the most foresighted and perceptive analysis of institutional adaptation was offered by David Riesman in his "Commentary and Epilogue" to a 1973 Carnegie report entitled *Academic Transformation: Seventeen Institutions Under Pressure* (Riesman and Stadtman, 1973). He essentially warned against overextending the institution's resources in order to be all things to all people at the expense of providing a sensitive and meaningful educational environment for students (p. 445). Although this advice is now twenty years old, it resonates well in the current environment of uncertainty and temptation. It is also very clearly a theme that ran throughout our site visits: being distinctive and purposeful is better than being all things to all people.

All of these studies converge on one key point: institutions experiencing fiscal stress are really facing the interaction of several forces. Market factors, evolution of ideas about how to educate, and financial trends all impinge on how an institution develops its identity and defines its particular competence. The stresses on our site institutions were more than just fiscal, and institutions that define their crises as purely financial deny themselves the opportunity to strengthen and sharpen their internal sense of cohesion and common purpose by facing up to the many threats and insecurities that challenge them. That sense is the most important resource—beyond the merely financial—that an institution can use to pull itself out of stress and decline (compare Chaffee, 1984; Finkelstein and Pfnister, 1984.)

In the case of community colleges, these findings should probably be applied with caution. Although these institutions do admit students from across the whole spectrum of academic preparedness and although they do emphasize diversity of clientele and programs, they perform a distinctive educational and social mission by serving the community of which they are a part. As far as we can tell, community colleges also provide an especially supportive and student-centered learning environment, which distinguishes them (dramatically in some cases) from other higher education sectors.

External Dimensions of Current Fiscal Stress

The Chronicle of Higher Education recently reported that the first-ever two-year decline in state funding for postsecondary education in the United States was recorded in 1992–93 (Jaschik, 1992). Although the general decline was on the order of 1 percent in current dollars, some of the specific drops approached dramatic—if not catastrophic—levels. The state of Virginia, for example, appropriated 13 percent less for higher education over the two-year period, and the University of Massachusetts lost 22 percent of its state appropriation.

The overall national decline amounted to 7 percent in constant (inflation-adjusted) dollars. By this measure, 36 states provided less funding for higher education over the two-year period. Among them were the megastates of California (–18 percent), Florida (–15 percent), Illinois (–8 percent), New York (–11 percent), and Pennsylvania (–7 percent). Other major states experiencing declines included Connecticut (–13 percent), Maryland (–10 percent), Massachusetts (–16 percent), Minnesota (–10 percent), Ohio (–13 percent), and Virginia (–18 percent).

The resulting problems have been analyzed from many different points of view. For the most part, these analyses have concluded that causes and consequences are related in complex ways. Predicting how many students will enroll and where they will go has long been a problem (Bowen and Sosa, 1989). The impact of increasing tuition and declining financial aid on access and choice has been interpreted from varying angles; some suggest that the growing gap foreshadows enrollment declines, yet previous predictions of declines have yet to be realized (Evangelauf, 1992). Defining and accounting for the productivity of colleges and universities depends on measures of faculty work and student learning that are still only crudely tied directly to outcomes (Johnstone, 1993). Predicting faculty retirement and turnover rates is an uncertain process (Lozier and Dooris, 1991). Forecasting state appropriations is unreliable as formula funding becomes more politicized (McKeown and Layzell, 1992). Certainly, conditions vary from state to state (for instance, the extraordinary fiscal crisis in California in 1992) and from sector to sector. *The Chronicle of Higher Education* notes as one example that community colleges have recently received an increasing share of higher education appropriations (Jaschik, 1992, p. A26). Indeed, as Bowen (1980) reminded us, in a pluralistic system conditions vary from institution to institution, and care should be taken not to overgeneralize.

The New Realities in State Funding

State budgets are, of course, showing symptoms of three kinds of severe stress. The first is residual downloading of financial obligations from the Reagan years. A decade and a half ago the federal government began to withdraw from aiding cities, the poor, and education, and from fiscal burdens it had once undertaken in the name of social responsibility. The overall strategy was to return funding burdens for health, safety, and welfare programs to the states and cities. The strategy worked, but the patient—state government—is now in worse condition than before the treatment, squeezed as it is between rising demands for services and increasingly strained fiscal resources. The November 1994 elections resulted in a Republican majority whose control of Congress has resulted in an intensifying trend to "devolve" federal responsibilities to the states. This devolution in its most radical form may eventually raise serious questions about the responsibility of federal and state governments for funding colleges and universities.

This inexorable trend to push responsibilities downward to the states has resulted in what we call "crowding out." Increasingly, state budgets are being overtaken by obligations that crowd out the discretionary portion of state spending—of which higher education is one major piece. This was a consistent trend among the states in which our case-study institutions are situated.

Crowding out is rooted in three interlocking factors:

- The relentless increase in obligatory spending for basic health, welfare, and safety
- The widely shared view that raising taxes is politically impossible
- The practical deadlock over cuts in "untouchable" discretionary budget items (which are often pork-barrel projects favored by powerful legislators)

State revenue streams are not keeping pace with the demands for existing (not to mention new) programs. Such issues as health care and corrections, as well as shedding of federal programs, have drawn resources away from these already thinning streams. Perhaps for the first time since the post–World War II buildup in state support, higher education is experiencing a structural displacement in its accustomed share of state budgets.

Gold and Ritchie's report on the fiscal crisis in the Northeastern states (1993) points out how colleges and universities in that region have had to shift dramatically the mix of their funding from state appropriations to a greater dependence on tuition. This pattern is one very stark symptom of how states have been forced to displace the responsibility for support of vital services downward—onto the consumer.

The existence of such a displacement is well illustrated by figures from the budgets of forty states for fiscal year 1992–93. The general-fund appropriations increased by an average of 4.8 percent, with increases in specific functions exceeding that average in corrections (5.2 percent), K–12 education (5.5 percent), aid to families with dependent children (6.5 percent), and Medicaid (9.4 percent). Increases for higher education averaged only 0.2 percent over the same one-year period (Eckl, Hutchinson, and Snell, 1992, p. 13). As the authors of this National Conference of State Legislatures (NCSL) report note, "Higher education's growth rate of 0.2 percent indicates how other areas of the budget are taking precedence. The effect is to reduce spending in real terms, since this amount is well below expected inflation" (p. 14).

It is important to keep in mind, however, that displacement of states' commitment to higher education is occurring in a broader context of severe stress for state finance in general. The grim picture is well summarized in the same NCSL report:

> The fiscal health of the states is not good and the outlook for improvement is not promising. . . . State fund balances have been driven far below a recommended level of 5 percent to only 1.4 percent of general funds at the end of FY 1992. Legislatures will address fiscal problems by cutting programs, reorganizing and reprioritizing services, [and] making marginal changes in tax codes while trying to avoid large general tax increases. . . . The states have enacted austere budgets that could easily come unglued if the economy falters further, or if federal mandates or other external forces drive health and welfare spending beyond budgeted levels [p. 17].

By mid 1994, more-hopeful signs that the recession had ended had appeared on the macroeconomic horizon—just in time, however, for one of the most stunning political reversals in recent memory, as Republican candidates and their "Contract With America" swept to control Congress.

Economic factors may suggest a period of relative prosperity and an enhanced capacity of states to raise revenue. But the public's reluctance to sanction new taxes, and its skepticism about the performance of higher education, make it difficult for legislators to commit themselves to expanded support for public colleges and universities. Great uncertainty about the future course of federal policy on many highly sensitive issues—including crime, health care, and welfare reform; developments in the highly volatile economic and political situations around the world; international trade and balance of payments; and unanticipated factors like natural disasters that affect all of these issues—contributes to a very insecure financial picture and very mixed signals at best about what lies ahead in the 1990s and beyond.

Impact on Higher Education: The Internal Dimension

This book is about how institutions have responded to the threat of structural change. Progress had been uneven, but we found an encouraging learning curve at most institutions we visited. We were struck by how different the circumstances and responses seemed to be from one campus to another.

Almost universally, those we interviewed at our site institutions reported (and lamented) that they had made too few hard decisions about their unique missions during an erratically but comparatively prosperous period of twenty or so years. The lament was frequently punctuated with one phrase: "We have tried too hard to be all things to all people . . ."—the unspoken trailer to which was, ". . . and we have become too diffuse to use our scarce resources well."

Causes of Stress

The sources of fiscal stress are complex. To some extent, external economic reversals and changes in public policy have seriously affected colleges and universities. On the other hand, some of our site institutions had neither planned nor managed particularly well as they faced inevitable challenges in their immediate environments. In many cases, two forces—an erratic and problematic environment, combined with a slow-moving and contentious internal decision-making process—made clear, intelligent, and timely responses difficult to achieve.

Effects of Stress

The effects of stress could be seen in all aspects of our site institutions' operations. The effects were also interactive: problems in one part of an institution typically affected others. The response of some institutions had been uneven—for example, academic programs had emerged unscathed during a period of budget cuts. This meant that faculty sometimes did not perceive the problem to be as deep and threatening as it really was, which meant in turn that little attention was being paid to how academic programs needed to change. In other words, we found that some institutions facing stress had responded constructively and strengthened themselves. But others were having more trouble—compounding the initial fiscal stress with problems in strategizing and managing change.

Responding to Stress

Adapting to fiscal stress required that each institution solve several very important problems simultaneously. The first and most challenging problem was that of "ownership." We found a considerable amount of tugging and hauling over whose claims to the mission and "products" of higher education should be given priority. Too often, the claimants confronted each other along adversarial lines. For example, while the legislature and the public demanded efficient service and effective undergraduate education, faculty may have put a higher priority on graduate education, research, and their own autonomy. These differing claims sometimes erupted into open disputes that had to be mediated by a governance process that often put the presidents and chancellors of the institutions in impossible binds.

Pressure to make decisions at the top inevitably produced resistance and reaction. Some institutions, however, broke this cycle of increasingly centralized decision making and conflict among interested parties. They engaged in what we call *simultaneous tracking*. Having reached an overall agreement about mission and focus, the leaders of the institutions delegated responsibility for change rather freely to individual subunits. They achieved a reasonably constructive balance between coming up with a grand strategy and giving individual units the freedom to solve their own problems creatively and realistically. Leadership and coordination were important to the process, as individual units needed to be drawn together around clear goals and values. But simultaneous tracking (which we will discuss in Chapters Five and Nine) also gave everyone enough freedom to work on the many different problems most of their institutions faced.

Reinvigorating Undergraduate Education

One of the most fundamental substantive issues our site institutions faced was how to reinvigorate undergraduate education—the economic foundation of the "business" of colleges and universities. We found very encouraging progress toward more outcome-based programs, toward programs that use classroom and extracurricular experiences, and toward interesting experiments in the assessment of student performance. However, we also found that faculty—by reason of their training and of reward systems that favored research and publication—felt that they were not particularly well prepared to address these issues. They were sometimes not convinced that it was either necessary or wise to devote too much energy to improving undergraduate education. But at those institutions where it had become clear that survival was the issue, faculty were deeply engaged in imaginative and promising innovations.

Solutions

Although our site institutions were diverse, and although the circumstances each faced could be described as unique, certain basic issues did emerge at each one, and these issues led us to see certain common tasks at which all institutions had to succeed. Most important, we suggest that colleges and universities can monitor indicators in four basic areas to sense when they may be headed into or out of trouble. These indicators help assess trends in:

• The external environment
• Financial patterns
• Management patterns
• The vitality of educational programs

Monitoring all of these trends simultaneously, and watching for their cumulative and interactive effects, can provide early warning signs of a developing crisis.

While an institution in crisis needs immediate guidance on taking steps to recovery, we also conclude that a longer-range focus is needed. Institutions need to be proactive in constructing their own futures. To do that, they need to strike a balance between strategic planning and continuous learning, between top-down management and a random trial-and-error approach. We suggest several steps along a route we have called *enlightened change*. This path includes generating good information, sharing it widely, and cooperating responsibly in framing new directions. Above all it urges that institutions make honest self-assessments and hold accountable those with a real interest in the future of the college or university for helping to secure it.

We noticed a quality of "resilience" in some of the institutions we visited. The leaders of resilient institutions seemed to us to be particularly secure about how they were going to meet challenges and survive periods of threat. We found that such institutions met three standards: distinctiveness, excellence, and continuous attention to quality. They differentiated themselves from other institutions, provided effective undergraduate education, and designed convincing ways of monitoring their own success. We think that resilient institutions are particularly good at reestablishing their social contract with students and the broader society. The fiscal health of these institutions is squarely based on providing an attractive product at a fair price—giving society value for its money.

Colleges and universities are being tested in the marketplace. The fiscal problems they face, in our view, are directly related to whether they offer good value to the public. The claim can no longer be made that such institutions "deserve" support because they have good reputations or big libraries or prestigious faculty. The inexorable changes we are now witnessing—both economically and politically—place the burden of proof directly on each college or university to show how and why it is worth supporting.

The financial health of virtually every American college or university depends directly on tuition-paying, appropriation-generating undergraduate students. Giving undergraduates good value for what they, their parents, and the public invest in higher education is the single most important thing that the institutions can do to get out of "the mess."

Conclusion

American colleges and universities have been affected by fiscal stress since colonial times. The stress currently affecting higher education can be traced to the following factors:

- Redirection of federal policies and funding patterns
- Displacement of higher education among the immediate priorities of state government
- Students' changing characteristics and levels of preparedness
- Shifting demand for academic degrees and other "products" of higher education
- Economic conditions in the nation and throughout the world

During several decades of expansion and comparative economic abundance (1950 to 1990), colleges and universities had become overextended and underfocused. Between the serious economic recession of the early 1990s and the landmark elections of 1994, most institutions unexpectedly faced an uncertain future in which they found themselves asked to do more with steadily diminishing resources. Although their methods for adapting varied greatly, the institutions in our study had begun actively to shape their new directions through changes in mission, in decision-making processes, and in approaches to undergraduate education—the core of each institution's economic health.

Chapter Two

Sources of Stress

The institutions we visited during our study were all reported to be in—or working through—a condition of fiscal stress. With hindsight, however, we now caution that "fiscal stress" is only a convenient label for a wide variety of problems that colleges and universities face.

We found that each institution we visited had reached a different understanding about its own situation, and that each institution's stress was—common shortage of resources aside—a product of its own history, circumstances, organization, culture, and location (market, geography, and political environment). In this chapter our goal is to illustrate how these factors act separately and jointly to affect an institution's financial situation. The factors we discuss affected all of the institutions we visited, regardless of type or location.

Understanding Stress

Institutions that reach a state of stress do so over time. None of the institutions we visited had made a single decision or commitment that had a catastrophic or even visible impact; nor did any of them reach a sudden realization that they were stressed. Stress happened cumulatively and incrementally at the institutions in our study. So did the process of understanding and diagnosing the source and nature of the stress. But the realization that the stress had gotten out of control and that a crisis was at hand sometimes came quickly and mobilized people on campus to act—sometimes too dramatically and sometimes without calculation.

The best way we can describe how stress affected our site institutions is to say that seemingly unrelated causes have resulted in unpredicted effects. This is not to say that leaders of the institutions are not ultimately responsible for their institutions' predicaments. But we do think that stress will happen because people often do not see the convergence of many unrelated trends and factors until they have reason to. They focus on their specific jobs and responsibilities within the institution, but they do not ordinarily need to sense and scan a wide variety of conditions beyond the scope of their work. In fact, converging factors are often very difficult to sense until well after they have begun to have an impact.

The things we saw converging on the site institutions were sometimes not easily foreseeable. In some cases political decisions affected the finances of both public and private institutions, while in other cases markets behaved unpredictably (even counterintuitively). People gradually lost resilience, and programs lost appeal. Economic conditions at the local level sometimes were headed in directions different than those at the regional or national level. Continuous changes in personnel meant that some institutions could not maintain the kind of stability or rational adaptation that takes years to achieve. Severe budget-driven cuts in personnel—often initially in support and staff positions—stimulated overload on remaining staff, coupled with leaving some important things undone.

No institution's stress could be traced to a single cause, and each institution's leaders understood that its current condition was a function of several vectors acting simultaneously on fiscal health. Sources of stress are simultaneously *external* and *internal*. They also occur at the *interface* between the institution and its environment, and they accumulate over time. In part, the sources also seem to emerge as a result of "loose coupling" within colleges and universities (Weick, 1976). Institutions may not command enough of their faculties' primary loyalty or of their attention and commitment to be able to respond to change. In other words, because a college or university affords faculty professional autonomy, it cannot get their attention as quickly or as substantially as it needs to in a time of crisis. When the institution cannot mobilize its internal resources to meet threats to its fiscal health, external forces have a better chance of doing damage.

External Sources of Stress

Colleges and universities rely on their environment for support. People buy or invest in higher education because they find some benefit in doing so. The only thing that higher education has to do, it seems, is sell its goods and services in the marketplace like other businesses. In fact, if it were as simple as that, perhaps the institutions would face far less stress.

The external environment is complex for most institutions, because colleges and universities draw their support from many different sources. These sources are both independent of one another and interconnected. If the economy of a state is in decline, for example, it affects that state's demographic patterns, choice of college, and state appropriations. Similarly, the politics of a state may operate to favor or disfavor higher education in a way that interacts with economic and other developments. Quite simply, the fiscal health of both public and private institutions is the product of a unique mix of such factors. Therefore, any useful estimate of a given institution's fiscal condition will account for external factors that act separately or together.

Economic Recession

The serious economic recession of the early 1990s was the single most powerful external force affecting the fiscal health of the institutions included in our study. Although each institution's financial health was affected by many other factors, all attributed a major portion of their fiscal problems to the recession.

Among our site institutions, the most dramatic example of the recession's effects was the University of Massachusetts at Boston (UMass-Boston), an urban commuter institution that was showing signs of stress at every level at the time of our visit. Readers may recall that Michael Dukakis, who was then governor of the state, ran for president in 1988 by pointing to the "Massachusetts Miracle," referring to a long period of expansive economic growth in the state. Very shortly thereafter, in 1989, Massachusetts began to experience a major economic reversal (Woolf, 1993). While the causes have been analyzed from different perspectives, the effects on the state budget—and on public higher education—are not in doubt (Penney and MacCormack, 1992).

UMass-Boston had absorbed fourteen budget cuts and midyear rescissions in the five years prior to our visit. These reductions had totaled $33 million, of which $17 million had been replaced by rapidly increasing tuition and fees. Higher education's more or less traditional 8 percent of the total Massachusetts state budget had by 1994 shrunk to about 3.5 percent. The net dollar loss to higher education in the state was 37 percent. In fiscal year 1987, UMass-Boston's state-appropriated operating budget was $62.1 million; by fiscal year 1993 the same budget had shrunk to $38.7 million.

Other institutions among those we visited—public and private alike—were affected to one degree or another by the economic recession. None, however, reported effects as severe as those in Massachusetts. However, fiscal stress was attributable to varied causes in other cases, and it was not much less severe than at UMass-Boston—it was just the product of different factors.

Demographics and New Demands

After the 1990s recession, the second most important factor affecting the site institutions' fiscal health appeared to be the size and composition of the market. Institutions in our study faced a market with widely varying dynamics at work. Some drew their students from a purely local or regional market, while others took a more broadly based approach. Some faced clear and obvious declines in the numbers of available prospective students, while others faced changes in the composition of their applicant populations as lower-income and less well prepared students replaced traditional students. Some institutions had experienced less decline than others but nevertheless expressed concern about the shifting interests and changing backgrounds of their market.

The direct impact of demographic changes is less startling than that of the indirect changes. That is, raw numbers of students are not the only way in which demographics affect what kind of business the institutions are in. A good example in our study is Bloom-field College. Founded in the 1870s to serve immigrants from Germany and Hungary (as an alternative to the elite Princeton), Bloomfield is located in Essex County, New Jersey, almost exactly on the dividing line between the predominantly minority (poor) cities to its south and east and the predominantly white (wealthy) suburbs to its north and west.

Bloomfield has adapted over the years to the locale and to the changing population. Today Bloomfield's student body is 48 percent African American and 38 percent white, with the remainder drawn from forty-eight other ethnic groups (with Hispanic and Caribbean origins predominating among these groups). Bloomfield has always educated first generations of college-goers and those mainly from the lower half of the socioeconomic scale. This has, for obvious reasons, handicapped the college in seeking alumni and other external support. Also, it has always been a relatively small institution, with about two thousand students, and its alumni have largely entered modestly paying service professions such as teaching.

The president of the two North Dakota institutions we visited was also acutely aware of the way in which demographics would affect the future of the two schools: "Our future is going to be shaped by North Dakota's demographics. There is an outflow of younger people, and lots of rural poverty. We need to get focused on the major community needs and develop programs to address these [needs]."

In New York State, similarly stark demographic trends were obvious at Syracuse University: "In the fall of 1991, the signs of a demographic downturn hit us. We could see we were going to have to restructure. There was a 20 percent fall coming in our recruiting base [over just the next few years]."

The recession of the early 1990s had struck New York and neighboring states with particular force, meaning that the institutions' smaller recruiting pool would also be less able to pay tuition and fees. One president analyzed the situation this way: "There is a real middle-class crunch in [this state], as recession and unemployment remain high by national standards and as major corporations lay off white-collar workers. The 'new' students coming through the schools are more likely to be from lower-income families and are in greater need of financial aid."

Decline in population base is only one source of stress. Other institutions had to cope with changes in demand for various programs and in the composition of their clientele while also being constrained to work within a budget that did not keep pace. At the ten-campus Maricopa County Community College District in Phoenix, for example, those we interviewed felt that the institution had an obligation to serve the needs of its rapidly growing Hispanic population, while simultaneously serving more traditional students, as well as the area's very substantial and politically powerful retirement community. As Maricopa has worked to serve these special markets, it has also been pressed to serve existing employers, to help new and growing companies determine and meet their work-force needs, and to contribute to the overall economic development of its community. Maricopa's ten campuses have all been affected differently as microtrends develop in the Phoenix area.

At Maricopa, the net result of these shifts has been a new set of demands on people and resources. Among the demands being addressed were the following:

- Emphasis on skills and knowledge needed by the "new" student population in a changing world (such as critical thinking, decision making, collaboration, and social responsibility)
- Early intervention to develop literacy skills in at-risk students
- Continuous recruitment of faculty who are prepared for the demands of teaching in a community college
- Development and implementation of a tracking system to analyze student progress and recognize where intervention may be needed
- Greater utilization of technology
- Implementation of programs to promote cross-cultural understanding and diversity
- Support for economic and community development

This array of new demands pulls the institutional fabric in several directions at once. It asks that institutions assume responsibility for ensuring both access and success for people with increasingly diverse characteristics—some of whom may not have the skills to cope with traditional college-level study. It asks that institutions reform and reorganize their curricula to focus on new and different outcomes above and beyond those they have emphasized in traditional programs. It asks that institutions serve their communities in a variety of ways beyond those that are purely educational. These pressures are not accompanied by new fiscal resources; they are add-on demands to what is already a tight fiscal situation.

Our site institutions were not experiencing the pressures of enrollment growth at the time of our visits, but is not difficult to imagine that such trends will turn upward in some regions in the near future. The State of Florida—perhaps an extreme case—projects an increase in high school graduates from 90,000 to 124,000 in the ten years from 1995 to 2005. While many of the new graduates will undoubtedly find their places at institutions in other states, there is growing political pressure in Florida to provide them with opportunities in the state university system. Unfortunately, this pressure is unaccompanied by the fiscal support needed to create such opportunities. As a prominent former legislative leader in Florida recently pointed out, the money for expanding the system to meet demand isn't in the treasury.

Multiple Funding Sources

Most colleges and universities are funded by a variety of sources; in each case, the balance among these multiple sources is unique to the institution. Although spreading the institution's funding sources across a broader and more varied base may be intuitively appealing—in the sense that there is lower risk when funding does not depend on a single source—budgeting becomes far more complex and problematic. In fact, almost *all* of the funding sources at our site institutions were affected by recessionary forces in the early 1990s.

Maricopa provides an interesting example of the problem. Its principal source of funds is the local property tax, revenue from which amounts to 60 percent of the college district's total income. In the three to four years immediately preceding our visit, property tax revenue had been increasing at between 2 and 3 percent a year—a dramatic decline from the 15 to 18 percent to which Maricopa had earlier become accustomed. Appropriated funds from the state comprised about 15 percent of the district's budget—and had not increased at all in the three- to four-year period prior to our visit. This, too, was a dramatic departure from earlier experience, when regular increases in appropriated funds had become a normal expectation. Tuition charges, although still low by national averages, had been increasing steadily: prior to our study, tuition collected had typically comprised 10 to 12 percent of Maricopa's annual budget; in 1994 it contributed about 20 percent. To complicate the situation, the district's enrollment at the time we visited was down approximately 2 percent over the two years prior to our visit; earlier it had experienced a fairly regular 3 to 4 percent annual increase.

Two other important—and quite unanticipated—developments have affected the income stream for Maricopa. The first was the defeat of a $340 million local bond issue in 1992. Although there is no way to determine why the issue was defeated, interviews suggested that it may have been directly related to the collapse of savings-and-loan institutions in the Phoenix area, and to fallout in the Arizona real estate market. Some of those we interviewed also suggested that the defeat may have partly reflected the financial concerns of the area's significant population of senior citizens—who often have problems with inflation and high costs, who live on fixed incomes, and who perhaps are no longer vitally interested in supporting public higher education. When the college district conducted a second campaign to get the bond measure passed it took a much more assertive posture in explaining the need and the benefits to voters. The bond issue then passed.

Maricopa may not be representative of any other case, but it illustrates how the interrelatedness of funding sources—in itself—can produce complicated effects. This is especially important in a time of shifting intergovernmental relations, when federal government is pushing responsibilities to the state level, and the state is pushing them to the local level. At Maricopa, the state's ability to appropriate adequate funding was reduced by competing demands, the property tax had come under pressure, and resulting tuition charges had discouraged enrollment. At the same time, fixed costs had not changed quickly enough to adapt, and uncertain enrollment figures compounded the problem.

Macropolitics

Public finance in some states is caught in the macropolitics of tax-limitation movements. California and Oregon have both passed propositions to limit property taxes (Proposition 13 in California,

Proposition 5 in Oregon). These popular initiatives have had the effect of shifting the burdens of public school funding to the state and displacing or severely limiting available funding for other programs, such as higher education.

In fact, we did not include California institutions in this study because the impact of Proposition 13 has been so substantial that the state's higher education system was in disarray over how to respond to the deep budget cuts. Southern Oregon State College was among the institutions we visited that had experienced the impact of the tax-limitation movement. Just before Proposition 5 passed, the college had initiated a strategic-planning process. While the plan did provide a guide to the college's future direction and priorities, it did not fully anticipate successive budget cuts of 7 percent, 11 percent, and (potentially at the time of our visit) 14 percent.

We observed a very similar situation at UMass-Boston. Strategic planning had established a set of basic priorities, but the plans became virtually irrelevant with the widely publicized "meltdown" of Massachusetts' economy.

North Dakota also experienced a popular tax revolt in 1989. One administrator recounted the story: "The December 1989 referendum knocked down a legislative reform in the tax structure that had included a sales tax increase. The public was in a "no new taxes/no new anything" mood and launched an initiative to repeal the tax laws. This meant tight fiscal times for social services, K–12 and higher education—the big three items in the budget."

The two North Dakota institutions we visited both reported that the "tax referral" had hit hard, bringing repeated cuts in appropriated funds in the ensuing years. (North Dakota had also based its education funding on oil taxes and faced the added burden of replacing those funds when oil prices declined in the 1980s.)

We will return to this theme at several points: the public funding of higher education is in flux. During the period covered by this study, a national recession was compounded by fallout from the shedding of federal programs during the Reagan era. The net effect was to drastically slow down the rate of increase in funding of higher education; in some states, higher education experienced unprecedented real reductions in its base support.

Micromanagement by States

While writing this book we learned that state governors, legislatures, and coordinating or governing boards may be part of the mix of factors that contributed to fiscal stress at the institutions we visited. While the scenario was unique enough in each state to make generalization difficult, state boards clearly deserve special attention. In some states they are in a position to exercise great power over the distribution of resources. In at least two of the states we visited, system executives exercised considerable personal power in attempts to limit the autonomy of institutions. We felt that these efforts went beyond what was needed to ensure a fair and effective distribution of the state's scarce resources and to ensure a reasonable measure of accountability. When leaders of an institution that is already in fragile fiscal health thinks it is coming under attack by its own system, morale suffers and energy is diverted from education.

Without a natural constituency, the boards and their executives depend on alliances. In three of the states we visited, it became fairly clear to us that boards gave rather broad latitude to the interests of older, wealthier, and more prestigious campuses in their systems. Perhaps these campuses were deserving of support by virtue of enrollment trends, ability to capture private funding of all sorts, and demonstrable academic strengths. But some decisions and policies of the boards seemed unbalanced and against the interests of urban populations, minority access, and the development of clear and distinct indicators of excellence among the more vulnerable institutions in the system. A community leader at one institution reflected rising frustration over the treatment of the smaller colleges and universities in the system:

We are enrollment driven and we have lost programs and students in recent years. This leads to lots of paranoia about whether the state is planning to close smaller institutions. We have bused people to the Capitol to protect [the college]. . . . The big guys were getting any programs they wanted. The little guys were getting pushed off the playing field. . . . Why, for example, should [they] be allowed to do teacher education? They aren't NCATE-accredited and we are. We even have to offer our elementary [education] programs on their campus! The state board bows and scrapes to [larger institutions]. After the tax referral, they didn't have to cut programs. We have to jump when told, though. The big guys bring political clout to the Capitol. They continued building, even though their campuses were underutilized.

In some cases, boards were passive in the face of clear threats. In others they took decisive action, but without warning and without building consent and understanding on local campuses. A faculty leader lamented the loss of a music program at a small, rural institution, indicating how much it had meant to both campus and community life. It was clearly a decision that led to great resentment of the state board's ability to dictate terms: "We are gunshy. . . . We lost our music program the last time there was a big change at the state board level; we need to build trust."

While it is hard to deny that "putting the skins on the wall" is a time-honored way to show toughness and decisiveness in crisis situations, it is also clear that some decisions are merely face-saving steps for system executives and may do long-term damage unless the consequences are carefully vetted. A faculty leader reflected on how a decision to consolidate administrative services at two institutions had been made and how it generated "anger" and "resistance":

The chancellor really didn't think this one out. He just wanted his name in the *Chronicle*. The process wasn't thought out; it all happened suddenly (he dreamed it up in his car one day!) and no one really knew what was going on. The transition meetings . . . were tense; no one knew why we were doing this. Was it money or something else? We heard both stories. We don't know if this is really saving money or not. There is lots of ancillary expense involved. We do see lots of opportunities for collaboration, but it isn't going to be easy.

By all accounts, great amounts of energy and time had been spent implementing the new arrangement—perhaps to good effect, but also at considerable cost in time and goodwill.

Do boards help solve fiscal problems by planning and rationalizing the distribution of scarce resources? Or do they contribute to the problems by generating backlash and resistance at the campus level? Obviously, the answer depends on one's perspective. We heard claims in both directions and saw evidence that could be used to make either case. We do think boards have become much more assertive and intrusive, though, and that they may overplay their roles in certain cases. As political players, the boards have learned to appear strong, decisive, and effective at times and on occasions when such traits enhance their role. But their decisions—perhaps made in good faith—do have the potential to stifle creative, timely, and nimble responses by local institutions.

Political Disaffection

Reclaiming the public trust is the theme of an article by Derek Bok appearing in a 1992 issue of *Change* (Bok, 1992). The implication, of course, is that the public no longer trusts higher education. Mythology holds that colleges and universities were once seen as pure, charitable organizations dedicated to the betterment of the human condition. Faculty were understood to be a humble and self-sacrificing nobility, moved by great ideas, moral wisdom, and a purely altruistic interest in teaching these things to a nation's future leaders. While both of us can remember a time when this view seemed to prevail in the public mind, it appears to have faded rapidly after the turmoil and upheavals on campuses in the 1960s.

Today, one is more apt to hear in the rhetoric of public officials and commentators a much less generous view of colleges and universities and their faculties. Our own experiences in (or close to) state government confirm that higher education is viewed with deep skepticism—even with a hard cynicism. Faculty who teach badly (or can't teach at all) and who are perceived to engage in the comic lunacy of "postmodernism" and "political correctness," presidents who squander or misappropriate funds, students who do not repay loans, athletic teams built on the violation of rules, tuition that increases above inflation rates without observable gains in quality or productivity, the inability of students to take required classes or meet with advisers, and institutions' arrogance in the face of demands for results are all part of the litany of criticisms most often seen or heard in the popular media.

In our study, we made a point of speaking with trustees, community leaders, and staff of state systems of higher education in an effort to assess how each campus was viewed in the external world. In the long run, the credibility of colleges and universities, and the public support they enjoy, may be more an issue than the current reversals in fiscal support—which after all may be seen simply as a proxy for public trust. As one of our informants put it, "The best way to get an increase in state support is to show them they are getting a big bang for their buck."

While we think there is diffuse support for the idea of "going to college"—and even very strong community backing for individual institutions—there is nevertheless considerable skepticism among the public about the value being returned to students and taxpayers. If college and university leaders cannot explain themselves, take responsibility for dealing with the public's concerns, or respond quickly and clearly to negative stories in the media, they will have brought a good part of the crisis on themselves.

Legal Requirements

The administrative burdens of meeting regulatory requirements and of managing risk emerged as stated concerns when we asked about sources of fiscal stress. In general, the people we interviewed saw regulatory costs imposed by state and federal governments as diverting funding away from program quality and toward administrative overhead. For example, as a faculty senator at one institution put it: "Administrative costs are too high . . . and faculty are suffering; we need to spend less on administration and more on quality people doing teaching and developmental education."

The president of the same institution acknowledged the problem, indicating that one major concern is the ratio of administrative expenses to the costs of instruction. The president of another institution had a particularly detailed grasp of the problems and related costs:

> The fastest rising costs [here] have been in the area of administration and state and federal mandates. For example, reporting requirements have risen exponentially. We now employ people to produce reports that are not really used in [the Capitol]. We estimate, also, that it would cost $200 million to come into complete compliance with ADA [Americans with Disabilities Act]. And environmental mandates are extremely costly. Monitoring old tanks, building holding ponds, disposing of waste now deemed hazardous, recycling, and so on, are all expensive, and these expenses have increasingly diverted funds from faculty salary increases and program development.

Most institutions could have benefited from a systematic attempt to understand how administrative costs may have contributed to their current fiscal problems. In general, however, we did not find such analyses to have been undertaken, nor were we wholly convinced that the impressions of excessive administrative costs were accurate.

Internal Sources of Stress

We think that the impact of external conditions on fiscal stress may be too easily overestimated. What institutions do with their funds and how efficiently and effectively they operate may determine to a large extent whether they are healthy or stressed. One very immediate and very obvious source of stress at the institutions we visited was the now-chronic practice of deferring maintenance.

Deferred Maintenance

As current funds have been increasingly stretched to meet existing needs, colleges and universities have in effect borrowed from capital—in the form of deferred maintenance—to balance their budgets. The vice president of one institution described the scope of the problem at his university: "We don't do the 1.5 percent funding of maintenance that is recommended—and now have a $70 million backlog in deferred maintenance! We have had a lot of capital funding, public and private, but haven't been able to keep up on the [operation and maintenance] funding. We have an infrastructure that is largely scar tissue from years of temporary repairs [without needed replacement]."

One concern about deferred maintenance relates to the problem of risk management noted above. At this particular institution, some of the deteriorating physical infrastructure was built long before modern building and environmental codes were enacted. Repair, replacement, and compliance with code standards (not to mention retrofitting to comply with ADA) are not just expensive: if such actions are delayed, they increase exposure to risk by an exponential rate. These risks—for example, spills from an underground tank whose existence and contents may not be known—are not carried in balance sheets because they are unknown. But administrators, particularly financial officers, understand that such risks are a basic part of the fiscal problems of virtually every institution. In other words, hidden risks are a far bigger part of fiscal stress than merely a matter of infrastructure decay from deferred maintenance and repair.

Discounting Price

Private institutions operate in a very competitive marketplace. Their tuitions are perceived as being high and have been widely reported as rising at rates above those of inflation for at least a decade. Although this is not literally true at all institutions, the public perception has affected behavior of parents and students in making choices about college.

In addition, as a matter of educational policy, institutions seek diverse student bodies and construct their financial aid packages to attract students with varied talents, varied ethnic backgrounds, and other qualities that may be valued. Merit-based scholarships and other forms of financial aid help to overcome concerns about high tuition among students whose qualities are sought by many institutions, and private colleges and universities widely offer such assistance to students. These institutions also, of course, participate in federal and state programs designed to help students who have demonstrable financial need offset high tuitions.

In most cases, merit-based aid must come from the institution's resources. This occurs in one of two main ways: either the institution's endowment provides income that can directly offset the tuition that is being forgiven, or the institution engages in direct "discounting" of tuition—so that each merit-based award is simply a decision to lower tuition for that student. Discounting requires that the institution's net income from all tuition remain high enough to meet the budget, so discounting requires that some students pay more to subsidize those who pay less. The extent of this practice and of its impact on private college financing has not been well documented, but we can say that it was a source of concern at the private institutions in our study.

People at private colleges also express concern about competing with public institutions for the same students. Administrators at one private institution that had been very successful in attracting minority students and providing them with a highly effective program were concerned that these same students were transferring to less expensive public colleges. In recent years the graduation rate of the minority students had been quite low—partly because students who gained skills and confidence during the first year or two felt that they could succeed in a public college while paying lower tuitions. In one sense, this institution had been a victim of its own success.

Such an experience may be somewhat unusual, but leaders of another private institution worried about whether the school could attract a sufficiently large freshman class while competing with a public system that had a good reputation for providing quality higher education with low tuition. The CEO understood clearly how changes in tuition discounting were affecting the budget: "The 1980s were good for higher education. We had lots of students, and funding wasn't a problem. We were able to raise tuition to keep pace with or do a little better than inflation, but the students kept coming, even when [federal] financial aid policy turned around and emphasized loans instead of grants."

In the 1980s only about one-third of all students got financial aid from this particular institution. Today, two-thirds get aid.

Tuition discounting concerned the private institutions we visited, but it is difficult to estimate the actual extent to which such discounting contributes to fiscal problems. Obviously, it helps to attract students who would otherwise not attend an institution, and—as with airline ticketing—it fills empty seats that would otherwise generate no revenue. Just as obviously, discounting can go too far and result in suboptimal income.

Analytical Capacity

Administrators of one of our site institutions were in the process of developing a financial analysis to determine how tuition discounting might be affecting its income. Although complex, the analysis essentially would examine which academic units were producing net income (including discounts) below their direct and allocated costs. (By allocated costs, we mean portions of the institution's overhead—including maintenance and the like—that is prorated to individual units.) Instead of focusing in the abstract on whether the institution is *generally* producing enough income, the analysis would look at each academic unit to see if discounts are necessary to keep some units alive. The weakest ones—that is, those with a record of excessive discounts—would be studied carefully to determine whether the institution can justify the subsidy.

With strong analytical capabilities, an institution can better see and understand the patterns—and potentially the causes—of stressed finances. Some institutions, however, do not have this capacity. Without it they are flying blindly into situations they do not understand. As one president pointed out: "We don't have any institutional research capacity—something we need. [Without it] there can be no grand design."

Analytical thinking is, of course, more than simply gathering data on past performance. It is also projecting ahead and developing scenarios so that decisions can be more informed and strategic and less immediate and incremental. A chief business officer put it this way:

> Our traditional strategic planning process has assumed a one-year horizon. There is a lot of immediate pressure on everyone, and we really haven't been able to get our perspectives focused on five or ten years out. We ought to have a vice president for planning to be thinking at this level. We can see that tremendous changes are coming. The [current strategic planning] process put teeth into our [two- to three-year] budget planning. It was a powerful exercise—but it would have been more powerful if we had thought even further ahead.

A chief financial officer at the same institution confirmed that "planning" had been largely incremental, although it had utilized good information. The information, however, simply rationalized the status quo. "People didn't have any incentive to change," said the CFO.

Management Problems

Some well-managed institutions were clearly pinched by external circumstances over which they had no control. But others got into fiscal trouble essentially because they were not well managed. The institutions we visited were selected because they had made substantial efforts to recover. At the time of our site visits, none appeared to us to be a poorly managed institution. In a number of cases, however, we were well informed of the *history* of past management problems that had led to crises.

At one institution, the litany of problems amounted to a textbook lesson in total organizational breakdown. Enrollment had declined to 230—well below the break-even point—and current spending was chewing into the principal of the endowment (half of the expendable principal was gone). The trustees had a "narrow business mentality," and the constant chase for dollars (by offering off-campus evening courses) had caused faculty morale to plummet. The admissions office had had eleven directors in ten years, and the development office had gone through seven directors in the same period. (All gifts and bequests were going into current budget accounts rather than into endowment.) Deferred maintenance was also a serious problem: several buildings were closed and unmaintained. The college had relied on short-term loans from local banks at high interest rates, and had essentially exhausted the goodwill of bankers. Financial management was under the control of a staff employee with no professional training in accounting, and payment of bills was being stretched out to the point that suppliers were essentially loaning money to the college.

Information had been tightly held by the president and an assistant, and faculty could not find out where money was coming from or where it was going. A "culture of mutual hostility" was reported to exist between faculty and administrators—a situation that ultimately led to open confrontation at a board of trustees meeting. The faculty had accused the president of lying, and they ultimately voted no-confidence.

Situations at other institutions did not reach this extreme, but there were nevertheless many signs of management shortcomings. Some were simply the endemic problems facing all academic institutions. One CFO rather colorfully and categorically expressed his impatience with what he felt was the amateur quality of leadership among deans and department heads: "[Some of these] . . . decisions can't be made by consensus. The faculty will talk it to death. Deans are selected from chairs and are trained as professors, and they excel in the art of academic politics and survival. In the next four or five years academic management needs to be looked at carefully, particularly faculty work load. The deans won't do this. These people were never trained to manage."

Another CFO expressed similar exasperation with the torpid response of academics to the urgent problems facing the institution:

Society isn't about to wait for higher education to figure out the solutions. The action will go to the people who can get the job done, the activists in corporations like NYNEX. . . . [O]ur structures don't serve us well, but we can't afford to stand back. . . . People say, "We need to go back to the way it was . . . ," especially faculty and the leadership of their governance bodies. But they have to learn that if they want to decide, they have to be informed, to know what the facts are. We have to rethink the relationship between the faculty and the CFO, and between the faculty and other administrative officers. As it now works, the faculty conduct their own "independent" review of administrative decisions. They tell us to decide, then judge whether it is "right" or not. They are "opposed." We need to find a more collaborative way to do business; the old adversarial process is flawed.

In addition to these problems, the same CFO perceptively noted how the separate jurisdictions of faculty and administration affect control over certain decisions with major impact on financial health:

> Colleges and departments have control of merit pay. The national disciplines effectively control tenure via their assorted gatekeeping functions. Faculty also control the search process, so we get more of the same. We have to find a way to break loose of this system and get faculty thinking about how to contribute to the university. The reward structure sets up a competition between interests of faculty and their disciplines and the university. . . . Management decisions frequently come up against what the faculty say can or can't be changed.

From the other side, faculty at another institution wondered if administrators could in fact take courageous and direct actions to solve big fiscal problems, or whether they would opt for a more ameliorative consensus-building process: "The management style here needs to be more than 'hold hands and drift into the future.' Some decisions have to be made, and the top people have to decide." The site institutions facing fiscal problems, in other words, often faced governance problems as well. For assorted reasons, they could not make valid, timely, and legitimate decisions that had the support of constituents on campus.

Leaders at many of the institutions we visited found themselves facing issues for which they had little professional preparation or experience. People of goodwill and high academic accomplishments might rise to occupy key positions. They would do their best—often in difficult circumstances—but they could do better with more support and preparation. This is one area in which added "administrative expense" would undoubtedly pay dividends. Creating a management team with the ability to plan and to understand institutional finance, principles of marketing, and human resource development would probably make for a more nimble and efficient organization—one that could use scarce resources to accomplish its work more intelligently.

Conclusion

"Fiscal crisis" describes a condition that has many causes, including:

- External economic constraints
- Shifts in public policy
- Demographic change
- Internal factors that combine to strain scarce resources

Fiscal stress, we now believe, is better understood as a general syndrome with many alternative causes. Although the causes of fiscal stress have usually been projected to the economy, to the legislature, to changes in technology, and to a host of other conditions, it is fair to ask whether the institutions themselves have responded effectively. In many cases, the people we interviewed told us that colleges and universities are internally divided and unprepared to analyze their own operations, to initiate change, or to act decisively.

As time passes, inaction (or unproductive action) may simply allow the effects of stress to multiply. We will further analyze what is happening inside institutions in fiscal crises, and how they deal with the serious dilemmas they face in choosing among alternatives.

Chapter Three

Impact of Stress

The institutions we visited were affected in many different ways by the financial stringency of recent years. Each of them differed from the others in their basic fiscal condition. They were all concerned, though, with certain basic issues, including:

- Mission
- Strategy
- Market dynamics
- Program quality
- Morale
- Organization and leadership
- The role of faculty
- Sources of income
- Budgeting horizons

All of these questions had to be dealt with simultaneously. They are all interrelated; change in one area directly (and sometimes dramatically) affects another. In some cases it was possible to "metamanage" these simultaneous developments, while in others institutions progressed "amoeba-like"—as one president put it. "They don't move forward in linear fashion, but send out pseudopodia and follow these where the environment provides least resistance."

In a human sense, fiscal stress has taken a toll on morale. At all institutions, we found people questioning the value of their work and the validity of their purpose. But we also found that fiscal stress had galvanized these same institutions into action. For the most part, we would characterize the stress as *eustress* rather than *distress*. Eustress is the healthy, motivating stress needed to stimulate growth and adaptation. However, growth and adaptation differed from one site institution to another.

Among the healthiest impacts, in our view, was the level of thoughtful introspection in which each campus was engaged. The status quo was widely perceived to be unsustainable, and—although different ideas were being floated about what to change and how to change it—broad and intense involvement had raised awareness and stimulated serious discussion of the future. These discussions, as far as we could tell, were rooted in good information that was being freely shared, and they were nonideological in content. Rather, they focused on realistic analyses and practical solutions.

This is not to say that there was universal agreement, nor even that some people did not look back with regret and wish for the return of the better conditions of the recent past. But it was our sense that there was no escaping the dialogue on most campuses, no way to retreat into a fantasy about how things would inevitably improve. For many of those we interviewed, the grinding effects of these realities—and the extended efforts to come to grips with them—had led to pervasive fatigue. But notwithstanding their weariness, people generally understood that the future could only be assured if they *changed*, and if the changes were real and substantive and valid.

One highly articulate and perceptive department chair told the story of his own unit in terms that we think best characterize this point. His department had previously been a separate college, and a high flyer in terms of external funding. Its recent history was one of reversals, though, and its status was seriously threatened by the institution's own fiscal problems:

We had been too theoretical. . . . We had high faculty salaries and lower numbers of students. We had to cut our budget 50 percent and lost five of our sixteen faculty to the voluntary separation program. [So] we agreed to switch; we became part of the college of ———, and actually only had to take a 42 percent cut. When we were folded into [the other college], our dean left because he couldn't take the demotion. Now we are not afraid to explore some of the alternatives. We want to find a way to remain a research university. So we have to reconsider things. . . . I want to do these things myself rather than let others do it to us. People are definitely more open-minded, more oriented to compromise, and thinking more creatively.

The purpose of this chapter is to describe the varying impact of stress on the diverse institutions we visited.

Mission

There was one astonishing consistency among our site institutions: virtually every interview we conducted reverberated with the refrain, "We can't afford to be all things to all people anymore." Institutions had added on and added on—except during a few periods of stringency—since at least the 1940s. Each institution had a clear sense of its mission, but that mission was based on a logic and a world that was rapidly moving ahead—one that most people feared would not wait for academics to catch up.

Missions that were developed in an earlier time now began to seem platitudinous, providing institutions with very broad umbrellas under which they could fit almost anything they chose to do. People had become committed to these platitudes, believing in them and using them as symbols of status and achievement—making it more difficult to dislodge the status quo. We think that this is a natural consequence of not having to worry about the flow of resources: when resources are easier to find, institutions can afford to be uncritically opportunistic. But when resources become scarce, mission and focus become far more important.

Two presidents of institutions we visited characterized the missions they had inherited as "platitudes" that gave real guidance to no one. As one of them put it, "This institution was trying to commit suicide; it did not have a clear mission beyond educating . . . students. Who doesn't do that?" At another institution, an opportunistic central administrator had—in the minds of faculty who lived through the period—diverted resources from the institution's explicit mission and "invested" in activities that the faculty felt were speculative and inappropriate. But as long as such institutions could evade financial crisis, they could afford to operate without focus. Nothing forced them to think seriously about what they could afford to do and what they could not afford to do.

Strategy

Growth was the one type of logic everyone understood; and growth, as long as it could be sustained, had driven strategy in the recent past. With few exceptions, strategy had apparently never really driven growth. Growth was occurring in higher education; it was not something that institutions did as an explicit response to a conscious plan. One of the consequences of "passive growth," of course, was that institutions became overextended—in some cases seriously so.

Although "planning" and "strategy" had become part of the vocabulary of institutional life, we found that the words were more likely euphemisms for indiscriminate expansiveness—whether to justify more of the same or to justify random opportunism. As a vice president at one institution pointed out, "The old strategic planning process . . . was mainly about how to hand out the new money that had been coming in each year forever." Institutions that had plans and strategies often could not focus on how to manage with declining resources until after it became absolutely necessary to do so. They had not, in most cases, engaged in serious strategic thinking about how and why they were doing all that they had taken on.

An interesting example of genuinely strategic thinking governed the unusual redesign of Trenton State College in New Jersey. The college negotiated a new role and purpose for itself as a quasi-elite public liberal arts college. In the early 1980s—an otherwise expansive time—Trenton State downsized its enrollment by about one third and eliminated many graduate programs. It did so in order to reallocate funding to quality improvement for undergraduate education. It now occupies a distinctive place among New Jersey's public colleges and has attracted a student body with unusually strong credentials.

Trenton State's leaders understood that the longer-term demographic trends were unfavorable and that funding would continue to be problematic. Instead of simply accepting that the college would likely have to educate fewer less-qualified students with a lower per-FTE funding base, Trenton State reinvented its mission and its image. It positioned itself differently to respond to obvious and inevitable changes in the marketplace. It anticipated stress and acted before the problem became acute.

Strategic planning was under way in one form or another at most of the institutions we visited. It was, for the most part, a serious, if very recent, activity in which the principal constituencies convened to consider goals, values, organization, and the overriding crisis in institutional resources. In at least several cases, members of the boards of trustees helped substantially by bringing their experience in corporate planning to the process. Healthy and substantive debate was emerging, for example, by considering what it would mean to be "smaller but different," or to make strategic (as opposed to incremental) reallocations in the budget. But strategy was being developed in reaction to crisis; it had, as a rule, not been a tool for anticipating or avoiding crisis.

Perhaps the most important perspective on strategy was well articulated by one president. After summarizing the planning that his institution had recently done, he said: "Now we have to take actions that are consistent with our mission. Strategic planning has to do with developing the principles and values that guide you; we are beyond that and are now making hard decisions."

Some institutions were still very much trying to get through the thinking and talking phases of planning. This president understood that strategy was not strategy unless it also involved making decisions and taking actions. In contrast, a vice president said that another institution had trouble taking specific actions: "We had a strategic plan, but we didn't bring it full circle to operation and closure. There was no structure for putting it into effect, no clear signal as to who was in charge or responsible."

But it is just as valid to point out that strategy is much more than courageous (but mindless) action—it is *also* thinking and talking. For the institutions we visited, involving the whole community in both thinking and talking about what was important laid the foundation for subsequent action. However, the time it took to think, talk, explore, and consider options was a luxury some of our site institutions did not have in abundance. To their credit, they took what time they had to do it; but in a few cases events simply bypassed them, and it became a matter of acting first and thinking later.

Market Dynamics

All the institutions in our study were dependent on undergraduate enrollment to drive tuition income and/or state appropriations. But fewer students were graduating from high school at the time of our site visits than had been the case five years earlier. Without planning to do so, most of the institutions had therefore experienced enrollment declines—either in specific program areas or across the board. In a few cases those declines were serious enough to raise questions about the institution's viability.

We observed three principal results of population decline: far greater attention to the recruitment (as opposed to the "selection") of students from traditional groups, far more interest in retention, and more entrepreneurial exploration of nontraditional "markets."

Tuition sensitivity was a matter of great concern to the leaders of the private institutions. In general, they felt that they had been adversely affected by the federal government's financial aid policy, which made loans instead of grants the principal form of assistance. Students and their families considering private institutions had become extremely sensitive to price. They were becoming far more analytical about competitive prices and discounts from colleges to which they had applied and more particular about the potential "value-added" return on their tuition investment that each institution could offer vis-à-vis its principal competition. The private institutions offered clear anecdotal evidence about the increasing competition with public-sector institutions on both value and price.

Tuition at the public institutions was on an apparently irreversible upward escalator, too. Consequently their leaders had begun to worry about the institutions' traditional mission to provide access to higher education. They were also deeply concerned about how the public would perceive the quality-and-price issue: Would they be more likely to opt for the perceived "quality" of a private institution as the price differential diminished?

It has become clear that state governments are less and less committed to public subsidy for institutions of higher education. Whether this is a conscious policy decision or simply the result of a zero-sum budget process, the effect is the same. Funding for public higher education has become a progressively lower priority for state governments, and tuitions have consequently been raised in order to replace operating funds once provided through state appropriations.

This means that both public and private institutions have become much more market-dependent and customer-sensitive in their recruiting and retention efforts. As one administrator of a private college noted: "Our goal is to make 'value' the target. We should be selecting good kids and satisfying them. We have to build satisfaction. . . . We can't get away with admitting great kids and [then] do nothing for them."

It may seem both incomprehensible and ironic, but in many ways becoming "student-centered" has been the most difficult change for colleges and universities. Finding ways to become more student-centered was a challenge our site institutions were working hard to meet, and we will return to this theme several times in the book.

Program Quality

The current wave of interest in "total quality management" has impacted institutions of higher education in many ways. The institutions we visited almost all had adopted one or another approach to quality management. Although each had, to some extent, home-grown its own version of this popular idea, the principles seemed to be broadly and well understood. The key idea is to focus on the "customer"—in this case students—and adapt the institution to meet their needs. While some of the faculty we interviewed expressed reservations (and even some concern about "hand-holding" students), there was nevertheless an impressive amount of rethinking and redesigning going on.

The institutions' leaders understood that tuition- and FTE-driven budgets depended directly on providing value to their student "consumers," and they were learning how to ensure a "quality" experience for each student. We observed a consistent trend toward making students' experiences exciting and challenging: getting them to participate, to engage in active learning, to work in teams on faculty research projects, to immerse themselves in a foreign culture, to lead community service efforts, and so on. As one senior administrator put it: "We are about to move from the traditional model in which we have 100 faculty 'partners' and 1,000 student customers to a new system in which there are 1,100 partners and involvement from the community as well."

With few exceptions, "quality" was understood to mean what

students got from attending the institution. It was also understood that "inputs" of money, books in the library, and faculty degrees and publications—all of which had traditionally been used as yardsticks by which institutions measured their status—were no longer as helpful in attracting students as they once might have been. In our sample of institutions, and probably at others as well, "quality" is being redefined to mean the intensity and impact of the college experience on students.

The most visible and far-reaching changes at most of the institutions we visited were program changes. We saw examples of three kinds of program changes: cutting, adding, and reshaping. The most obvious problem that the institutions under fiscal stress faced was how to cut losses and find new resources. Most could easily see that across-the-board budget moves would leave weak programs and financial drainage points in place—that without structural change the existing fiscal strengths and weaknesses of an institution would remain very much as they had been. Therefore, there was no hope of a "cure," or even of incremental improvements. As one faculty leader put it, "The only way to find new money is to cut from the old; all new program money is now going to have to come from internal reallocation."

Virginia Commonwealth University had set a goal of discontinuing or merging programs and restructuring its administrative functions to recover 15 percent of its budget. The president reported that "savings from this process will support our strategies over the next several years."

So the leaders of the institutions were taking much harder looks at programs than they had traditionally been accustomed (or willing) to do. They were becoming aware of how indiscriminately they had conducted their business during a period of comparatively plentiful resources. The chief financial officer (CFO) said: "[We] had lived from increase to increase every year, and had just let all the programs and functions accumulate without ever thinking too critically about them."

Criteria such as "centrality," "quality," "demand," and "relation to mission" were being used to assess the viability of programs. Programs that could not support themselves with enrollment, and/or that were not considered vital to the overall mission of an institution, were being selectively targeted for closure or realignment. One common dilemma added stress to the process: if strict cost-accounting and "productivity" standards were used to decide whether programs should be kept, then institutions risked losing some of their essential parts and fundamentally changing their missions in ways they might regret later.

The "classical" example is the classics department. While it may not be an institution's most productive department—nor its most popular—it nevertheless represents the institution's basic commitment to preserving the culture. Do you kill classics to ride the wave in business (or engineering, or education)? What happens when enrollment cycles reverse themselves and the institution has simply lost its competence in some core areas? Some of our site institutions had learned bitter lessons from earlier efforts to benefit from such cycles. What may be "up" today may be "down" in a few years. Making quick and opportunistic moves may look smart in the short run but may damage the institution's position in the long run.

At some institutions, refocusing of programs and reallocating of resources was profoundly changing both the programs that had traditionally been offered and the institution's image among its traditional clientele. At one such institution, for example, a state official made this point: "——— has cut its service-oriented programs and is pricing itself out of the graduate education market. Local professionals and adults with educational needs aren't able to get what they want. You can't enroll for a degree on a part-time basis anymore!" While this change in the institution's service commitment was generating some backlash in the community as well as at the state level, the institution defended its strategy as a conscious (and largely successful) attempt to refocus its scarce resources on high-quality, residential undergraduate programs.

However, institutions also understood that they needed to seek out new opportunities, generate new interest and sources of enrollment, and find new sources of income. They were not just cutting and shrinking; they were trying to focus their identities and be more entrepreneurial. In some cases, they could take advantage of state incentive programs to do so. In others, they simply had to become much more self-reliant and entrepreneurial than they had ever been.

A particularly interesting approach at some institutions combined a searching look at economic development needs with a thorough assessment of the institution's strengths. In one case, this meant strategizing about how to pull together faculty who had the relevant expertise so they could focus on three "hot" areas for research and professional training: health, the environment, and materials research. The leaders of this particular institution believed that it could best redistribute scarce funds by investing them in interdisciplinary work on these three themes. In the smaller institutions, weekend, evening, and other programs for adults were being tried as a way to generate more income from their existing facilities and faculty. In some cases, tuition assistance provided by corporate employers helped attract new working adult students.

Morale

Two very important correlates of fiscal stress are anxiety and suspicion, both of which can have a serious impact on morale. At one private college, a senior administrator said:

> Most [faculty] were actively looking for work elsewhere, anticipating the imminent demise of [the institution]. They saw the adult/evening program as a separate profit center that was actually siphoning money away from the college. This program had been farmed out to a private marketing firm that took about 60 percent of tuition revenue as its fee for service. Faculty felt they had no control over what was going on in this division and didn't approve, either.

Two themes emerged when we discussed morale in our interviews. One theme emphasized action, and the other emphasized appearances. People felt better when they thought that action was being taken—that someone was doing something constructive about the institution's problems. But it was also important to attend to the way people saw themselves and the institution. As a department chair said: "Be careful about the labels you use. Don't call budget cuts 'restructuring.' People get tired of clichés and shell games. Morale here is low already." But a president was praised at another institution: [He has done a] good job of selling the message that 'we're good and we can be better' to the faculty. National publicity and ratings are good for faculty morale. This may help us get through tough times."

"Message" seemed to be as important as substance, and each institution was grappling with the delicate balance between acknowledging the depth of its stress and reaffirming the competence and worth of its people. An institution in trouble, we found, goes through a subtle process of parsing out the blame and the hope. The psychology of the organization is affected, and the symbolic and emotional content of communication have a greater impact to the extent that people are aware that the institution is under stress and have realistic hope that it can recover.

Organization and Leadership

The focal point of organizational psychology in times of stress is clearly the top level of leadership. Presidents and other central administrators are watched more closely and judged by harsher rules when resources become tighter. Potential conflicts among constituencies become more serious, particularly between internal and external constituencies. These pressures can produce some clear (and consistent) organizational changes.

Most noticeable at the sites we visited was the shift in overall initiative and strategic decision making to the central administration. As the availability of surplus or uncommitted resources declined, pressure grew to generate a strategy, to define options, to establish procedures, to work out decision rules, and to choose solutions. The more serious the fiscal problem, the greater was the pressure on presidents and their immediate staff to *do something*. But just as the pressure grew, so did the potential for conflict and disagreement over which specific "something" to do.

In addition to the obviously increased pressure to act, fiscal stress clearly brings a need to change structure. Stress is a sign of mismatch between resources and demand on those resources—or to put it another way, stress may be a symptom of inefficient organization. In fact, this was well understood at the institutions we visited. They knew they could not continue to operate the number of different programs they had, nor could they do it in the same way they had operated comfortably for years. Things had to be changed.

Organizational changes were under way at most of the institutions. Among the most important changes was the far clearer articulation of goals and objectives of each unit. Less duplication and more cooperation among units might generate efficiencies, and some institutions found that some unfamiliar ways of doing business could be remarkably productive. At Bloomfield College, for example, student-affairs and academic-affairs units were working very closely together to create a common educational focus and a cooperative approach to the student experience.

Mergers of organizational units were also being initiated. The most dramatic effort we observed was the sharing of central administration between Mayville State and Valley City State universities in North Dakota. At the time of our campus visits, they had a single president, one provost, and one vice president for administration. Although both colleges were still in the early stages of their experimental partnership, they had begun to unify some operations such as financial aid. By collaborating, they could in theory achieve economies of scale and efficiencies that neither institution could achieve alone.

While that effort had a certain dramatic appeal, other institutions were looking closely at what they could and could not do within existing or anticipated funding levels. Although very little had actually been done, some were aggressively investigating "outsourcing" of services. Institutional control of printing services, food service, bookstores, computer services, some physical plant operations, and other specialized services was seen as potentially inefficient when the cost of providing them was compared with purchasing them in the open market. We did not find much real experimentation with contracting these services out, but it was certainly a matter for discussion in many cases.

At the institutions we visited, there was a marked conservatism about cutting or closing academic programs; more likely, the administrative and support side of the house was the principal target. One result was that faculty had commonly learned to think that academic programs were immune, and that "cutting waste" meant cutting *only* administrative and support services. This made it far more difficult in the long run to initiate changes in academic programs.

The Faculty Role

One of the principal questions that arose at all site institutions was the extent to which faculty understood and appreciated the nature of the fiscal problems their college or university was facing. In some cases, we were informed directly and bluntly by faculty that they did not believe what they were being told—that there was no crisis and no need to respond. In many cases, faculty may have understood but did not have enough information to respond with specific ideas or suggestions.

Faculty have been largely conditioned to endure minor changes in budgets and the year-to-year incremental budgeting process. At many institutions, faculty understood that they had to be entrepreneurial in order to support their own research, but felt confident that the institution would reward them for their successes. The system had grown reasonably predictable and familiar.

For most faculty, therefore, the appearance of fiscal crisis was a blow to their sense of living and working in an ordered and secure world. One dean characterized their reaction this way: "The faculty we recruited came here to move [this institution] ahead as a research university. The budget restructuring meant 'backing off' [from] this commitment, and many faculty felt they had been betrayed." He anticipated having to make a fundamental "cultural change" that would foster among faculty "more allegiance to the institution and to the students, as opposed to our traditional focus on the conventional indicators of competitive excellence." His biggest challenge: "We have to get the faculty turned around"—a view that was reaffirmed by the president of student government at the same institution.

Overcoming faculty resistance to change may be more than just a matter of communicating and informing them. It may require overcoming strongly rooted cultural values. For example, the new president of one institution saw the depth of the problems he faced and called a retreatlike meeting of all the major constituencies. Faculty union leaders, who were in the process of negotiating a new contract, boycotted the retreat, thereby limiting faculty participation.

During our interviews at the institution, the three most recent presidents (as well as the current president) of the union expressed considerable wariness and ambivalence about the college's future as well as its strategy. Acknowledging the president's success in attracting new programs and grants, they nevertheless worried openly about whether "we are degrading ourselves to chase small market niches." They went on to question "whether change will be fundamental or only at the margins." They clearly felt beleaguered and had weathered a great deal, including the institution's historic bankruptcy in the 1970s. This was but the latest crisis in a long history of crises, so the union leaders felt that the best they could do was to watch and to question—while clearly hoping for the best. But they also saw themselves as the faithful defenders of the main values they thought the institution had stood for over the years.

It should be acknowledged that faculty and support staff—especially in the smaller institutions we studied—had felt the painful impact of recent economic reversals during the five years preceding our site visits. Not only had they endured salary stagnation, they had also seen their work loads increase. As one president acknowledged: "Faculty here are working at their limit. One of the keys to innovating is to help the faculty get time. They are desperate now, carrying twelve-hour loads and trying to be creative on top of that. . . . People are very tired. [This campus] is in fragile condition. There has been a real overload on the system."

But faculty at some institutions had responded to crisis with admirable grit and determination—even at the expense of their most sacred traditions and values. At Tusculum College, the many changes included a new faculty constitution that eliminated tenure. The constitution was developed as an outgrowth of a new commitment to "civic arts" as the college's core curriculum, and it was seen as a defining moment in the affirmation of certain values the faculty felt were at the heart of their "self-governing community." An administrator summarized the change this way: "If you are going to model civic responsibility [for students], then you need to practice it in governing yourself, and you need to include everyone in the campus community—students and staff as well." The new constitution was more than a symbolic gesture; faculty leaders acknowledged that "this reform has pulled a previously factional faculty together and given them real authority."

Elsewhere, faculty had been active in pursuing grants for program development and in coming up with new ideas for teaching and learning, for research, and for public service. One provost praised the faculty's "work ethic" as the bedrock for getting through tough times. In other cases, faculty had been looking ahead and taking responsibility for making changes *before* the current situation became painful. A faculty leader at Valley City State University said: "As far back as 1989, some faculty leaders [here] saw a financial crunch coming. . . . We thought it would be a good idea to begin clarifying our mission and doing our own thing. Instead of fighting each other for nickels and dimes, instead of continuing to cannibalize existing programs to fund new ones, we [decided that we] should scan the environment, find partners, and start being more proactive." In this case, the faculty at Valley City State University in North Dakota succeeded in setting up a model program that now serves as a showcase for instructional technology and that has received new state funding.

Faculty have obviously been the carriers of institutional values—and obviously are aware of their ownership of and interest in the institution's future. Their role has varied: in some cases they have clearly been responsible for carrying the institution through a crisis, while in others they have made a more conservative effort to preserve what they valued from a time when resources were more plentiful. This is a positive—not a negative—contribution to change. It gives the institution core values, continuity, and a basic resistance to impulsive change. While it may dampen risk taking, it does so in a way that forces the institution to confront its own identity, and to sharpen the questions it asks before simply scattering its energies in pursuit of ephemeral new directions.

Sources of Income

One of the major changes imposed on institutions has been the need to find new sources of income. Radical changes in the flow of income streams are now occurring. We do not know precisely how these changes will turn out or precisely what impact the changes will have. But a general outline can be drawn.

Public institutions are clearly facing a future in which state appropriations will make up a declining share of their general operating revenues. We were told repeatedly about the scarcity of state funding, the increasing demands on those scarce resources, and the low importance of higher education on the scale of legislative priorities. Rescissions, both temporary and permanent, have been made in university budgets during recent fiscal years. In one of our site institutions, this even occurred without any advance notice to the campus. Base budgets have also been cut; the recent experience of a vice president at a major research university tells the story of many: "The state rescinded 5 percent of the university's budget at midyear in 1990–91. It was to be a temporary rescission and amounted to $12 million. Another temporary rescission of 3.7 percent was made in 1991–92, amounting to $9.5 million. Then for the next fiscal year, the governor wanted to make the $9.5 million [rescission] from the previous year a permanent budget cut. It was [our] first base reduction . . . in fifty years."

The university's situation was complicated by political constraints to hold down tuition increases. The CFO summarized the squeeze this way:

> Tax revenues were obviously not going to increase. The [state's] economy was flat. And appropriations were not going to increase under any scenario we could imagine. State government was sending very clear signals about the situation. The governor put pressure on [us] not to raise tuition more than 4 percent. We had gotten 9 percent in 1991–92 but have held increases to 4 to 5 percent since then. Tuition is now high—approaching $5,000 a year. So with no new appropriations and limited tuition increases, we could see that there was no place to go for quality enhancement. We would have to recycle [or] reallocate existing funds to do new or better things.

This public university embarked on aggressive capital fundraising drives as a way to finance initiatives it considered important but for which public funding was clearly out of the question. Private institutions similarly turned to more-aggressive campaigns for private giving.

However, private institutions do draw public funding—to an

extent that may be underappreciated—so the crisis in public finance affects many of them. Public funding in New York had been an important source for that state's private institutions until it was dramatically reduced during the early 1990s. Private institutions elsewhere have seen their state supplements rise and fall; in Pennsylvania, for example, several lean years were followed by restoration of aid to an earlier level—perhaps at the expense of state funding for public colleges and universities. The results on this front are clearly mixed, as they vary from state to state and from year to year. Nevertheless, the impact of cuts in state funding are serious for some private institutions.

Private colleges, however, are more tuition-dependent than public institutions, and are also more dependent on annual contributions by alumni and friends. For some institutions, cultivation of private gifts has literally meant the difference between survival and failure. One CFO noted that a substantial operating deficit at her institution had been cured by the receipt of two estate bequests—one each in succeeding years. Although unanticipated, the bequests were apparently the result of continued attention to and cultivation of potential donors.

This institution had learned its lesson from a series of recent turnovers in the development staff. This lack of continuity and stability had not only led to reduced income from current gifts, but it may have damaged the institution's long-term relationship with potential donors of large gifts. As the board of trustees chair noted, "The development staff has to focus on making friends for the long run, not just raising cash in the present."

Otherwise, private institutions were obviously concerned about pricing themselves out of their traditional markets, especially at a time when tuitions could not be adequately met with financial aid. An administrator at one private institution said that it had been able to raise tuition to "keep pace with or do a little better than inflation" during the 1980s. But the institution had fallen into an apparently unsustainable cycle of "discounting." As the president noted: "We have gotten on an escalator in terms of providing institutional financial aid. We were spending 5 cents on the dollar of tuition for financial aid at the beginning of the 1980s, but that has now risen to 28 cents on the dollar." The president of student government at the same institution expressed concern about escalating tuition: "From the students' view, the public universities are competitive on quality, better on price."

Budget Horizons

Budgeting is becoming more sophisticated as well as more problematic—more sophisticated in the sense that institutions are generating more information and doing more-substantive analyses of their operations than had earlier been the case. We found that institutions were building capacity for budget analysis and institutional research so that they could answer very refined questions. Specifically, administrators were finding that "every penny counts," and that they needed to tie expenditures to productivity. Knowing where to find the unproductive activities gave institutions the ability to "find" resources and move them to areas of need.

Budgeting has become a far less theoretical and far more urgent process. The time horizons are shorter—in some cases less than a full fiscal year. In fact, for some institutions, "budget" has become a meaningless term to the extent that it may be defined as a plan for spending during a given fiscal year. Faced with appropriations that bear no discernible relationship to actual need, and/or with rescissions imposed during the budget year, institutions have taken to conserving money at every opportunity in order to preserve as much flexibility as they can. This is as close to rational behavior as one can expect, but it has also led to spending patterns that have less to do with educational judgments, or with the actual needs of students and programs, than might be optimal.

One of the fears expressed on campuses is that these patterns may become cumulative and do real damage to them if continued for a period of years. Some feel that the institutions have become too accustomed to short-term palliatives. They are concerned about how these decisions are shaping their futures. As one faculty senator put it, "We need more direction, research, [and] planning, and less pressure to move for the sake of moving; we're getting the 'innovation of the week.'" In this case, the senator was pointing out the apparent disproportionality of administrative budgets (even after major cuts) to expenditures on direct instruction.

At another institution, a recurring theme had to do with the appearance of the campus: "There is a lot of deferred maintenance; the place looks bad. We take lots of money from our students and then turn around and cut the services they need." Maintenance was an easy target for spending cuts, but the appearance of buildings, public areas, and classrooms were depressing for faculty and staff, and alienating to the public and to prospective students. Unfortunately, these kinds of accumulated problems did not pass the threshold of consciousness until they had become so recognizable and painful that the costs of doing something about them were prohibitive.

In a few cases, fiscal stress had essentially resulted in "nonbudgeting." Since funding bore only a tenuous relationship to goals, needs, and plans, spending decisions were made with the most immediate concerns in mind—usually with the feeling and hope that corrective actions could be taken later. But for the institutions we visited, funding became increasingly tighter from year to year, and needs for correction simply accumulated. The danger of this pattern was clear: something—a program, a computer, a building—would weaken to the point of serious damage before anything could be done. For the most part, institutions would have to exhaust all uncommitted resources and deplete any reserves, leaving only incidental savings and random windfalls as their cushion against emergencies and/or the cumulative effects of deferred maintenance.

Conclusion

The immediate effects of fiscal stress were apparent in all parts of the colleges and universities we visited. Leaders found themselves questioning and reassessing their institutions' identities, values, and customary ways of doing business. They also had to cope with the substantive and psychological impact of budgetary and financial shortfalls:

- People were working harder under more pressure.
- Physical plants were declining.
- Classrooms and libraries were more crowded.
- Students were taking longer to complete their degrees.
- Costs to students and families were escalating.
- Conflict among stakeholders in the institutions' futures was more frequent and intense.
- Uncertainty about the future was increasing.
- Morale was low.
- Faculty and staff were questioning the validity of what they were doing.

But as long as fatigue and morale problems had not overtaken their institutions, the leaders felt that the stress had a galvanizing effect. Given a crisis, they could mobilize people, generate ideas, and undertake challenging new agendas. The institutions could start redefining their roles and, as more than one person put it, "seize the opportunity." Some of the institutions had begun transforming themselves into substantially renewed entities.

Part Two

Searching for Solutions

Chapter Four

Mission and Organization

This chapter will explore how institutions define "the business they are in" and what the current round of fiscal stress is doing to their concept of mission. For some of our site institutions, the stress had created deep uncertainty about the validity of their missions. In several cases, that uncertainty had been converted to an extraordinary commitment to redefining and reinventing the institution; in others, the process of rethinking had only begun. Although new directions were being considered everywhere, readiness to consider long-term changes varied among institutions and among constituents. We will base our discussion on decisions that our site institutions said they would be making about their missions in both the near term and the long term.

Two striking themes emerged from our discussion of the future. With some notable exceptions, the people we interviewed wanted to focus on the goals and methods of undergraduate education. They also repeatedly addressed the extent to which faculty roles, rewards, and careers would have to be redefined.

In this chapter we will look closely at:

- The two faces of mission
- The content of institutions' missions
- "Ownership" of those missions by assorted constituents
- The impact of public and private investors on higher education
- The constraints and opportunities of the marketplace

- The dynamics of changing mission
- Commitment to a new or more-focused mission

The Two Faces of Mission

Mission, especially in distinctive institutions, plays a powerful role in getting the college or university community to focus its energies and creativity on the special qualities that make their college or university unique (Townsend, Newell, and Wiese, 1992). Yet there are perils in becoming too "distinctive." By focusing on too narrow a mission, an institution rejects alternative roles and in a sense limits the marketplace in which it competes. An institution therefore faces a dilemma in clarifying, focusing, or changing its mission.

On one hand, in a battle for survival or advancement an institution needs to commit people's energies to a clear objective, and it needs to create powerful bonds among faculty, students, and staff. If the institution has a distinct sense of itself and a clear mission, it can do this. On the other hand, in committing to a particular mission, the institution also risks becoming too specialized and limited in its appeal. In other words, by deciding to be *something*, an institution may default on opportunities to be something else. In the worst case, these kinds of decisions can prove economically unsound because they narrow the economic base of the institution (Townsend, Newell, and Wiese, 1992).

Institutions of higher education are often driven by diverse and divergent goals of their subunits (usually departments). For this and other reasons, developing an overarching strategy for a college or university has long been recognized as a problem (Keller, 1983). One of the other reasons has to do with vigorous resistance to change among faculty, whose academic culture typically values independence, freedom, and opportunism. Some have argued that such freedom of action may stimulate creative and energetic adaptation to turbulent environments (Weick, 1976). But others have noted that faculty sometimes focus their considerable energy and creativity on preserving their autonomy as an end in itself—instead of doing productive and creative work (Bok, 1992; Mooney, 1992; Sykes, 1988).

When this occurs—as it seemed to have done at some of our site institutions—faculty may resist efforts to strategize. This means that the institution devotes more energy to resolving internal conflict than it does to adapting; that is, by attempting to change, an institution may actually generate so much internal resistance that it paradoxically reduces its ability to change.

During our site visits, we frequently observed the institutions' leaders grappling with these two faces of mission. They saw clearly the need to frame and clarify the institution's overriding purpose— they could not otherwise focus on the way they budgeted and allocated increasingly scarce resources, nor could they maintain the commitment and energies of faculty, students, staff, and other constituencies. But strategizing generated resistance and involved taking risks. It also mobilized the many different "owners" and "investors"—stakeholders—who tried to protect their vested interests and resisted change.

We will now examine how institutions balanced out the search for a useful and energizing mission.

The Content of Institutions' Missions

With or without public sanction—and perhaps substantially without it—colleges and universities have evolved into complex entities with multiple missions. They are far from simple "teaching" institutions; rather, they have become intertwined in fascinating ways with the culture, economy, government, and social life of the nation. As vividly foreshadowed by Kerr (1966) in his portrayal of the emerging "multiversity," this quintessentially American institution might today better be called the "interversity." It forms and facilitates connections among people and institutions in all strata and arenas of society. More than ever, it is a meeting place, a cross-roads, an intersection.

The institution's mission has solidified around teaching, re-search, and public service. But subunits and individuals place dif-fering priorities on these functions, and lines among the functions are not always clear, as Birnbaum notes in referring to "overlapping yet competing structures" (1988, p. 12).

To begin with, we found a weak or conflicted sense of mission at some of our site institutions. This was partly a reflection of the times: growth had come naturally and without internal confronta-tion over purpose, strategy, or objectives. It had once been possible for a college or university to become stronger by default as long as the environment continued to provide support. But having a dif-fuse mission was also a product, perhaps, of what Keller referred to as a culture of deference, caution, and conservative incrementalism in managing fiscal matters (1983). One president described what he found upon assuming office: "The institution needed to reclaim its identity. It was doing too many things not connected to its roots—just trying to stay afloat. Alumni had largely lost confidence, and the donor ratio was down to 8 percent, a very low proportion." At another institution, the president reported: "[This institution] couldn't have been in worse condition and still been here. . . . There was platitudinous talk about mission, but nothing that gave specific direction to the institution and its programs." A subtext that ran through our interviews at a third institution repeatedly cited the lack of image, mission, or distinctiveness as a contribut-ing factor in precarious public support: "People don't know exactly what [this institution] is; surveys show they have no opinion when asked about [it]."

The idea of mission did not even come up explicitly during our interviews at one research university. Although the institution had engaged in "strategic planning" for years, it was generally acknowl-edged that this term had become largely a euphemism for incre-mental budget allocations. The president reported that the process was going forward "without a sense of reality," meaning—from his point of view—that political and other environmental changes were being overlooked in the interest of maintaining the status quo.

In comments about recent history at his institution, one dean reflected how academic culture had been allowed to defeat efforts to develop a coherent mission: "You can't function if you behave like a herd of cats . . . with senior faculty just making lots of chaotic choices to do whatever they want." Perhaps equally frustrating was the almost willfully unrealistic effort of some faculty to preserve traditions and/or aspirations that might have been appropriate for an earlier time. As one CEO put it, "The liberal arts faculty want to be like what they think Harvard is like. . . . This just isn't realistic anymore." Another administrator at the same institution pointed out that "the [senior] faculty of the campus has dug in heels trying to preserve the Harvard . . . mentality, and this is a totally unrealistic posture for [us] at this stage of history." The administrator added that if the institution could get past the "egos and self-preservationist instincts" of the senior faculty, perhaps it could begin to construct a mission appropriate to its situation.

These institutions had been unprepared for the impact of fiscal stress. They did not have a clear sense of what they were and where they were going, or why. Indeed, they had no reason to know these things: under "normal" conditions, evasion of such existential questions had been much easier than confronting them.

This is essentially what Keller observed—and warned about—in citing "inertia and chaos" (1983, p. 27). Although he suggested that new efforts to develop strategy were at the nascent stage, he also castigated the shortsighted and vacillating leadership of American colleges and universities: "Presidents can't act and faculties won't act. This, at the very time that higher education faces the most serious enrollment, financial, and public confidence crises of the century, as well as radical changes in program demands, the use of technology, and client markets" (p. 172). If this was true in 1983, we think that the condition has persisted well into the 1990s and has worsened.

And in the 1990s we have observed a far less benign external environment. The public (and political leaders) expect far more of higher education than merely the self-important preservation of the status quo. Pressure is mounting for evidence that public money is being spent responsibly and that colleges and universities are producing real and valuable outcomes. So the appearance of paralysis or failure to change is, by itself, creating additional stress in the form of more demands for accountability.

We should tip our hand here, however, and point out that we have observed cases in which presidents *did* act and in which faculty *did* put aside their vested interests in the status quo. Later in this chapter, we will point out that severe stress does eventually move people to think about mission and to work through potential or actual conflict so they can converge on clear goals and objectives.

Mission: To Do . . . What?

What is a college or university for? Whom does it serve? What should it do—or not do? More to the point, *what* is Syracuse University or Tusculum College or Mayville State University or the University of Texas at El Paso? How does each institution define itself, its work, its niche, its product?

The range of American higher education—even among the thirteen institutions we visited—is little short of astonishing. Colleges and universities serve local, regional, national, and international markets. They are public and private (although distinctions between the sectors are blurring). They conduct cutting-edge research with broad significance for all the fundamental activities of human life. They provide the most elementary kinds of service and support to the rural and urban poor. They teach and socialize each generation's cohort of intellectual, political, and business leaders. They enrich their local communities through art, sports activities, youth development, extension services, short courses, and continuing education.

In short, colleges and universities have become focal points for what it means to be human: no question is too small or too large or too challenging to be contemplated at one institution or another.

But with such a broad canvas on which to paint its own self-portrait, each institution looks at the problem of mission with more questions than answers. The freedom to be whatever the imagination suggests is also the freedom to be nothing in particular. And this is the fear that haunts institutions that are stressed. Their leaders sense that they have perhaps squandered opportunities to make clear choices about their institutions' identity, focus, and distinctive qualities—and that it may be too late to make these choices.

We heard many times some variant of the complaint "We have become everything in general and nothing in particular." But crisis had forced *all* of the institutions we visited into thinking about choices. Some had made their choices, others were able to talk through the options that seemed reasonable, and ambivalence was clearly complicating the process for a few. For the most part, they all knew the value in differentiating themselves from other institutions—in defining their missions more clearly, in developing a distinctive identity, and in focusing their programs to serve a clearly identifiable market.

The campus of one site institution had galvanized into a state of heightened attention when it became apparent that the state was considering closing it. A member of a faculty planning committee said, "The main issue is to find our niche. We have to identify real needs and decide what we can do together to meet those needs." Noted a vice president at the same institution: "We had been a very defensive institution. We'd been battered a lot. Now we see that we need to be more proactive. We have to show that we have earned support, that we deserve it. We have to carve out our own niche instead of just 'keeping on.'"

For some of those we interviewed, attempts to make their institution emphatically different sometimes seemed too risky and counterintuitive. Commenting on one public institution's move to differentiate itself from others in the state, a system head noted that "the other [institutions] . . . were more risk averse. They focused on the middle 50 percent and *safety*" (emphasis added).

Among the institutions we visited, those that had decided to focus and distinguish themselves almost invariably did so by identifying a clear niche and a definitive philosophy that emphasized undergraduate education. (*Niches* are combinations of geographic, economic, and programmatic openings that institutions can fill. Community colleges, for example, have clear geographic niches.) Many public institutions serve commuting populations of low- and middle-income students, and most institutions develop at least one distinctive program or curricular identity that draws a certain kind of student. Some institutions identify their niches in very general terms; as one chief student affairs administrator said: "Our niche is [looking for] new ways of delivering undergraduate instruction. For example, using performance-based assessment [and] using innovative and flexible teaching strategies. The idea is to give students a good experience."

Other institutions reflected a far more focused commitment. The president of Tusculum College recounted how the school had remade its program:

> These meetings [with faculty] got into deeper things, too. We read current critiques of higher education—for example, Bruce Kimball. We read Cicero on civic virtue and traced the history of the liberal arts. One of the understandings we came to was that the influence of the German university in the 1800s led American colleges away from their historical focus on liberal arts. Going back into history helped us "remember" how, as far back as Cicero, [the purpose of] education had been to prepare people to contribute to the civic good. Several things ensued, but the centerpiece was [our] adoption of Cicero's "civic virtues" as the core of our mission.

Geography was important, too; even the more nationally known universities understood that their market niches were geographically bounded. In some cases, those boundaries were very close to the campus. "The traditional and current mission of [this institution] is to serve kids from —————— County [and its immediate environs]. . . . We focus on working closely with counselors in the local schools, bring them to campus, work with them to identify the potential winners."

Three of our site institutions defined their niches in terms of the opportunities they provide to minority students. Ethnically diverse Bloomfield College, which serves a predominantly urban population, offers programs that focus on preparing students to assume leadership roles in a multicultural society. The University of Maryland-Eastern Shore is traditionally a minority campus that has attempted to prepare students for civic responsibility and for professional fields that have not drawn the interest of proportionate numbers of minority students. The University of Texas at El Paso orients its programs to the needs of the predominantly Hispanic population it serves, focusing on preprofessional preparation for fields like health care and law, as well as other fields for which a regional need can be identified. And the population within Maricopa County Community College District's service area is also heavily Hispanic, so there is a need to teach classes in Spanish and a need for faculty who can appreciate the heritage and educational preparation of students from different ethnic and cultural backgrounds.

Virginia Commonwealth University defines its niche as being "a national leader among urban universities." Several striking program initiatives support its mission. For example, the university's primary health care initiative operates through a community-based collaborative program designed to improve the accessibility and quality of care for underserved and underinsured populations. It also has started up a multidisciplinary center for people with HIV/AIDS that deals with both social and medical aspects of the disease.

In another case, the institution's competition is such that no "escape" from its defined niche is likely. An alumni leader at an urban institution described the position of her alma mater this way:

"We are perceived as a 'Sears Roebuck' of the local higher-education market. We offer lots of programs, but none is the best. . . . There is no student union, no 'home away from home.' We also lack dorms. This hurts recruitment because one reason kids go to college is to get away from home! But our students are wonderful. We have to focus on our urban mission in [this city]. We can't do everything."

Significantly, some institutions struggled with ways to keep their options alive and to find, perhaps, a new role to play. One institution was struggling with the realization that its fiscal viability depended on undergraduate students, while its faculty were oriented toward graduate education and research. Recognizing that he had radically changed his own perspective, the provost acknowledged: "We can't afford to continue equal emphasis on the traditional trinity of teaching, research, and service. . . . Now we have agreed we are going to be a 'student-centered research university'. . . . We have to get faculty to see survival in terms of their students."

This effort to redefine the university's mission struck us as more than a ploy to create a larger umbrella for multiple and conflicting subcultures within the institution. It appeared to have substance and stimulated serious thought and discussion about how to put a novel idea into practice. A veteran administrator observed that the operational changes would be significant: "This is going to mean changing the primary loyalty of the faculty from their disciplines to the institution. We need smaller classes, better teaching and advising, opportunities for active learning. These are the things we mean by 'student centered.' "

One particularly aggressive and optimistic dean had seen the new direction clearly and had begun to act: "We have to do fewer things and do these well. I have set up six institutes and centers. . . . These support important activities. If you want to do something outside these areas, you are on your own. We just can't be all things to all people anymore. . . . You have to say clearly what you want to be doing."

Residual doubts and ambivalence surfaced, however, when the institutions confronted the need to change and to leave behind past successes. For one thing, as a planning director pointed out, identifying programs or activities that might be cut or eliminated involves a real risk: "Making public confessions of weaknesses is really hard." For another, institutional inertia can be substantial, as a department chair noted: "People—particularly faculty—don't really want to change. They don't want to perceive the real scope and depth of the problem." And substantial risks are involved in making big changes; at some point the institution is irrevocably changed—and the change may not make it a "better" institution. Considering the income-producing assets—tangible and intangible—of his institution, a CFO remarked: "We need to preserve [our] identity. . . . We have to be careful not to take strengths away from the campus."

In the end, each of our site institutions was reexamining its place and its role. They were all able to see that undergraduate education was central to their survival. And they could all readily understand the concept of niche—offering a distinctive product to part of the larger market. They varied widely, however, in the extent to which they had moved away from "softness" of mission— being all things to all people—to "hardness"—moving resources from one thing to another in the interest of building on strength and seizing a clear niche.

The smaller institutions were able to deal with the issue of mission and identity more nimbly than the large institutions. The smaller schools were often under much more severe financial pressure, and each could more readily decide as a community what it wanted to do about its situation. But the more complex the institution, the more difficult it was to achieve an overarching consensus.

Stakeholders and Their Interests

One of the principal impediments to establishing a clear, hard mission is the multiple ownership of colleges and universities. Multiple owners exercise a microcosmic version of the special-interest politics that have so overtaken public policy debates. Boards of trustees, state political leaders, community and business leaders, professional associations, alumni, presidents, faculty, and students are among those who have vested interests and who—by asserting those interests—make it more difficult to close off debate and agree on directions. Public and private institutions alike have to deal with the problem of multiple ownership. Like public colleges and universities, private institutions are affected by public policy at the local, state, and federal levels. Similarly, public institutions court corporations, alumni, and foundations for gifts, contracts, and grants.

Every CEO we talked with during our site visits felt simultaneously hamstrung and whipsawed by the divergent interests of powerful constituencies. Most expressed increasing exasperation with and fatigue from the continuous assertion of veto power by one or more key constituencies. In some cases, multiple ownership resulted in virtual paralysis of the change process.

Politicians or system bureaucrats clearly obstructed decisions in a few cases. At one institution, a strategic plan resulted in a decision to close a program. Although the campus process ran its course, and administrators took the risk of adopting a recommendation to the board of trustees to close the program, the decision was stopped by the state legislature. A different solution—merging the program into an existing department—had to be found.

The CEO of another institution drew a particularly compelling picture of the constraints placed on his school by political interests. Appropriations were flat, tuition increases were being controlled, and both legislative and gubernatorial staff intervened when program changes were considered. In at least one case (confirmed by several people we interviewed), a program slated for closure was saved when students and alumni mobilized to lobby key legislative and executive staff for a reprieve. In our view, the institution was facing a Hobson's choice: it could exercise its discretion and close the program, but in doing so it faced the unacceptable alternative of having its budget held hostage by committees and agencies in state government.

"Balkanization" by special interests paralyzes the institution's ability to harden its mission. In many cases, this is precisely what got the site institutions into difficulty. As a CFO pointed out: "We were an institution out of control. You had to grow in order to add dollars, and stay grown to keep it. We tried to get the whole system to downsize to protect the available but increasingly stressed pool of state dollars. But the other presidents wouldn't do it." A trustee of the same institution was blunt about why presidents are reluctant to take risks on mission: "We have been the one to stick our head up over the trenches, and we get shot at by the others." Being bland, diffuse, and accommodating has its rewards in safety.

Faculty are among the most entrenched of the recalcitrant special interests. In a colorful aside, a veteran administrator advised, "Don't get the troops [faculty] to hemorrhaging too much, or they'll create backfires against change." Faculty at several institutions had created those backfires with considerable vigor. At one institution, both the union and senate had called for the president's resignation. At another, an ad hoc petition had been circulated declaring that the CEO's performance was poor.

In a third case, the president announced his resignation shortly after our visit to the campus; while he had told us of the many pressures he faced, he had not signaled his intent to resign. When we visited another site institution, we heard faculty union leaders compliment the president on his willingness to clarify and focus the mission. But they nevertheless remained wary and skeptical. Others at the same institution suggested that the faculty were "in denial" and rooted in a "culture of antagonism" with the administration.

Faculty do have a stake in the status quo. They are, after all, the longest-serving and most heavily "vested" employees of the institution. The most senior faculty are tenured and have long memories of previous presidents, crises, and efforts to change. In some cases, they have been badly hurt by arbitrary, authoritarian, and horrendously misguided leadership. Faculty at one institution we visited had within the past few years confronted and overthrown a president whose financial strategies they viewed as suspect. Faculty are not only "risk-averse," as one faculty leader put it; they also often have good reason to question and resist.

That resistance, in our view, can be pathological—and has become so at some institutions. "Process fatigue" was cited by several of those we interviewed as a probable cause of resistance to change. Process fatigue seems to set in when people are distracted by a continuous, open-ended search for new ideas and change. With no prospect of real decisions and some kind of closure, they begin to resist further movement.

We think that another root of pathological resistance is simply insecurity. People who face potentially major changes—who will need to learn new skills, whose prior investment in professional development is negated, and whose status is threatened—are fearful and defensive. It is not hard to empathize with a faculty member who has lectured to a passive audience for thirty years and then resists the introduction of new ideas about interactive, cooperative learning. Or with the faculty member who has taught biology and is now being asked to teach "critical thinking."

But there is a general understanding among those who are pivotally responsible for planning that changes in faculty's role are inevitable. One CFO put it this way:

> We need to redefine the role of the faculty if we are going to change. While teaching, research, and service are all important, we have to teach here since it is the base of our support. Management decisions frequently come up against what the faculty say can or can't be changed. We have now cut administration beyond the limit. But faculty are still just coming in to teach on Tuesday and Thursday . . . and the place looks like hell from deferred maintenance. We have overinvested in research and service; we are [overspending] on fac-

ulty salary, part-time faculty, and grad assistants [when you consider that the state expects salary dollars to go principally to teaching and not to research].

Students, too, can behave like a vested interest group. At one institution that had recently gone through a serious planning exercise, student government leaders with whom we met remained skeptical: "The students were unconvinced that there were any real and permanent cuts being made—or that [this university] was actually facing some kind of fiscal crisis." They saw their interest in quality education being affected by the proposed changes: "We don't want 'fast food' education via distance learning and other technologies crammed down our throats! We also don't think the [total quality management] metaphor is a good idea if it means turning out the most product at the lowest cost and selling it for the highest price!" They could see (correctly, as it turns out) that this institution was likely to increase tuition, squeeze more efficiencies out of undergraduate education, and concentrate on building graduate programs. They opposed moves in these directions.

Students at other institutions had some of the same concerns. They wanted quality in undergraduate education, and they wanted it at competitive prices. One student government president lamented what she saw as a low priority given to investment in the student experience, and she placed the burden squarely on research-oriented faculty: "It is not clear that the faculty yet believe the need for reform is real."

In analyzing what the various constituencies want and expect, some clear lines of conflict emerge and major divisions over mission become clear. The external community wants a responsive institution that is committed to economic development and to the professional preparation of graduates. The faculty want to advance knowledge in their own individual disciplines, as well as maximize their own individual professional rewards and mobility. The students want a useful and efficient education, but not necessarily at the expense of a well-rounded collegiate experience. Administrators are acutely aware of the inconsistencies and tensions among these constituencies in what they want and expect from their institutions.

At some institutions, mission has therefore become not a clear, concise, valid, and accepted mandate, but rather a highly tentative political compromise among the competing claims. This presents leaders with a serious challenge. Mission can be represented neither as the received wisdom of tradition nor as the product of a clear and powerful consensus. It has rather to be intuited and constructed over time in the excruciatingly incremental process of coalition building. And even when one might imagine that a workable consensus is in place, it often appears that the center will not hold against the second thoughts and individual preferences of key players.

Because it has become so much a vehicle for the advancement of individual interests for both students and faculty, higher education is having increasing difficulty performing a social mission of any real substance. This leads to our next point: the tension between public and private claims on mission.

Public and Private "Investors"

For what and for whom does higher education work? Is it for the provision of opportunity to students? For the career and professional advancement of faculty? For the production and/or application of knowledge on behalf of economic development interests? For the allocation of privilege? For the enlightenment and enrichment of the community? All of the above?

Our analysis of the many competing interests suggests that the issues surrounding mission can be boiled down to a relatively simple dilemma: balancing the returns to public and private "investors." Public investors include the federal government, which underwrites massive research, development, and service enterprises and promotes access and opportunity through programs of financial assistance; the state, which builds and operates institutions with appropriations from tax revenues; and the varied array of donors who subsidize colleges and universities through annual, special, and capital campaigns.

Private investors include those who pay for or "purchase" specific services at prices they consider to be reasonable. For example, students (and their parents) purchase degrees with tuition. Business corporations purchase research with grants; government agencies do the same.

These competitors have become players in the internal economies of colleges and universities that, instead of allocating resources to the achievement of rational plans, are consumed by competition among many interests. Faculty, for example, are paid from public funds to produce public "goods": literate citizens with the ability to reason and contribute to both political order and economic development. However, faculty are also often paid what might be considered bonuses from private funds (if not in salary, then in other tangible incentives such as research assistants, laboratory equipment, secretarial help, computers, and travel funding) to produce knowledge and expertise that may benefit private interests.

It is often argued that teaching and research are "joint products" of faculty work (Volkwein and Carbone, 1994, p. 148). That is, when faculty teach they enhance their research productivity, and when they do research they enhance their teaching productivity. This more or less traditional conception of academic work suggests that mixing the public and private interests (and investments) in higher education creates a higher level of "output" than would be possible if only one or the other prevailed.

The alternative view is that incentive systems have increasingly drawn faculty toward a concentration on research at the expense of teaching. Massy and Wilger describe this gradual shift in faculty effort as "output creep" (1992, p. 367). Output creep, they suggest, has resulted in faculty that spend a declining portion of time on teaching and an increasing portion of time on research and/or "self-selected activities" (p. 367).

In other words, instead of producing balanced returns for all parties with an interest in the "product" of higher education, there has been a subtle but consistent shading of effort and a return to activities that favor private investors. Fairweather (1993) showed a correlation between faculty effort in research and the distribution of rewards. Also, in a national study of social science faculty, Fox (1992) showed that "those whose publication productivity is high are not strongly invested in both research and teaching. Rather, they appear to trade off one set of investments against another. This finding is contrary to the mutuality hypothesis" (p. 301).

The balance of evidence strongly suggests that faculty do not invest equally in teaching and research; they make the choice of (or are rewarded for) spending a balance of their effort on one or the other. This does not address the question of whether good teaching and good research go together—it only addresses the issue of whether faculty work is truly a joint product. It appears not to be. And if it is not a joint product, then when decisions are made—individually or organizationally—about the work that faculty will do, they are really decisions about whose investment will be rewarded.

We were struck by the extent to which people we interviewed were familiar with the ideas developed by Ernest Boyer in *Scholarship Reconsidered* (1989). Boyer argues that the research/teaching dichotomy oversimplifies the range of legitimate scholarship in which faculty engage. He advocates that rewards for faculty be distributed to encourage productive work in knowledge discovery, knowledge synthesis, knowledge application, and knowledge transmission. A balanced institution needs faculty who can do all of these things.

We think that decisions about what faculty do and how much they do of teaching or research have a direct impact on the kinds of investment that government, business corporations, and foundations are willing to make in a college or university. By strategy or by default, what faculty do is what the institution becomes. An institution in which faculty effort is focused on purposeful and effective undergraduate education is likely to secure for itself a tuition income stream. Conversely, an institution in which the faculty focus on research will perhaps be successful in attracting grants and contracts, but may find its student "market" unpersuaded to pay the tuition being charged.

Breaches of trust appear in both directions. That is, faculty at teaching institutions elect to spend time on research, while faculty at research institutions convert their contracted time into teaching. Up to a point, investors—both public and private—appear willing to tolerate this benign "double billing" on the theory that joint production does take place, or even that it is desirable. But there is great concern in the literature (see Johnstone, 1993, for example) and among those we interviewed that a certain amount of goal displacement has infected the system. This shows up in an academic culture that shifts rewards almost exclusively to faculty who spend more time on (and produce more) research, at the expense of those who spend more time teaching.

The fiduciary responsibility that faculty are supposed to exercise for the public investment is—it is alleged—being breached. The returns on time spent doing research *when that research is paid for out of public appropriations* go principally to the faculty themselves, rather than to the investor; such returns, therefore, amount to self-dealt gains. This has been the subject of scandal-mongering books (Sykes, 1988) and has also been a concern of legislatures (Layzell, Lovell, and Gill, 1994, p. 12).

The point we wish to make is that decisions about what faculty do are decisions about the institution's mission. There are competing claims on mission by reason of different interests of different investors, and institutions have conflicting fiduciary responsibilities to their various investors. Unfortunately, this fiduciary conception of mission has, in some cases, not been carefully nurtured—or it has been glossed over by holding to the joint-product idea.

The choices are much clearer and much harder in times of fiscal stress. Massy and Wilger (1992) pointed out that growth serves as a cover for failing to make such choices. But institutions we visited were finding out that fiscal stress simply magnifies the impact of decisions—especially those about faculty work. A vivid example at one institution illustrates the point: "In physics we [are] shooting for national recognition. This will take a major investment in new labs for new faculty, but the university expects a return on its investment in labs through the grant process. It takes close to [half a million dollars] to set up a new faculty member's research program."

The dilemma, of course, is whether the "fronted" half-million dollars at a public institution relying on higher and higher tuition ever does get returned in fact or in kind. Given this investment in a faculty member's research, what kind of effort to teach well could one expect from that faculty member? How much of the faculty member's salary is coming from public appropriations or from tuition? Is the faculty member's performance providing commensurate returns on these investments? Whose investments (and interests) are being given short shrift?

And so we return to the question at the top of this section: What is a university for? We might rephrase the question and ask whether an institution's mission can or should be conceived in a fiduciary sense. At the very least, there are clear consequences in taking money from investors and in deciding how to produce returns on those investments.

It has been difficult for colleges and universities to make these decisions in a coherent and rational way. The problem faced by most institutions in our study was that these decisions have been made by default over the years, and it is now "payback" time as investors become increasingly concerned about what returns they can expect. This is a question that academic institutions have not confronted squarely. The easy way out is to constantly seek new investors and thus evade real accountability. But there is only a limited pool of investors in higher education, and they are getting impatient.

Constraints and Opportunities of the Marketplace

How free are colleges and universities to seek out new investors? Or how freely do investors seek out institutions of higher education? How are their markets affected by current economic conditions?

Realistically, the institutions we visited did not have a wide variety of options. They were bound by place in more than one sense of the term. Institutions of higher education occupy comparatively narrow markets, and their economic health—at least in our study—closely mirrored the economic strength (or lack of strength) of their customary fields of play. In good economic times, that relationship translates into an excess of demand and an expansive concept of mission. In tight times, demand is more variable—it is not always lower but may be of a different kind. In either case, stress results. Institutions also have to deal more directly with competitors, a challenge that only becomes more intense when the economic pie is shrinking or not expanding.

Ambitions, self-concept, and reality are not always well aligned. We found that fiscal stress had generated identity problems for most of our site institutions. Their leaders grappled with the idea of expanding their missions to broaden their bases, but they also grappled with the idea of making their institutions more focused and distinctive (reasoning, perhaps, that a clearer image would draw people from a broader market).

The choices were not always easy to make. The experiences recounted at our site institutions were replete with cautions about the perils of expanding mission and adding programs. One group of faculty leaders worried about the diversion of resources involved in developing adult education programs and corporate training agreements: "[Doing] more nontraditional programs for nontraditional students . . . only tears resources and energy away from the core." At another institution, though, an adult education program was reorganized and now serves as a "cash cow."

Focusing

Many of our site institutions had either narrowed or focused their missions. For example:

- Trenton State essentially eliminated graduate programs and community service programs, instead concentrating its resources on establishing itself as a highly selective residential college emphasizing undergraduate arts and sciences.
- Tusculum College redesigned its curriculum and reconstituted its whole structure to concentrate on (and exemplify) the "civic arts."
- Bloomfield College focused on preparing its graduates to live and work in a multicultural and multiracial society.
- Syracuse University is developing a "student-oriented research university" mission.
- The University of Massachusetts at Boston is focusing its developing graduate programs on interdisciplinary approaches to urban problems.

In each of these cases, the decision to focus was part of a strategy. (We should caution the reader that not all of the plans we learned of have been fully implemented as this book goes to press; we have tried to report those ideas that were at least in the early stages of implementation. We acknowledge the likelihood that ideas and plans may have been somewhat ahead of the realities on campus.) At each institution, the strategies resulted from a sense that it had been too diffuse—trying to do too many things, and presenting an unclear image to the public.

The marketplace is not really a wide-open, blank slate. For most institutions in our study the opportunities were quite limited. They each had to calculate the costs of adding new programs and clienteles, and they had to balance those costs against savings from doing fewer things better. In previous eras, these same institutions had tended to be expansive, and uncritically so. But adding here and expanding there had gotten most of them into unsustainable commitments. So they had learned to be far more selective and careful about what to undertake, and they became far more conscious of doing those *more carefully selected* things well.

External Perspectives on Mission

While most of the institutions had canvassed their constituencies for perspectives and viewpoints on what their mission should be, we felt they had been most successful in understanding and articulating the insiders' points of view. Conspicuously less evident were the points of view of clients and external interests. We attempted to interview trustees, community leaders, and others who were outside the institution because we wanted to see if contrasts existed between the internal and external interests.

People with whom we talked often knew that their institutions needed to do a better job of relating to and informing local, state, and regional stakeholders. This is not to say that presidents and other key administrators were not conscious of or did not work hard at developing good relationships. But these relationships were often not as substantive and productive as either side might have wished. Signs of weakness in external relations with communities, with other levels of the education system, with the business sector, and with government were all called to our attention at one institution or another.

Parents, business and industry, state and local governments, and citizens/taxpayers in general do not understand the mission of higher education in the same terms that those in the academic community understand it. What the general population does understand about mission, it learns through not entirely complimentary media stories and anecdotes from personal experience. People at one institution had a very clear awareness of the damage done to its image through accumulated (and not completely fair) media attention: "We found that we don't have many friends and that the environment is substantially hostile. We have critics among our own . . . faculty, and among the media. We are getting spilled on by troubles in the K–12 sector, fair or not. We can't just go out there and ask for more in this environment."

Coverage of higher education in the press can be a drumbeat of bad news. At one institution, the need for better press was recognized: "Negative publicity in the media hurts us. We have had to dig in and promote ourselves. Prospective students worry if programs and sports will be cut. Politicians here feed [bad] images to the media." This statement came from a staff person in media relations, who worried that students and their parents would become concerned about paying steadily increasing tuitions and fees for a constantly declining level of service from the institution. (Although this fear was partially manufactured by the media, it was not entirely unrealistic, either.) But good news is seldom published. An admissions officer was keenly aware of the impact of news reports on the image of higher education: "The public gets news on high salaries, waste, and politics when they read about public higher education; they don't see what we do for our students." The media were also cited at several campuses for coverage of athletic scandals, scientific fraud, student and faculty misbehavior, crime on campus, bizarre incidents of so-called political correctness, and the perceived peccadillos of the professorial "leisure class."

Image and press coverage, while often not seen as a serious issue by faculty or even by key administrators, may nevertheless greatly affect an institution's ability to attract students and money. One trustee we interviewed noted: "A lot of marketing is perception and image. For example, no one went to ———— in the 1950s, but it is now one of the hottest schools going. . . . [Whether I like sports or not], athletics helps our image, results in more applications, and supports the local economy. And people don't give to [institutions they perceive as] 'dogs.'"

This trustee candidly professed to disliking college football and didn't want to spend the time it took to attend games and related social events. But he understood the image-making value of football and understood that image making was part of his responsibility as a trustee. (He noted that it came with the job description!) On the other side of the equation, we should note that "image" problems do tend to result from media stories with bases in fact—something educators may be tempted to overlook.

We also heard substantive concerns about mission that suggested real disjunctures between what colleges and universities do and what their constituents and clients expect of them. These concerns are far more worrisome than image problems. Business and government leaders want to get a real return on their investments in higher education. They do not have a great deal of sympathy or patience with institutions that cannot articulate a clear mission and demonstrate that they are giving "bang for the buck." In the estimation of one administrator at the state system level, future funding levels will depend on how institutions in his state satisfy an increasingly skeptical array of public authorities: "[The state higher education] board wants to see success on instructional technology and innovative instruction—since this is the focus of special program funding; the legislature wants to see success on course sharing and cost cutting."

But leaders in the external community want more than just efficiencies. One business leader wanted far more applied research and development, as well as advanced training in management and technological studies: "The big issue is increasing the size of the economic pie so everyone benefits. [The university] should be working with business and industry toward this larger goal."

On one hand, if an institution responds uncritically to every external demand, it risks becoming too diffuse. If it does not at least show good faith in trying to meet society's needs, on the other hand, it risks being perceived as arrogant. But certainly, if there is no working consensus about mission, the institution has no way to sort and prioritize the most pressing or most promising overtures from the outside. A coherent sense of mission serves as a filter and helps leaders decide which options to pursue aggressively, which to decline, and which are worth negotiating.

Theory and Practice: Focusing Mission

Although a great deal of inspirational and quasi-spiritual rhetoric has been disseminated under the guise of mission statements—and although a large literature exists on developing mission or vision or strategy—we were struck by the hard, pragmatic realities that went along with institutions' attempts to get focused. This is not a romantic quest of some kind, nor is it a process that comes to closure in any textbook fashion: just getting a modicum of consensus and a reasonably stable truce among the contending stakeholders took a great deal out of the key leaders at our institutions. Even when some consensus is achieved, it is not always apparent that good, valid decisions have been made. The process has clearly been dominated by "incrementalism," as one state official put it.

Nevertheless, several of the institutions we visited had adopted clear visions and explicit mission statements and were following through with assertive action plans. The value of having clear directions and a working consensus around a set of core ideas was evident.

In several of our cases, a CEO who could deliver a clear and consistent message about mission helped focus both internal and external audiences. One CEO indicated that the most important lesson in emerging from fiscal stress is "to create an identity . . . a really strong sense of mission." She further pointed out, "Everyone on campus needs an opportunity to understand the mission and to become a part of it. It's then important to communicate [it] to the outside world." Where consensus had been achieved on mission, a communication-rich process simply served to reinforce that consensus and to mobilize people to work on its behalf.

At one institution, we concluded that—for reasons quite beyond the control of campus leaders—no stable consensus on mission had emerged. This meant that the "message" to both internal and external audiences about whom the institution was serving, how it was serving them, and with what impact could not be clearly framed. Instead, the image that most people we interviewed reflected back to us was of an institution moving from crisis to crisis. It was surviving, but it was doing so in spite of considerable conflict and uncertainty.

However, an institution that had weathered a virtually annual set of fiscal setbacks over the past five years had used an earlier long-range plan as a way of keeping its mission in focus during these periods. As its chief financial officer pointed out: "You can't let a fiscal shortfall dictate how you plan or decide. We've stuck with our 1987 long-range plan and evaluated decisions against that. We have kept the five major goals of that plan up front as our guide." Each successive fiscal crisis had spawned a new process of planning and deciding at this campus, but the results of these processes were variously characterized as "ad hoc" and "incremental." In the end, the earlier strategic plan had set the important boundaries and pathways by which consensus was guided. The value of the plan was described by one administrator in this way: "The 1987 plan guided us through short-term moves during the succeeding crises. It told us how and what to slow down—not what to cut out, but how to stretch it out pending better times. This kept us focused on the long-term goals."

Certainty and consensus were responsible—in large measure—for the fiscal turnaround of another institution. The president, summarizing the impact of the planning process, said, "We know that our survival depends on doing something distinctive, on filling a particular niche." The institution adopted a new curriculum, established a set of common outcomes that undergraduates must achieve, developed an innovative calendar, and revised the governance structure to emphasize participation and responsibility on the part of all campus "citizens." It has also paid close attention to how these steps are perceived by students, parents, and alumni. Good ideas are not enough if they do not produce applications, enrollment, and tuition income. At this institution, enrollment doubled in about three years, and fiscal stability was restored.

The institution's success was partly a matter of identifying a valid mission, but also a matter of bringing people together into a working consensus. This is a good example of a case in which the "powerful bonds" we mentioned at the beginning of the chapter were realized. The faculty and administration built trust and commitment to the institution through what became known as "side porch" discussions at the president's home. Unstructured and existential in character, these discussions caused people to interact with each other on a personal and human level. People discussed the nature of the institution, its fundamental philosophy, and their personal commitments to it.

The intimate character of this process could not easily be replicated at larger, more complex institutions, but that does not invalidate the general idea: colleges and universities, no less than other organizations, are human creations that require a certain degree of psychological and social maintenance. In our view, if people know that they share a commonly understood "mission," they feel they have a direction that guides their work and helps them maintain a satisfying commitment to the institution.

Interviews at institutions that had not achieved as strong a sense of shared purpose showed that people felt that too many individual actors were pulling in too many different directions, and that this lies at the root of fiscal problems as much as funding does. As one dean noted, solving fiscal problems requires that "You have to have a sense of responsibility to the larger university."

Conclusion

We began this chapter by discussing how institutions realized they could no longer be indiscriminately opportunistic. We also noted how difficult it has become in the larger, more complex institutions to construct some kind of working consensus about mission. Multiple ownership and the diverging interests of internal and external constituencies have created centrifugal forces working against focus and direction.

Institutions that deal successfully with these issues, though, create both clear directions and the human commitments to follow them through. Successful institutions define and control their own identities, and they succeed largely because they fill a need that others do not fill.

Chapter Five

Decisions and Conflict

In this chapter we will explore how fiscal stress has affected the way institutions make decisions. We will also look at how the methods that institutions use to decide can affect their fiscal health. We found that the culture of decision making is thoroughly entangled in both the processes and the substance of strategic decision making. Institutions may consider some possible courses of action because of the way they make decisions, but they may be blinded to other possibilities because the decision-making process simply screens them out.

We interviewed as wide a range of people on each campus as possible because we wanted as many different perspectives on the process as we could get. While it was clear that each interviewee brought a perspective and a certain amount of self-interest to the interview, we found general agreement about the core facts of decision making and the processes that had been followed. People differed in their interpretations and appraisals of decisions, but not in their reconstruction of events.

We found a broad dispersal of power and a narrow range of options. In other words, many hands left prints on the decisions, but they made choices from a middle ground that proved acceptable to a viable coalition of interests and forces. One theme ran through all of our discussions about decision making: *conflict*. The strategy on which our site institutions finally settled—or were struggling toward, since not all the institutions had achieved consensus at the time we visited—was shaped by how the process handled conflict among all the interest groups with a stake in the outcome.

With this in mind, we have arranged this chapter to cover:

- Decision making during fiscal crises
- Defining the situation and promoting understanding
- Ownership of and commitment to the institution
- Balancing leadership and involvement in decision making
- Consistency of environment
- Internal communication
- The emergence of conflict over strategies
- Use of "simultaneous tracking" in adapting to stress
- The CEO's role in simultaneous tracking

Decision Making in Crisis

In the institutions we studied, fiscal crises tended to shift the burdens of decision making to the CEO and a few other key leaders. Decentralized management worked when institutions had surplus or uncommitted resources with which to fund programs and invest in new activities. But when the scarcer resources had to be stretched further, the pressure on presidents, vice presidents, and boards to make hard, authoritative decisions was inescapable.

In some cases, presidents tightened their control and became more directive. In others, they reached out by sharing information, communicating openly, and seeking advice and alliances. In either case, some of the traditional organizational lines changed—at least subtly. For example, open forums or hearings gave people from all layers of the hierarchy access to those at the top. Memoranda and planning documents circulated widely, making information and perspectives accessible to everyone on—and beyond—the campus. (We have even been able to follow developments at one of our site institutions by reading current status reports on the Internet!)

This process, quite naturally, shortened the distance between the top and bottom of each institution's campus hierarchy. It served to speed up the achievement of a common definition of the situation, and it got people throughout the institution to focus on solutions. In some cases, it also reduced the latitude of discretion for vice presidents, deans, and department chairs: with so much public dialogue going on, their voices had less clout and they had less freedom to produce their own independent analyses and plans. In a few cases, this led to departures.

In other situations, presidents tightened their control. Although this meant less sharing of information and less public dialogue, the impact on structure was similar: middle management had less discretion and freedom. But this also meant that presidents took bigger risks. They risked taking sole responsibility for the validity of their ideas and plans, and they risked moving ahead without the support of potential allies. Some, however, felt that there was no option under the circumstances.

Making hard, authoritative decisions at the "top" of the organization is counter to the culture and traditions of higher education. In effect, the greater the need for hard and clear decisions, the greater the resistance to the central administration acting alone. Uncertainty and conflict therefore make it difficult for presidents, vice presidents, decision-making committees, and trustees—to move freely in any direction.

We found that political interests simultaneously demand change *and prevent it*. The public institutions we visited almost universally reported that they were under pressure from legislatures and governors to be more efficient, more accountable, and more responsive to increasingly diverse clienteles. Yet when they attempted to make specific changes, in some cases state officials intervened directly or indirectly, often in response to pressure from an interest group mobilized on behalf of faculty, students, or alumni. Some of these interventions were benign or helpful to the institution, but some obstructed change.

Our site institutions made liberal use of the "joint big-decision committee" (JBDC), a committee with members from assorted constituencies that has a broad mandate to consider the institution's future and to recommend strategies for achieving agreed-upon goals (Schuster, Smith, Corak, and Yamada, 1994). At Pennsylvania State University, for example, the president appointed a "Futures Committee" composed of twelve members who represented various constituencies. The Futures Committee operated outside the existing governance structure and had a very broad charge. A similar "Long-Range Planning Committee" was appointed by the chancellor at Syracuse University. Three successive JBDCs, each with a slightly different purview, advised a succession of two chancellors at UMass–Boston.

Each of these processes was initiated by the institution's president. But the committees' charges and functions differed. In some cases, the CEO chaired the process; in others, the JBDC presented the CEO with a set of options; and in still others, the CEO received reports but reserved the right to develop a strategy independently.

Defining the Situation and Promoting Understanding

Whether by committee, by community forum, or—as in some cases—by executive leadership, visibly centralizing the tasks of planning, analyzing, and deciding served to redefine the situation. These different processes all called attention to the fact that the institution was facing a serious problem or a crisis. The attention and energies of constituencies were turned from daily routines to higher-level issues: mission, survival, the future. But defining the situation and refocusing people's attention was only a first step— one that initially produced more conflicts than it resolved.

If step one was to raise consciousness and redefine the situation, then step two was to promote understanding of the problem's dimensions. Although each institution approached this in its own way, and although some had more analytical capabilities than others, all had done some kind of intense analysis of existing programs, operations, students, staffing, and funding.

Traditionally, financial information had been tightly held at many of the institutions we visited. To some extent, they had all engaged in the urgent public rhetoric of crisis. But because that rhetoric had sometimes been unaccompanied by either hard data or sound analysis, and because reality was perhaps more forgiving than people had been led to believe, it became difficult to convince anyone that *this time* it was real. Faculty, particularly, had become immunized to "the sky is falling" speeches.

A chief financial officer at one site institution said that "there has been a common view that we can muddle through because that's the way we have always done it. But there are no more pockets to raid to make up cuts. It is going to start getting really painful now." So when the sky really did begin to fall in the early 1990s, presidents and other leaders (who in many cases had only recently been appointed) found they needed more than the standard rhetorical ploys to get the attention of key stakeholders such as faculty.

They needed to paint a realistic picture, and they often did so by opening up the books. A faculty budget committee chair pointed out how important this had been at his institution: "Openness has been the key to change here. The Budget Committee under the previous CEO didn't know what was going on. Now we know the data and we have been able to educate ourselves. We have had open forums, group discussions. There has been an effort to share the broad picture, the trade-offs involved in making key decisions, and opportunities to suggest options."

A CFO from another institution put it in similar terms: "Be honest about the state of the institution's finances and about other things, too. Lay the story out as it really is to the faculty, to the trustees, and [to] other constituents. Get the problems stated as clearly as you can. People will pitch in and help if they know what the problem is. You have to know how much of a hole you are in before you can devise a way to get out of it."

The data by themselves are important to the process of promoting awareness and understanding. But the capacity to analyze and compare performance of individual units—both within the institution and with similar units at other institutions—is also needed. At least two of our site institutions were working on "benchmarking" studies—using data to assess their own performance in comparison with peer institutions. Given the radically individualistic patterns of finance in higher education, we are not convinced that benchmarking is as applicable as it might be, say, in the manufacturing sector, where unit cost really affects competition in the marketplace. But the analytical spirit in which the benchmarking is being done is certainly worth applauding.

Results of information sharing and analytical studies were sometimes unsatisfying because the understanding achieved was incomplete. One CEO, who had been immersed in two institution-wide efforts at strategic planning, expressed considerable frustration about getting people to understand fiscal realities: "The earlier strategic planning process hadn't produced a sufficient sense of reality. . . . The [trustees on the committee] felt we had always 'done more with less' and that this was more of the same. . . . The [committee] was making largely incremental—not really strategic—decisions. I sat in on all the budget hearings and there was a lack of realism about the long-range constraints."

We found this varied sense of reality at all the institutions we visited. Understanding was clearest and most comprehensive at the top of an institution's hierarchy, and became a good deal more tenuous and fragmented closer to the bottom. External people, beginning with trustees, understood in general terms but lacked a feeling for operational detail and the impact of budget cuts on the organization. At a few institutions, students were the most difficult to convince; they simply did not believe that a crisis existed or that budget cuts were necessary. Even after cuts had been made, students expressed skepticism about whether the cuts had really been made or whether the institution was creating the *appearance* of cuts ("smoke and mirrors") to position the administration advantageously before the next budget was published or the next legislative request made or the next tuition increase proposed. The students saw (or perhaps imagined) the political maneuvering involved, and they elected to defend their own bread-and-butter issue: keeping tuition increases down.

Ownership and Commitment

In the battle to achieve consent and momentum for change, our site institutions had tried very hard to promote understanding throughout the campus community. But in no case were they able to saturate the major constituencies with enough information to win them completely. In part, communicating budgetary and financial information in easily understood language is hard to do effectively. When this kind of information is presented in the arcane technical jargon of accounting, it can generate more uncertainty and suspicion than understanding—or, if it is oversimplified, it may be perceived as patronizing and uninformative.

Problems of communication aside, the various constituencies themselves are only marginally aware of the larger organization and its operational intricacies. They lack a context in which to interpret financial information and may not be knowledgeable or experienced enough to reach the same level of understanding and sophistication as, say, a CFO has. They are also not necessarily committed in the sense of feeling they have a permanent stake in the institution's future.

Typically, faculty and students serve fairly short terms on university-level committees and councils. They are also shielded by layers of administration that sometimes intentionally bottle up the flow of information. As one dean said, "I protect faculty as much as possible from all this strategic planning and futures stuff; they have all they can handle with their teaching and research." Trustees and alumni leaders are predominantly volunteers and of necessity concede great latitude for decision making to the professional judgment of administrators. More than anyone else, central administrators can communicate the big picture throughout the campus and keep that picture in focus no matter how often membership on committees turns over.

We found a very uneven sense of ownership and commitment to advancing the health of an institution. We found the most profound commitments at the smaller institutions, where fiscal conditions were truly marginal. At Tusculum College, for example, the faculty had faced up to the prospect of seeing the institution closed and losing their jobs. They clearly understood that the future of the college would depend on whether they individually and collectively played a direct part in saving it. This was largely a result of their extensive involvement in a communal exercise in rethinking and recreating the institution during a period of serious decline. The CFO described the feelings of the faculty during that period this way: "The Tusculum faculty had become extremely alienated from the administration—to the point that the campus was characterized by a culture of mutual hostility. The faculty lost all sense of ownership and all sense of hope."

The new president, alarmed by both the fiscal and human condition of the college, concentrated on several fronts simultaneously—one of which involved returning a sense of ownership to the faculty. He described his approach this way:

> Faculty and staff ownership of the mission is crucial. The campus culture has to be one of collaboration. You can't do this from the top down, and you can't go look at what someone else did or borrow their "package." The faculty have to have control of the process. We have invested a lot in faculty development, training, and recruitment. New faculty are now more often older, experienced people who want to commit themselves to something different. They are more interested in teaching and in investing their time and effort in a place like this [that has a clear set of values and educational goals].

In addition to giving faculty more control over curriculum development, Tusculum has also immersed them in budget-allocation decisions—a move that appears to have greatly advanced faculty's knowledge and understanding, as well as having increased their sense of ownership and responsibility for the college's future.

At the larger and more complex institutions, we think that this sense of commitment and ownership varies from college to college and from department to department. Some units cooperate and work together in figuring out how to adapt. We think it is important for each unit to develop this sense because it is better that larger institutions frame global strategies and leave implementation to the subunits.

Balancing Central Leadership and Communal Involvement

Obviously, not all institutions can operate in the same communal way as can a small institution with twenty-five or thirty faculty. Sometimes it falls to central administrators to develop effective communication and decision-making strategies. Our site institutions differed substantially in how they chose to go about this process, and the differences had very pronounced effects on how their various plans emerged.

One constant factor was common to all of the site institutions: *presidential leadership*. Making allowances for differences in style and in the seriousness and immediacy of fiscal problems, each of the CEOs in our study had been open, forthright, and candid with the campus community. (In a few instances where they had not, the process was at least temporarily impaired and valuable time lost.) The CEOs saw their roles realistically, appreciating the need to educate and to encourage problem solving. This does not mean that the presidents played a passive role; they just carefully mixed the degree to which they challenged and nurtured. In some cases they had very clear ideas of what to fix and how to fix it, while in others they genuinely believed they should broker the best ideas that bubbled up from elsewhere. But none was willing to let matters drift or to admit publicly that the problems could not be solved.

The presidents and chancellors paid great attention to media as well as messages. They put themselves on the line both symbolically and substantively. Communication strategies at all of our site institutions were generally similar. As we noted earlier, the three common steps the institutions took were redefining the situation, sharing financial data, and promoting understanding of the implications. The next step was to identify alternative solutions and to explore the feasibility of these alternatives.

At almost all of the site institutions, the CEOs had issued letters or reports that thoroughly and candidly framed issues they felt had to be faced. They also carried the burden of public relations—dealing with the press, with government, and with donors and partners. They immersed themselves in the flow of information and campus politics—if not directly and personally, then via proxy: a trusted vice president, a director of planning, or another close associate. In some cases presidents chaired campuswide committees or forums in which to consider strategies and plans. They sometimes encouraged others to take this role but stayed in close touch through formal and informal channels.

The CEOs thoroughly understood the strengths and weaknesses of their institutions, and they usually had more-concrete information about those characteristics than any other single actor we interviewed. They could relate program to finance, and finance to planning, and planning to politics. While others might have had depth of knowledge in one specific aspect of an institution's assorted dilemmas, the CEO was usually one of only a few people who were in the position to orchestrate whatever responses the institution might make.

Orchestration then became the toughest part of the CEO's job. The presidents worried about whom to push, what to push, when to push, how hard to push, in what order to push, and which "carrots and sticks" to use when pushing. They also understood that while their institutions were already stressed, there was a very fine line between nurturing the process and waiting too long to make decisions.

There is no "science" involved in weighing how much change is needed versus how much change would simply traumatize and weaken an institution. Also, no particular science is involved in recognizing and seizing opportunities when they appear. In a crisis, though, it is often the CEO who first sees opportunities. Failing to act may result in missing something really important, so timing is an important part of orchestrating strategy.

One institution's CEO, by common agreement among those we interviewed, "wanted a smaller, more focused university." To get there, he started by charging the planning committee with seeking 10 percent cuts from all units and with evaluating proposals to redistribute those cuts. Almost everyone we interviewed at the institution agreed that the target had been too low. A typical assessment included these remarks from a faculty leader: "The process probably didn't go far enough. We had a window of opportunity, but the surgery we performed wasn't major enough. We could have done more reorganization . . . perhaps initiating some mergers or restructuring."

Calibrating the strength of "push" is perceived as balancing between two poles, according to one vice president: "If you think you will be second-guessed by the legislature and trustees, you won't go far enough. But the risk is that people will not want to throw anything out. We are pushing the walls and know we have to operate differently now. This threatens people and creates unease. We can't keep thinking the same old way. . . . We really face hard decisions."

Pushing "hard enough" can be "too hard" in some cases, resulting in low morale and fatigue—"process fatigue" was mentioned several times during our interviews. A steady dose of bad news and the constant pressure to cut expenditures, programs, and people damages the resilience of an institution and the creativity of people at just the time when these qualities are most needed. Comments from one institution's staff advisory committee reflected clearly how the members felt they were being ground down by constant pressure:

> We would like to sustain the "family" culture we've long had, but this might not be possible. We are stretched to the limit. . . . It is tough to have to keep working harder and harder just to stay alive. After a while, you are just fighting fires; the creative juices don't keep flowing. Actually we are stretched beyond our limits. We are always doing more with less. It is harder because we are such a small place. You can see who is getting the money, and this heightens the sense of competition and increases the emotional toll.

This "emotional toll" was most noticeable in cases where the institution did not or could not reach agreement about strategies. We turn next to internal and environmental reasons why such agreement was difficult to achieve.

Consistency of the Environment

The most exasperating problem at our site institutions was the fickle and uncertain policy environment. This made it difficult to frame and define "the problem" and to convey a coherent analysis to the attentive constituencies. About the only truthful message one could send in most cases would be: "Things change; they change quickly and randomly. We don't know what the next change will be because everything relates to everything else in ways we don't understand." Obviously, this is not an effective call to arms.

But shifting realities are a serious problem for institutions that depend on predictability in their environments. For example, two of our site institutions—Bloomfield College, a private institution, and Trenton State College—were located in New Jersey, and both were dependent on stable state policies. In Bloomfield's case, state subsidies for poor urban students played a big role in the college's solvency. With Trenton, state appropriations, the balance of each public college or university's share of the overall appropriation, and the level of tuition charged were—as is normal in public institutions—subject to political decisions. But shortly after our visit to both campuses, New Jersey's new governor abolished the state's department of higher education and set up a new structure for coordinating policy for higher education. She also embarked on an aggressive plan to cut state taxes substantially. Overnight, a totally new equation had to be calculated—with many unknowns.

Similarly, in North Dakota the state commissioner for higher education had departed for a new job shortly before our visit. This left many policies and commitments—both programmatic and budgetary—without their principal champion and with a very uncertain future. The public colleges that had committed to new initiatives were suddenly much less certain about which course to follow—and whether they would ultimately be rewarded or punished for doing so.

At other site institutions, both public and private, a similar litany of policy reversals and inconsistencies brought uncertainty. Public colleges and universities worried about whether they could depend on commitments made by one regime when an election changed the governorship or legislative leaders, or when the head of a state board departed.

In situations like these, "rational" planning was extremely difficult. In fact, to be rational in the face of such a volatile environment may require that leaders not waste too much energy trying to predict and control various factors. Asking people to find and pursue new directions and behavior requires something like a plan. Management theorist Henry Mintzberg has argued that organizations need strategy to "set direction, focus effort, define the organization, and provide consistency" (1987, p. 25). But knowing in what direction to head, defining themselves in clear terms, and achieving consistency are tasks that assume that leaders have enough knowledge, that people involved trust one another to behave predictably, and that rational choices will actually result in some degree of control over the future. In many of our cases, these conditions simply did not exist.

There is a considerable body of experience and theory that suggests how to cope with great uncertainty. We will return to this issue in Chapter Nine, where we offer suggestions for an idea called *simultaneous tracking* that we introduce later in this chapter. In general, we believe that rational strategy—like "vision"—is an overworked concept: both ideas can mislead people into grasping for a solution that is too "rational."

However, we believe that strategies or plans are important as *one part* of a constructive response to crisis. On one hand, some mix of strategy, opportunism, and continuous adjustment to turbulence—if guided by an enlightened consensus among key stakeholders—is the most likely path to realistic change. On the other hand, to face a turbulent environment without a clear sense of identity, values, direction, and commitment is genuinely risky.

Internal Communication

The external situation is only one problem, however. Internally, colleges and universities are composed of easily mobilized and vocal people. Achieving the working consensus to which we referred depends on how people bring these assorted voices into some kind of harmony. Among our site institutions, there was no single, simple solution.

We found that without a structured and consistent message, a kind of free-floating opportunism reigned. In one institution, this drew complaints about the "innovation of the week" approach to crisis. So great was the need to establish an appearance of action and progress that even relatively trivial victories were recognized as steps forward. The risk, of course, is that an institution that is too laissez-faire about experimenting may well waste scarce resources on a lottery of both good and bad ideas. Some will hit and some will miss, and too many misses waste valuable time and money. It is easy to see how scattered activity contributes to fatigue and lowered morale.

We should add that such scattering was occurring at one institution *notwithstanding the efforts of central administrators to focus*. A senior faculty member suggested that communication was a problem: "Rumors, miscommunication, misunderstanding, and conflict have blown efforts to make strategic change work." Variants on the same theme emerged elsewhere. An especially perceptive junior faculty member at another institution was asked how he thought the planning process had come to enjoy as much support as it appeared to. He replied: "Plan strategically. *Talk* about how the plan is developing. *Be honest* about what is being done and what is not being done, about what is working and what is not working. The good thing here is that the administration listens, consults, facilitates, and solicits feedback. Communications are open both laterally and vertically in the organization. It is also important to keep lines of communication open across divisions" (emphasis supplied).

While open and honest communication may go a long way toward moving all the actors toward a common understanding and a clearer focus, it is perhaps equally true that it can simply lead to more conflict. Citing anxiety and "negative anticipation" about what might result from a strategic planning process, a dean pointed out that a great deal of "political back-pressure" had been generated at his institution as rumors emerged.

This particular episode illustrates our point rather well. The strategic planning committee tried to be extraordinarily open by holding hearings in various venues on campus, and by encouraging as much input as the schedule would tolerate. However, the committee's substantive deliberations and decision-making proceedings were closed. So although extensive communications and exemplary openness succeeded in getting a wide array of ideas on the table, they did not succeed in framing a clear direction or getting people to focus.

In this case, one reason for so much uncertainty was a wide misunderstanding about what "on the table" really meant. For some it meant that ideas had been accepted by the committee; for others it meant that the ideas were merely on a longer agenda of things to be debated. The committee had not succeeded in gaining broad understanding about the ground rules for its proceedings—and thus sowed more confusion than closure.

This case illustrates why process alone is too neutral. If the process results in a clear sense of direction—the development of clear markers by which to gauge progress and closure—and if it helps participants understand the context of the problem they are trying to solve, it can produce useful results.

Conflict: The Shape of the Field

We observed a fairly regular sequence of events among institutions that were facing up to their fiscal problems. They were able to:

- Develop forums in which ideas could be explored
- Realistically assess their market and their role
- Consider the needs of their clienteles and communities
- Develop and nurture creative program ideas
- Open themselves to partnerships, external support, and involvement of students and other stakeholders

The process had a galvanizing effect on people, but it also brought further conflict over the value of tradition and past experience, "ownership," and the process itself: who decides, how much is enough, and how quickly should change be introduced?

Breaking with the Past

Coming out of an era of comparative comfort, our site institutions seemed psychologically unprepared to deal with the new financial crunch. To a varied extent, people were in denial about the realities that faced their institutions and about the implications of those realities.

On one level, this was simply a matter of vested interest, as one might readily expect. As one faculty member said, "There is lots of tradition here and we are slow to change." A vice president specifically mentioned "turf problems" as the root of resistance to change at her institution.

But serious political and public relations problems come up when an institution tries to make a candid assessment of its own strengths and weaknesses: "Assessing what is good and what isn't is hard to do, especially for unit heads who try to be really candid. If they confess to weaknesses, they may take a hit." Such assessments were especially hard, as pointed out by a senior dean at an institution that was about to embark on a capital campaign: "If you are open, though, you have to also avoid giving the perception that the ship is sinking; we are about to embark on a [large capital] campaign, and you don't want potential givers scared away with the notion that all they are doing is filling a sinkhole." A faculty leader at the same institution said that too much publicity can also affect the recruiting base: "Going public with information about finances . . . is risky. Prospective students and their parents may interpret this as a weakness."

However, setting the agenda and moving realistically toward solutions requires honesty, clarity, and authenticity in framing the message. As one senior planner said: "How you define your crisis makes a big difference. Be sure you get your questions framed in the right way at the start. It makes a big practical and political difference. You can't stand political heat unless you have a real crisis."

Faculty Responsiveness

Obviously, colleges and universities cannot change unless faculty are motivated and have incentives to change. When they clearly appreciated the severity of the problems their institutions faced, faculty at our site institutions responded well. But without a perspective on the overall situation, faculty sometimes got caught up in an effort to stall or defeat proposals for change, in the guise of debates about faculty autonomy or academic freedom.

Faculty sometimes make vigorous and vocal arguments that colleges and universities exist to advance the disciplines and/or professions to which faculty have devoted their lives. The consumers of higher education—students, parents, employers—make competing claims and demands. These conflicts are sometimes waged over ideology, sometimes over programs, and sometimes over money.

Ironically, the conflicts seemed more intense at site institutions with more resources, and less intense at those institutions facing serious threats to survival *and* whose leaders had begun to deal with the threat in a way that allowed the assorted claimants a place at the table. Working out these conflicts involved a surpassing measure of patience and endurance; but once the stakes had become clear, the players could see the overriding common interest and move forward.

At an institution that had succeeded in turning around a grim fiscal situation, we asked what the most important variable had been in achieving the changes. A group of faculty leaders agreed that the factor was the depth and seriousness of the crisis they had faced: it was so severe that the faculty knew radical changes had to be made. This reality forced them to face the issue of their common survival. Conversely, a sense of crisis at other institutions—albeit one at a less severe pitch—might have led instead to open conflict and competition.

Process

Sometimes people perceived that the decision process had simply gone too fast and too far. For them, a kind of "last stand" approach was the only logical tactic. In a few cases, this meant formal or informal expressions of no confidence in administrators, while in others it meant seeking support from alumni or legislators in a campaign to save programs. Rallies and protests were held to call attention to issues and gain support for causes.

In another set of cases, the resistance to change was less public but no less firm. In instances in which the process seemed timid or what we might call "negotiably incremental," we found that positions had hardened and that movement was slow at best. One result was that people learned not to agree—at least not as a first response. As a chief academic officer at one institution noted: "We have generally held academic programs harmless, and this may have made it harder to change. The only time faculty faced up to the possibility of change was when the [planning] process led to rumors about cutting tenured faculty. So planning here has been generally at the cosmetic level, and [it] has been crisis oriented."

By attempting to hold cuts largely to administrative and support services, this institution had essentially conditioned its faculty to dig in their heels whenever a threat was rumored. A little resistance went a long way, and administrators then felt that more substantial and painful cuts would have to be made on the academic side than might have been the case if a more balanced and forceful approach had been taken from the beginning.

Dysfunctional resistance to change was one of the main byproducts of too much pressure for change on one hand, and too little pressure on the other. Dysfunctional resistance occurred when people felt that they had to raise barriers to protect themselves and their programs. But they also raised barriers when they had learned not to expect that crises would touch either them or their programs, and that all they had to do was resist change.

Open/Closed

Behavior was also affected by whether the change process was perceived as open (participatory) or closed. Among our site institutions, a process that was perceived as too closed engendered paranoia—and in one case, even open resistance. Although extensive open hearings were held during the planning process at this institution, the committee that held decision-making powers worked in closed sessions. Participants were not always clear about what the committee members were thinking, perhaps especially as the open hearings generated questions and impressions about which alternatives were actually being considered. One close observer thought that the process was partially self-defeating: "It was an open process with lots of input. Maybe it was too ad hoc at the beginning. Colleges might have needed more time to think through what they were doing and how. If anything, I would open the process up more. We did take lots of political flak, whether threats to specific programs were real or not. Some things were saved because the political heat was turned up too high." In this case, the political temperature went up when the committee began its own deliberations.

Processes that were too open, conversely, stimulated a chaotic and frenzied level of activity. A member of a faculty committee involved in planning at one site institution offered several observations about why its process had not reached closure:

> Right now, there are many groups all simultaneously throwing balls into the air to see if they can get them on the "list." But ideas change as they are considered by different groups. What starts out as someone's good idea gets "translated" as it moves from committee to committee—sort of like a shaggy-dog story! It is unrecognizable eventually. Great ideas are being floated, but it is not clear how they are going to get developed and implemented. The process needs to legitimize them, accept them, and find the money to implement them. Otherwise, the ideas and the enthusiasm behind them go away and the people behind them get deconditioned to proposing things—because there is no reward for doing so.

Conflict is inevitable in making change. But it seems to be exacerbated—and acted out—where change is either too forced or too restrained, or where the process is either too open or too closed. As we said earlier in this chapter, decisions are entangled in process. The process itself determines to some extent which solutions to fiscal stress an institution can realistically consider. If it pushes hard and moves quickly, it risks open conflict and resistance. If it fails to move quickly or assertively enough, it will almost certainly foster a culture of delay and evasion from within and allow external events to control its fiscal condition from without.

Avoiding Entanglement: The Simultaneous-Tracking Alternative

At some site institutions, we observed a kind of forward motion that attacked a number of issues and problems simultaneously and seemed to solve the "fast/slow" dilemma in promising ways. We have come to think of this approach as *simultaneous tracking*. It is a way of dealing with separate components of a problem *nonsequentially*, *nonhierarchically*, and in a *nonlinear* way.

None of the institutions we visited had consciously adopted this way of dealing with their fiscal stress. Some simply had so many problems that they had to fight crises on several fronts at once. Others recognized, more or less intuitively, that the different pieces of their fiscal problems could be addressed simultaneously and that the connections among these pieces were not necessarily tight.

Two old ideas support the simultaneous-tracking approach. Bowen and Douglass (1971) showed that there were no clearly superior efficiencies to any given arrangement of curriculum and instruction; outcomes and efficiencies were basically acceptable across a rather broad range of alternatives. So, they wrote, funding and programs may not need to be tightly related; decisions about one can be made without serious consequences for the other.

The other important idea comes from several sources. Karl Weick (1976, p. 3) is often credited with introducing the idea that colleges and universities are "loosely coupled" systems—that there is no necessarily unifying logic to the way they behave. The parts of a loosely coupled system act with relative independence of one another, and their independent ability to adapt strengthens the overall health of the institution. Earlier, Cohen and March (1974, p. 2) used a slightly different label, calling colleges and universities "organized anarchies"—a term that has not been especially popular for obvious reasons.

Whatever the label, the idea is that what happens in one part of a college or university may not be very tightly linked to what happens in another part. The idea of loose coupling, however, suggests that relatively autonomous subunits can and do develop good solutions to their own problems. If those solutions are guided by an overall sense of the institution's direction, the organization as a whole can solve its big problems by allowing each subunit to work on little problems. Leadership in this kind of organization requires continuous reinforcement of the overall direction, provision of information and feedback, and support for the subunits that are making progress. The slogan "Think globally, act locally" captures this idea.

By any objective measure, the problems that our site institutions faced were of radically different urgency that had nonparallel solutions. Some things (such as fundraising) could be done fairly quickly and in a rational sequence, but others—downsizing a department, for example—could not.

Here is a quick example of rational planning's shortcomings. Suppose that an institution took a year to plan a new approach to undergraduate education so it could occupy a new market niche. This niche would yield a steadier flow of tuition-paying students, and it might attract philanthropic support as well. But if the institution then laid out a plan to design and implement the program, market it, and raise new funds to support it—and if these things were to happen in that order—the institution would probably die before it could implement all the pieces of the plan.

We were very impressed with a few cases in which an institution—partly out of desperation—simply tried to solve a number of problems at once. We stress that this did not happen by design; it was just a pragmatic way of moving ahead in the face of problems that demanded immediate action. As long as the process had been kick-started by the institution's leaders—and as long as it was informed by a clear sense of context and of the problems being addressed—it seemed to be an approach that avoided the worst effects of inaction or top-heavy (and slow-moving) efforts to bring everyone together on one grand strategy.

One institution in particular struck us as an interesting example. It had major problems in five key areas that needed to be addressed. First, it had spent down its endowment and experienced frequent turnover in its fundraising staff; it needed to stabilize its development operation and work toward a major improvement in annual giving; and it had to rebuild its endowment through a capital campaign. Second, the institution had experienced declining enrollment—in part because no effective recruiting strategy existed and in part because of admissions staff turnover. Third, the institution's financial accounting was chaotic. Fourth, the physical plant was in disrepair. And fifth, it had no coherent academic program or philosophy.

While there are obvious and real connections among all of these problems, the institution's survival required that at least the first four be solved *simultaneously*, not sequentially. As it turned out, by the time of our site visit substantial progress had been made on each of the issues. Perhaps the most interesting result was that as each subunit of the institution worked toward its own goals, it expanded its capacity to help and support the other parts. Without taking the time to design and implement one central strategic plan, the whole institution had become stronger.

But this was a small institution with a serious crisis, and everyone involved clearly understood how important it was to move ahead quickly and effectively. This level of cooperation might not have been as easy to establish at a larger institution that wasn't facing a serious threat to survival.

Certainly there was coordination and leadership on the part of this institution's president and other central administrators. But it was the kind of leadership that fostered communication and cooperation rather than the kind that directs and controls. At a different institution, a more directive kind of leadership might be necessary.

In either type of situation, as one system-level administrator said, "You have to have a vision, but the actual innovations have to grow at the local level." Those who were simultaneously tracking had simply started working on each unit's problems before and during the period when a consensus about "vision" was emerging.

Simultaneous tracking places responsibility with each subunit for its own success. Assuming there is a generally understood direction and real discipline among the subunits, we think the simultaneous-tracking approach involves less of the rather substantial "overhead" that is measured in lost time and resources when institutions wait to act on problems before they first try to produce a strategic plan.

We do acknowledge that letting each unit go its own way can be overdone. We are not advocating anarchy and dismissing the need to plan! In fact, each of the subunits in the case we have been discussing worked very hard to develop its own plans. And the institution had *reached a very clear consensus on certain basic values and program directions*. But we think that an institution can become too entangled in one overarching effort to produce a unified strategic plan. When it attempts to do so, it entangles itself in a range of new issues and problems that act to slow down the decision-making process. The system simply has to start solving a host of dilemmas that arise when strategic planning adds another layer of procedure and conflict to an already very complex organization.

Simultaneous tracking does not happen of its own accord, nor does it produce change by some kind of magic. It is a learned process. Even those institutions that were experimenting with simultaneous tracking clearly had much to learn, and the whole process was subject to serious errors. But serious errors committed at the unit level can be absorbed and corrected, whereas the same errors at the institutional level may be fatal.

Most of the institutions in our study had faced their fiscal crises as unique and threatening events. In some cases, they had short memories and short horizons. We saw that there was real danger in assuming that "strategy" involved ensuring that an institution survived one episode of fiscal stress. One senior administrator noted that a continuous process of questioning and monitoring would keep the institution from accruing liabilities between crises: "We need something like a five-year sunset provision for all programs to be sure we . . . are investing in things that add value."

The people we interviewed at the site institutions also tended to assume that their problems were unique, that other institutions could not possibly be facing such an exasperating and humiliating experience. So they were often surprised when we were able to tell them about how similar their experiences actually were to those of others. In fact, if this book accomplishes nothing else, we hope that it will convince trustees, administrators, and faculty alike that they should learn from others' experiences. Perhaps it is a case of misery loving company. But if there were more candor and openness about the real problems facing institutions, people could avoid making mistakes that others have learned from. To this end, we urge that national organizations provide forums in which such open sharing can be done in a nonjudgmental setting.

The CEO and Simultaneous Tracking

Chief executive officers of institutions may at first view simultaneous tracking as a distressingly sloppy way to solve critical problems, but they should give the process a chance. Among other things, simultaneous tracking allows great discretion at lower levels in the organization (this is also true of the total quality management process). It assumes that deans, directors, and department heads will understand the overall picture and can put aside their self-interests. It also creates problems in coordinating the flow of information and communication, in monitoring the pace and adequacy of change, in constructing a coherent public relations strategy, and in controlling costs. It may, in fact, not be a workable method for situations in which an institution's leaders must direct immediate action in an emergency (for example, when state appropriations are rescinded during the budget year).

We will return to the idea of simultaneous tracking and continuous attention to quality when we make recommendations in Chapter Nine. We also want to call the reader's attention to the qualities of what we call the "resilient" institution. To us, such qualities seem to invite the best uses of simultaneous tracking in a crisis. Resilient institutions develop clear values, programs that add value to students, and measures of progress toward achievement of outcomes. Given that such overall directions are clear, subunits in resilient institutions can operate more freely but, paradoxically, in more-purposeful ways.

Conclusion

We wanted to look at how crisis affected decision making and at how decision making affected the way that site institutions tried to get through fiscal crises. We found, basically, that crisis put powerful pressure on the institutions to centralize their decision-making processes. But we also found that a more centralized decision making process did not necessarily produce better decisions or acceptance of those decisions by stakeholders.

Some of our site institutions—in a few cases out of sheer desperation—elected to start fixing problems and initiating change *before* they had formulated an overall plan or strategy. These institutions were simultaneously tracking—accepting the loosely coupled nature of their organization and giving each unit its own opportunity to work out adaptations and solutions. Simultaneous tracking seemed to multiply good solutions and build capacity in a quicker and nimbler way than the more heavy-handed approaches to centralized strategic planning.

Within the boundaries of an overall vision for the institution, and with a minimum level of discipline among subunits, we find much to recommend in an approach in which units are given the opportunity to work separately but simultaneously toward their own solutions.

Chapter Six

Teaching and Learning in a New Era

By far the largest portion of money spent on higher education provides for teaching and learning. When money is tight, colleges and universities inevitably think seriously about how well and how efficiently they are educating students. The institutions we visited were addressing these questions, and they were coming up with interesting experiments in new ways to be both more efficient and more effective.

We have organized this chapter around three basic questions:

1. In what ways are fiscal pressures motivating changes in teaching and learning?

2. What kinds of changes in teaching and learning have emerged at colleges and universities adapting to stress?

3. What effects are these changes having on people and programs?

We conclude the chapter with a look at four institutions that have initiated major changes in their philosophy and curriculum.

The core business of higher education is now—and has always been—undergraduate education. Notwithstanding the intense focus on the production and application of knowledge over the past few decades, the foundation for society's support of colleges and universities lies in a social contract. That contract requires that students and their families make considerable economic and psychic sacrifices and that colleges and universities provide a powerful and effective environment in which young people can come of age intellectually, morally, emotionally, psychologically, and vocationally. While it is assumed that this means that teachers will teach and students will learn, history suggests that there is a good deal more to the relationship—and that the expectations of both sides have transmogrified with each successive generation.

The teacher-student relationship is clearly colored by the high expectations and substantial investment of students, their families, and the public. "College" is widely perceived as the essential rite of passage into the middle (or upper) class, into economic security, and into adult roles. Increasingly, the college experience has come to determine a young person's life trajectory. This has become especially so as opportunities to attend college have opened up to those who once found the doors to education closed.

The relationship may not be as direct or clear as is generally believed. For example, Geiger pointed out in 1980 that "the traditional relationship between a bachelor's degree and the preferred occupational slots in the nation's labor markets [has] weakened or collapsed in numerous fields" (p. 16). But Grubb's (1992) study of 1,972 high school graduates confirms that over the long term there are very substantial returns on the investment in college, especially in certain fields. Recent studies are also showing a comparative advantage of an associate degree in high-demand technical fields.

Our study brought to the surface a realization that fiscal stress is testing this social contract and producing both impetus for change and wrenching pressures on how institutions conduct undergraduate education. We found some clear markers in the process of change, and we suggest that three basic trends are now in motion:

- Uncertainty about the "payoff" of a four-year undergraduate degree is increasing—especially as the tuition burden increases.
- There is increasing diversity among institutions in the content and process of undergraduate education.

- New models of outcome-oriented education are emerging and may redefine what "quality" means.

Richer and Poorer: Unequal Pressure for Change

The institutions we visited occupied vastly different niches in the larger academic marketplace. Some were tiny, poor, and fearful. Others were large, comparatively wealthy, and fearful. All were under serious pressure to attend to the quality of undergraduate education, but the source and nature of the pressure varied. Among the smaller institutions, it came from real concern about survival. Among the larger institutions, especially those in the public sector, the concern came from the perception of eroding confidence and interest on the part of business leaders and policy makers.

In all cases, however, the institutions' leaders felt that the legitimacy of their role and the reliability of their market appeal were threatened. They sensed that the public was not as supportive as it had once been, that more questions were being asked about the merit and value of a college education, and that answering those questions would require more-substantive proof of "effectiveness" than most institutions could provide.

Pressure was being put on the site institutions to assess outcomes and to prove that tuition and state appropriations were being responsibly invested in programs that produced results. The smaller institutions operating with a thinner resource base very clearly recognized that their financial health depended on retaining tuition-paying students from admission to graduation. This, it was obvious, would require an increased level of attention to the quality of the undergraduate experience, as well as its worth or value to graduates.

"What constitutes a viable, effective, and legitimate undergraduate education?" was the most current and urgent question our site institutions were asking themselves—and there was a marked convergence in their answers to this question. They chose different ways to redefine their programs.

The "Worth" of a College Degree

No serious question exists about the general economic value of a college degree (see Breneman, 1994, for example). But there is considerable anxiety among both public and private institutions about *which* institution's and field's degrees may be worth more than another's. Institutions appear to be scrambling (in their various ways) to differentiate their identities and thereby create competitive niches for themselves. Grubb (1992) has noted that the economic payback of attending one institution as opposed to another is not as great as might be expected. But at some institutions in our study, we sensed a great uneasiness about these issues:

- Are private colleges really worth the much higher tuitions they charge?
- Will any institutions be able to maintain quality in the face of eroding state and federal support?
- How can real access to college be maintained in an era of shrinking support and with the changing nature and preparation of nontraditional students?

The institutions we visited fundamentally served local and regional markets with unique social, demographic, cultural, political, economic, and educational profiles. A public institution in rural North Dakota, for example, must deal with a radically different clientele and context than a private college in urban New Jersey—even though the two institutions may be similar in size, and even though their programs may not differ greatly in form and structure. Similarly, issues facing research universities do not arise in community colleges.

So the "industry" of higher education is naturally segmented into geographical and functional strata. However, with the rise of more-universal norms and standards (see Jencks and Riesman, 1968), these fundamental differences seem to be masked by similarities in form. To an extent we cannot estimate, some real convergences in substance have also marked the last two decades. Institutions intent on mainstreaming their programs and identities have simply followed educational fads, trends, and fashions. But it has become obvious to us that an approach might make sense at Harvard or Stanford precisely because it addresses the needs, abilities, and interests of the unique (and elite) clienteles at those institutions.

The rhetoric of an institution in trouble reflects a basic ambivalence. On one hand, it wants to show all prospective students that it is au courant by mimicking the forms and appearances of the elite institutions. On the other hand, it wants to signal that it is both safe and a good value for its "real" clientele. For the vast majority of institutions, that real clientele is a broad swath of humanity—the middle class that sells real estate, brokers soybeans, staffs government agencies, teaches, nurses, and consumes. And this clientele largely expects a conventional, useful, and fungible set of credentials in return for the tuition it pays and the effort that students make.

The surveys of college freshmen conducted annually by the Higher Education Research Institute at the University of California at Los Angeles show that in recent years the most salient reason for deciding to go to college has been "to be able to get a better job" (82.7 percent, 75.4 percent, 78.3 percent, 78.6 percent, and 78.5 percent in the most recent five-year period); a close second was "to be able to make more money" (76.5 percent, 75.6 percent, 73.2 percent, 74.7 percent, and 73.3 percent over the same period) (Astin, 1989, 1990, 1991, 1992, and 1993a). These motives are remarkably stable: getting a better job was also the top motive among entering freshmen in 1982 (77.9 percent). The 1989 study of faculty by the Carnegie Foundation for the Advancement of Teaching confirms this orientation: 84 percent of faculty agreed that "undergraduates have become more careerist in their concerns" (p. 12).

The views of faculty seem dramatically at odds with the motives of students and with the desires and values of those who provide political and financial support for colleges and universities. A majority of faculty (56 percent) responding to the 1989 Carnegie Foundation survey agreed that "undergraduate education . . . would be improved if there were less emphasis on specialized training and more on broad liberal education" (p. 2). Two-year colleges aside, fewer than 25 percent of faculty think that preparing students for careers is very important (p. 11).

These national data were largely replicated in our interviews, although we do recognize substantial variation both among and within institutions. The trap into which institutions fall, and that most of our interviewees recognized, is that the institutions have been able to survive because they have sufficient demand on one hand and sufficient resources on the other. Few have actively considered how to achieve vocational preparation in the liberal arts setting, or how to achieve the ends of liberal education in vocational programs, although good ideas are readily available (see Stark and Lowther, 1989).

One dean recognized that the "value" calculation that students make was critical to the institution's survival: "Our goal is to make 'value' the target. We should be selecting good kids and satisfying them. We have to build satisfaction with [the] education [we offer]. It is probably not worth the $100,000 investment [if we] do nothing for them. We have to ratchet up on quality—both in admission and [in] the education we provide. We are evolving on quality. We have to start working on student-centeredness, focusing on caring and responsiveness."

The faculty at this institution were in some cases oriented to a totally different concept of education, and they expressed opposition to the idea of student-centered reforms. In their comments to us, they talked disparagingly of "glorified high school" models of education. The dean recognized that faculty were going to have to change in fundamental ways: "Doing research on the backs of tuition-paying undergraduates isn't going to hold up over time. Students are more than customers."

We should add, though, that this institution is recognized as a leader in using Ernest Boyer's ideas about a broadened definition of "scholarship" (1989). It has, among other things, developed a new model for socializing graduate students to understand that faculty are expected to teach well while also advancing knowledge through research in their disciplines. Using Boyer's "scholarship of teaching" and "scholarship of application" ideas, the graduate students are participating in a national project to design and test a model program for a new generation of faculty more oriented to teaching and to the institution.

All of our site institutions were trying to refocus faculty attention on how to teach undergraduates effectively. At one level, they understood that their viability required them to return value to students. At another level, it was just as clear that faculty culture would resist both the demand for institutional loyalty and the idea that education should be centered on students rather than knowledge.

Three recent research efforts confirm that changing faculty's orientation to education is difficult. Lattuca and Stark (1994) explored the intellectual and substantive divisions among faculty; they point out that the structure of different academic fields makes cross-disciplinary conversation about things like curriculum difficult, although we found interesting examples of such conversations (and new program initiatives) at a few of our site institutions. Pure-science disciplines, according to Lattuca and Stark, are just organized differently from fields such as social sciences. Massy, Wilger, and Colbeck (1994) confirm the isolation of faculty from one another by a number of critical barriers—specialization, politics, generations, and so on. They point out that the effects of limited resources and a reward system that emphasizes research at the expense of teaching serve to harden these divisions and make it more difficult for faculty to agree or cooperate among themselves.

Burton Clark's seminal work on "the academic profession" (1987) showed that disciplinary loyalty is more influential than institutional loyalty on faculty ideas about the goals of education.

Notwithstanding that such divisions exist among faculty, a basic and serious dilemma lies in the degree to which faculty have been socialized and conditioned to put the highest value on competitive excellence. For example, we heard variants of this comment at several institutions: "Search committees tend to look for traditional sorts of things." The comment was offered to describe the control that faculty exercise over the selection and appointments of new recruits, as well as the selection of new department heads and deans.

The academic value system appears remarkably resistant to change, whether due to self-perpetuation in the selection process or for other reasons. When faculty are so committed to knowledge-centeredness and to universal norms of competitive excellence, they vigorously resist efforts to differentiate their institution from others, especially when it might mean becoming too student centered. So perhaps open competition has actually helped to make institutions less different from one another, because faculty think it is important to be mainly knowledge-centered and to use other knowledge-centered institutions with similar definitions of excellence as their benchmarks.

It seems to us that these points at least partially explain how institutions get into the bind of trying to emulate "better" institutions by doing more research and rewarding students who are more likely to go to the "right" graduate schools. Both kinds of behavior put strains on the fiscal health of an institution—either by overextension or by diversion of faculty effort to activity that does not add value directly to tuition-driven undergraduate education.

In other words, we can see that a major difference in value systems is driving a wedge between what colleges and universities do and what consumers and supporters want. The responses of the most stressed institutions are instructive. The first step, they pointed out, is to be utterly candid about students. They could report that

"77 percent have to take developmental courses," or "we don't get the straight-A students," or "our population base is eroding and we will see many more nontraditional students in the future." Recognizing who their students are and what they need has led to serious soul-searching and analysis of program goals.

We think a substantial advantage will go to institutions that take this more realistic view. They can more clearly identify a market for the education they offer. The population these institutions serve will be more responsive to the value returned on the tuition it pays. And by focusing faculty effort more fully on activities that do add value to students, the institutions will enjoy an efficiency advantage over institutions that have not reined in the diversion of faculty effort to research and other nonteaching activities.

We appreciate the idea that teaching and research go together and form "joint products." But we are mindful of the serious consequences of "output creep." Most faculty simply do not do enough research to support the argument that this should be their primary activity. Indeed, new data from a national survey of faculty show that 86.5 percent have published ten or fewer articles in refereed journals over their full careers, and 58.7 percent have published none at all (Zimbler, 1994).

In the same survey, only 25 percent of faculty said that opportunity for more research would be a factor in looking for a new job. Half of all faculty teach at least 60 percent of the time, and half spend less than 5 percent of their time on research. So we think that there is a much greater potential return on *how faculty use the time they teach* than on how they use their time to do research. If we were to suggest where to invest surplus funds, it would be in developing faculty skills to enrich the educational experience of undergraduate students, and not in releasing more time for research.

Student-Centered Programs

The institutions that have broken from the pack chose to define themselves in terms of what they do for their students—and they

have very specific programs to do it. They have also embraced outcome assessment as a way of monitoring their own performance and
of accounting to students and the public. Among our site institutions, the most dramatic cases involved turning from faculty- or
knowledge-centered values to those oriented toward students, outcomes, or processes. Each of the cases involved a unique, self-
defining idea and acts of singular courage and persistence—often in
the face of odds that, if rationally analyzed, might have argued
against going ahead. While each case constitutes an experiment with
$n = 1$, and while the "data" are still coming in, these cases are important for what they show about shifting the focus to the student and
to outcomes of the student experience. This is where we think that
institutions in stress see the route to survival. It is now virtually a
cliché to say that "focusing on the customer" is the most important
thing, but this is an inescapable lesson in the cases we observed.

Trenton State College

We briefly discussed Trenton State's transformation in an earlier
chapter. But the example is worth looking at more deeply for what
it shows about how to change an institution by starting from the
bottom and from the outside—rather than from the top and from
the inside.

Trenton State College (TSC) had 11,000 students in 1977.
Facing looming downturns in public funding and student demographics, its leaders made a strategic decision to become a smaller,
more academically demanding institution. They cut enrollment to
7,000, focused on recruiting and selecting students with care, and
transformed TSC from a commuter school into a principally residential campus. Its entering students now have among the highest SAT scores (averaging about 1100) of New Jersey state colleges,
and the school has been able to level a surcharge on tuition for the
last few years.

The TSC strategy was formed by agreement among top-level

administrators and had the approval of the board chair and state political leaders. The president personally began hosting an annual event for high school counselors, conveying a simple message: "Come to our campus and see why we think you should send us your best students." The college set aside funds for merit scholarships that were awarded to students that scored 1200 on their SATs and were in the top 10 percent of their high school class. At the same time, TSC began a long-term program to create a "pedestrian-friendly" residential campus with a centrally located student center, residence halls, recreation facilities, and attractive academic buildings and landscaping.

A third part of TSC's strategy focused on creating high expectations and a set of clear campus values for entering freshmen. The school holds a convocation, for example, at which the president speaks about values and traditions and tells students why Trenton State College is "a special place." The convocation is followed by a mass walk across campus and a candlelight ceremony at the campus lake. This ritual welcome into the TSC family is designed to generate a shared ethos among new students. The president also systematically addresses ten smaller groups of entering freshmen and their parents. He tells the students to take responsibility for their own education and for making the school a better place, emphasizing that TSC has high expectations for itself and for them.

Trenton State College follows up with a concentrated effort to develop among students a series of shared experiences and a sense of community. Virtually all students (96 percent) live on campus for the first two years, and transfer students go through a student government orientation that is peer to peer and student to student in nature. The staff of the dean of student affairs have worked hard to generate a sense of a single student community in the residential context, rather than the fragmented subgroups that tend to characterize a commuter school. The staff find ways to get students involved and to provide services that pull students together. Activities, for example, are built around the student residences, and the dean reports that he thinks about his work in terms of "student community development," rather than of individual students. He stresses the need to keep students active and involved through leadership roles.

Students are also required to engage in community service activities and in multicultural and life-skills experiences. The staff believe that such involvement and active learning inside and outside the classroom create a strong student culture, lead to learning, and give students a stake in improving their school.

In effect, Trenton State College simply stopped admitting the bottom half of its applicant pool and concentrated on developing the kind of campus and student life that would be highly attractive to "achievers." Students themselves now carry a strong set of values and are—by common agreement—the college's best recruiters, passing on the word to prospective applicants. The retention rate was reported to us to be over 95 percent in recent years.

The sequence of change at TSC began, interestingly enough, with recruitment of certain kinds of students. Their interests drove later changes in academic and extracurricular programs. The steps in the process were as follows:

- Recruit the best students.
- Develop the student experience with close-to-the-ground, hands-on involvement of the president and other key administrators.
- Improve the campus infrastructure.
- Attract faculty with an interest in undergraduate education.
- Reform the curriculum to emphasize involvement and active learning.

Recognizing the central role of faculty, TSC's academic vice president noted that faculty are selected "with extreme care" and that reappointment and tenure decisions are made with similarly exacting attention to performance. Faculty's teaching performance receives the highest priority in all faculty personnel decisions, and prospective faculty are asked to teach a real class while being observed by the search committee. New faculty are mentored, evaluated by peers, and oriented to good teaching practice during retreats. We were told that TSC's promotion and tenure committee looks "meticulously" at all student course evaluations.

There is a general consensus among TSC's administrators that students with high expectations have pushed the rest of the college to respond. As one administrator said: "An institution that expects a lot from its students has to give them a lot, too. Everyone has to meet high expectations—from the secretaries who see students every day all the way up the ladder. The whole act has to hold together."

One of the central elements of this story is Trenton State College's refocusing on undergraduate education. It has essentially dropped its programs for graduate students, community service, and continuing education. This move has not been politically popular, and it has put TSC at some risk in its relations with the community and with state government leaders. However, it has allowed the entire institution to focus on doing one thing well.

We do not wish to imply that TSC accomplished all this change without significant conflict or friction. The school has faced disruptive controversies—over, for example, a faculty housing program, over relations between the faculty union and the administration, and over the role of TSC as a public (as opposed to quasi-private) institution. Faculty leaders told us that they felt that much of the change had been accomplished without their substantive involvement.

All we wish to illustrate with this summary is the extent to which one institution focused totally on its undergraduates by investing in the quality of the student experience. The measures of change on this one campus are striking.

Tusculum College

A small, independent school in Greeneville, Tennessee, Tusculum College was founded in 1794—the first institution of higher education west of the Appalachian Mountains. Between 1816 and 1818 Samuel Doak, a protégé of John Witherspoon (then president of Princeton), used Witherspoon's ideas about education to found Tusculum Academy. (*Tusculum* was originally the site of Cicero's academy in Roman times, and the college's focus on "civic arts" actually has its roots in Cicero's ideas).

The current president of Tusculum College arrived in 1989, and found an institution in serious distress. It had only 230 regular-session students, low morale, and a history of recent conflict between the faculty and the former president. Under the new president's leadership, the Tusculum faculty developed an outcome-based curriculum. They identified 15 competencies that would reflect the "civic virtues" as outlined by Cicero. Students would live and study in a community in which everyone shared the pursuit of civic virtue, and graduation would require that each student complete an assessment to confirm achievement of the competencies.

At the same time, Tusculum adopted an innovative calendar similar to one originally developed at Colorado College: students take one course at a time, concentrating for a month on that course. This has allowed great flexibility in teaching. For example, one course on the New England transcendentalists was taught in Boston, while another was taught in Costa Rica. The new calendar has forced faculty to replace lecturing with new and more effective ways to get students to become active learners and has been helpful in attracting student interest. Three core courses—largely interdisciplinary—are required in each year. The junior-year core courses, for example, include "Athens," which tracks perennial problems in republican self-government; "Jerusalem," which juxtaposes religious beliefs with contemporary problems; and "The American Experience." During the senior year, each student undertakes an independent community-service project under faculty supervision, and also completes a "Seminar in Practical Wisdom."

Tusculum's clearly framed and distinctive program has galvanized the faculty and has successfully attracted the interest of students and parents. The president noted that Tusculum now receives 18,000 inquiries a year—about six times the number it got in 1987. There is a general feeling on campus that this kind of curriculum demands more of students and that selection must be more precise. Tusculum has conducted considerable research on its applicants and has clearly identified its targets, geographically and otherwise. But Tusculum's leaders and faculty are also convinced that the school's program is the principal attraction, and that the framing and successful operation of a distinctive, student-centered, and outcome-based program has been crucial to the flow of applications.

The Tusculum experience, however, is one in which the entire community of faculty, trustees, students, and staff rediscovered and reclaimed their institution's authentic historical identity. The college faced a bona fide threat to its survival and had to confront the most basic questions about its role and about whether to go on. The president noted that this was a collaborative process in which the faculty and staff generated their own ideas and felt a genuine ownership of the solutions: "You can't do this from the top down, and you can't go look at what someone else did or borrow their 'package'; the faculty have to have control of the process."

Considerable effort has gone into faculty development at Tusculum, including the funding for a resource center with a foundation grant. The center has supported projects on collaborative learning, civic education, and critical thinking, and faculty workshops have been held in competency development and assessment.

At Tusculum, ideas were framed, debated, and refined during a long period of development. Adopting outcome-based education and developing an assessment strategy required research and time, as well. Among other things, a major culture shift accompanied the adoption of the new program. Since "civic virtue" carries with it the norm of self-government, the faculty at Tusculum have adopted a new committee-based structure, and the college now functions without a dean. By all accounts, the process requires heavy involvement and a deep personal commitment on the part of all faculty. In addition to self-governance, faculty are involved in the continuous development of their courses so they can provide students with opportunities to achieve the required competencies.

Following the example of Alverno College, the entire Tusculum curriculum has been placed on a grid that cross-tabulates courses with competencies. Students can tell at a glance which courses provide opportunities to develop and "test out" all fifteen competencies required for graduation. Competencies are assessed by faculty: they check off each validated competency and provide a narrative comment on what the student has achieved. A permanent binder containing the record of each student's progress is kept in an assessment center.

The changes have yet to fully penetrate the student culture at Tusculum, because the idea of competencies and the unusual calendar are radical departures from convention. Students, for example, are slow to understand that competencies are separate from course requirements, that in effect they are being graded on two separate measures: whether they achieve course goals and whether they achieve the competencies on the required schedule. But the assessment center staff see changes in student attitudes: "As more students go through it, they become 'survivors' and initiate the newer students. They are beginning to see that this program adds value to their education, that they are getting something students at other schools aren't. So there is also a payoff in increased self-confidence."

There are direct and indirect benefits from introduction of Tusculum's new program:

> [Faculty engage] in more talk about teaching and learning. Students
> have to talk with each other about learning the competencies, and

faculty have to talk with each other as trials and errors produce feedback. The system is maturing incrementally, but it depends on people working together. Faculty are learning to explore different ways of teaching in order to help students learn the competencies. Also, students learn to take responsibility for their own learning. They have to go to the center, check out their progress, assess themselves, and figure out what the next steps are.

The Tusculum case involves a great deal more than curriculum reform, but this reform obviously has drawn students to the institution (and, incidentally, has helped in recruiting new faculty). The specific substance aside, people had agreed on a simple mission—to produce graduates who are better citizens—and on a variety of innovative and stimulating ways to achieve it.

As with the Trenton State College case, the most interesting point of the Tusculum experiment seems to be the clear commitment of the campus community to refocus on the student and the student experience. While Tusculum has introduced many meaningful and essential *management* reforms, all of those reforms would have had little impact if the student base had not been rebuilt. Tusculum's plan was, as people candidly admitted, partly homegrown (the civic arts theme), partly borrowed from Colorado College (the calendar), and partly borrowed from Alverno College (the outcome-based program and assessment scheme).

In truth, the substance was less important than the commitment, and the commitment stemmed from a realization that Tusculum College would close unless it rebuilt its enrollment.

Bloomfield College

In many ways Bloomfield College's fiscal situation was similar to Tusculum's; in other ways the two institutions could not have been more dissimilar. One was located in the pastoral foothills of eastern Tennessee, the other in the heart of densely populated and heavily industrialized New Jersey. While Tusculum looked to history and ancient civilization for inspiration, Bloomfield looked to its immediate environment—a multiethnic community heavily populated with immigrants and first-generation college students. Most came from poor academic and economic backgrounds and needed all kinds of support in making the transition to college. As had Tusculum, Bloomfield was functioning with an utterly minimal faculty, a temporizing search for cash-generating program ideas, and no sense of mission or of the future.

The catalyst for change was the same: appointment of a new president in 1987. He launched a strategic planning process that produced a clear and realistic analysis of the setting in which Bloomfield's future would largely be determined. Because New Jersey provided generous tuition assistance to students from low-income families, as well as per capita support to institutions enrolling them, Bloomfield (and its new president) concluded that it could focus on the needs of the local population by preparing its students "to live and work in a multiracial/multicultural society." Like the Tusculum approach, this idea has now been fleshed out in substance, and the institution is small enough to engage in a communal effort at reform.

Bloomfield's many problems were captured in a single statistic: its six-year graduation rate was 9 percent—a catastrophic number when about 70 percent of the school's budget comes from tuition. The chief academic officer analyzed Bloomfield's program in this way: "The curriculum was not clearly organized around any goals or competencies. The students had no clear view of what they were supposed to get out of their education. . . . There was a need to rethink and redesign [Bloomfield's] education from the ground up."

Examining the student population and its needs led the CFO to recognize that "we have to deal with the whole student, to bring both academic and student affairs closer together so they are coordinating their approach to the student experience." The chief student affairs officer realized that "our students would not ordinarily be well prepared to live and work in a competitive society. . . . They need to change their lifestyles. Faculty should be teaching the competencies [they will need to be successful]." Bloomfield refers to its several simultaneous attacks on this problem as the "student advancement initiative."

Bloomfield began doing "formative" assessments to find out who the students are and what they need so that programs could be shaped to the population the school serves. Since Bloomfield could find no model programs dealing with a similarly situated population, it decided to "home-grow" its own student-advancement initiative. At the core is a set of all-college competencies that are derived from an effort to characterize the ideal graduate of Bloomfield. While the explicit text of the plan focuses on "how to live and work in a multiracial/multicultural society," the practical meaning for Bloomfield's predominantly minority student body can be summed up as, "You can enter and succeed in the mainstream."

Development of the program, which took two years, was carried out by first interviewing all faculty, representative students, and others. From the results of the interviews, an original list of about thirty competencies was identified; these thirty were subsequently boiled down to twenty-two, then twelve, and finally seven. Bloomfield is developing an assessment strategy to monitor students' status on these competencies at the time of admission, and to follow progress in each of the four undergraduate years. Standard academic assessment measures will be supplemented by a "student development transcript" that assesses how experiences outside the classroom have contributed to achievement of the competencies.

The intense involvement of the students in pursuing the competencies—and of Bloomfield in tracking and supporting students—will presumably help retention rates, although there is a general acknowledgment of the difficulties in such a radical reorientation of the college. One part of the theory stresses the need to simultaneously support and challenge (or "disturb") students. As at Tusculum and Trenton State, the developers of Bloomfield's program theorized that asking students to achieve specific competencies will engage them more deeply in learning and promote growth.

A major grant has provided faculty at Bloomfield with opportunities to rethink their disciplines and teaching strategies in light of the need to integrate competencies into their courses. They have been given time to study and to redesign courses, and they have been asked to help develop assessment strategies.

Bloomfield is trying to focus and coordinate the efforts of both academic and student development sides of the institution on the needs of its specific student population. The CAO described the rationale for coordinating change this way:

> The faculty need to acknowledge the reality of our students' deficiencies, to understand what they need, [such as] skills in self-presentation. [But] we are beginning to recognize that the classroom experience has a [relatively] minor impact; we are shifting our focus in recognition that we need the help of the student affairs people to do the job. The student life staff can address some of the biggest needs our students have, and therefore we need a team approach with them. In order to cooperate on this, we need to be clear about the outcomes we are pursuing. We recognize that faculty are not the "sole provider" and that all of us need to be working in concert.

We were urged not to "romanticize" the Bloomfield story. It clearly had taken a great deal of focused and dedicated effort, as well as candid self-examination, to reach any kind of working consensus. The issues of academic freedom and faculty prerogatives had not been fully resolved at the time of our visit. There was also uncertainty about how serious the institution would be in enforcing progress toward attainment of competencies. For example, would achievement be required for graduation? Might students be required to take additional course work? Could faculty learn to teach both their disciplines and the competencies effectively in the same course?

But there was a rather broad consensus among those we interviewed at Bloomfield about the realities the institution was facing: "This is not going to be a place that ever takes a highly selected student body. . . . But it will be a place where they can get a tough and challenging education to make up for their deficits and become well prepared for graduate school and work. Our job is to add value for those who haven't had an equal opportunity up to now." The spirit of this mission, we were told, was well articulated by a student at one of the planning retreats. He responded to rhetoric about "celebrating diversity" by saying, "I don't want to be celebrated, I want to be educated!"

Mayville State University/Valley City State University

A small public college, Mayville State University (MSU) is located in a rural farming community in eastern North Dakota. Valley City State University (VCSU), some 85 miles to the southwest, is in a similarly rural location. As North Dakota has experienced serious financial problems—substantially related to the collapse of energy prices in the 1980s and a tax limitation referendum passed by voters—leaders at both institutions have periodically felt that their colleges might be targets for closure by the state. However, both colleges have begun a collaborative relationship as leaders in redesigning the undergraduate experience.

MSU and VCSU are both led by one president and one chief academic officer. Other elements of the administration are being restructured into a more consortial arrangement, and the two institutions are experimenting with jointly offered academic programs that make use of distance-learning technology.

The collaboration between MSU and VCSU has focused mainly on strengthening undergraduate education—not specifically for the purpose of saving money, but to provide leadership on issues related to quality. The colleges have received external funding from the Fund for the Improvement of Postsecondary Education, the

National Science Foundation, and the Bush Foundation, as well as from the federal Title III program to strengthen developing institutions and the state department of public instruction.

Through ad hoc working committees, the two institutions are experimenting with "total quality learning" and instructional television. The Bush Foundation grant is providing funds to experiment with cooperative learning.

The goals of these several experiments converge on one theme: to create a student-centered environment. As MSU's chief student affairs officer put it: "Our niche is in new ways of delivering undergraduate instruction—for example, using performance-based assessment, using innovative and flexible teaching strategies. The idea is to give students a good experience." A team of faculty and students from both colleges are looking into innovative programs at other institutions. For example, the team took a bus trip to Alverno College, Milwaukee, Wisconsin, to study this national exemplar of student-centered, performance-based learning.

The two institutions differ in many ways, though, and the collaboration has required considerable nurturing. VCSU has a liberal arts tradition, while MSU has been oriented more to career and professional education. And while MSU faculty have more experience in coordinating instruction, faculty at VCSU have tended to work more independently. MSU has put its emphasis on cooperative education and clinical experience, and it takes a more hands-on approach to teaching and learning. Conversely, VCSU received funding for a center to experiment with instructional technology. The colleges have offered joint televised courses, and at the time of our visit they were continuing to explore new ideas for teaching and learning that would work on both campuses.

Essentially, both institutions understand that their futures depend, as one former administrator put it, on "entrepreneuring ourselves out of the mess we've been in; we have to find services [that] others want and will pay for." Although the collaboration is very much in its early stages, leaders on both campuses seem to understand clearly that innovative undergraduate education is their special niche, and that finding strength through this unusual partnership is likely to produce results that neither school could do alone. As difficult as some of the joint effort has proved to be, several of our interviewees spoke to one theme: "The collaboration will work if both schools look for win-win situations. . . . The one with the most partners wins."

Intense and Effective Undergraduate Education

While we have focused on four specific case studies in this section, we should point out that we have heard about similar reforms being attempted on other campuses. These reforms all acknowledge that the core of the higher education "business" is providing an intense and effective undergraduate experience. Good ideas being tried at some of the campuses we visited are converging around that theme: outcome-based education, cooperative learning, experiential education, student-centered learning, technological innovations, and the integration of in-class and out-of-class experiences are all part of this apparent movement. Underlying this trend is an emerging sense that, as one CFO put it: "Students are going to have to take more responsibility for their own learning, too. They will have to become more innovative themselves. Ours aren't the straight-A kids, so we have to put a different twist on how we engage and educate them."

Focus: Pains and Gains

There are two sides to the refocusing being done by institutions working their way out of fiscal stress: pain and gain. On the "pain" side, institutions are delimiting their purposes to niches and realigning their programs to address the needs of target populations. This is painful because instead of trying to advance in status by competing with institutions in a higher tier, these institutions, we sense, are making a more mature and realistic effort to differentiate from other institutions on the grounds of their own strengths. They are beginning to see that they can redefine quality as the specific "value-added" dimension to which they are committed. Quality is then something quite different for each institution (rather than something measured by one common standard) and reflects the ideas and programs that a college or university adopts to achieve its own particular market edge.

This is not quite the same as claiming "uniqueness"—a cliché that colleges and universities have used rather indiscriminately in their public relations materials. We found that institutions engaging in a serious effort to differentiate themselves from others clearly identified their population base and designed specific value-added programs to serve that population's needs. Furthermore, these institutions were developing specific outcomes—and methods for assessing those outcomes—partly as a way of validating their own programs, and partly to demonstrate that they are living up to the expectations of consumers and the broader society from which they draw support. In general, they are trying to focus on doing fewer things better.

But there are costs associated with such changes. Faculty have to understand that they have a stake in the fiscal health of their institution and commit themselves to that end. This is a more traumatic change than one might first expect. Faculty have been socialized to maximize their own autonomy, marketability, and mobility—perhaps at the expense of the institutions employing them at a given time. Part of the logic of a successful faculty career lies in accumulating credit toward upward mobility. So faculty may be more disposed to leave one institution for better pay, more research time, and other perquisites at another.

Putting their present institutions first and their careers (or research or disciplines) second is—for many faculty—a wrenching psychic change. It is a painful problem for institutions, too. As one seasoned department head put it, "It may well be difficult to hold good faculty if we can't support their research agendas." A vice president noted that faculty simply respond to the reward structure as it exists and that the current system won't help turn faculty loyalties inward to institutional survival: "Faculty are rewarded first for doing research. Tenure as now awarded is archaic, not responsive to our current realities."

This is, of course, only one painful element. Faculty at institutions that turn attention to student needs and to an outcome-oriented approach have to become much more skilled at diagnosing and addressing student needs. As the student population becomes more diverse and its learning styles more varied, and as K–12 schools continue to search for better ways of preparing students for college, faculty will find that they must orchestrate instructional methods to help ensure that all students can progress. (For an overview of studies on learning styles and the need for a greater variety of approaches to the learning needs of "new students," see Schroeder, 1993.)

On the "gain" side, we noticed three general effects. Most important, institutions are refocusing on the main bread-and-butter issue: attracting and retaining undergraduate students. Second, a basic (and very promising) reconceptualization of the undergraduate experience is under way. And third, institutions have begun to see that committing themselves to a distinctive value-added mission is a more effective competitive strategy than emulating other institutions.

These three developments, we think, show real promise for helping institutions recapture, hold, and satisfy their market share of undergraduate students. And this, along with strengthened public credibility, should help institutions secure their financial base. Our view is that money follows excellence; the schools that develop the best programs will attract students and donors. Certainly, good programs require a certain minimum level of funding to succeed. But ideas and commitment are what kick-started the programs that we think have the best chance of success. To be sure, our site institutions have benefited from big grants or other private sources. But they got the money because they demonstrated that they had a real chance to do something different and valuable.

The academic community may have been framing its general strategies for managing and conducting business in precisely the wrong way. Considerable conventional wisdom in higher education has been built around the idea that "richer is better," so institutions with more money per student are generally perceived to be "better." This idea has been roundly critiqued by Astin and others as the "input fallacy." The fallacy is that more money and other resources will result in better education. Astin has long been arguing that what happens during the educational process is more important than how "rich" the institution is (see, for example, Astin, 1993b).

In other words, it isn't how rich the school is in traditional terms, but what it does with its resources and how resource allocation affects the student experience. This is where the institutions in our study were making the most significant progress: their strategies for fiscal recovery emphasized redirecting resources to effective undergraduate education.

Conclusion

In this chapter, we examined how institutions are redefining their approaches to undergraduate education. We found a real tension over ownership and control. On the whole, the academic community has been converging through several decades on increasingly homogeneous models of status and "quality." This has meant diverting attention away from undergraduate education. But among those institutions with serious concerns about survival, we observed a refocusing of attention on the "core business" of higher education— namely, the reinvigoration of undergraduate education:

- Faculty roles are being redefined.
- Institutions are defining quality in their own terms.

- Undergraduate programs are being designed to add value.
- Outcome assessment is being used to monitor effectiveness.

We also learned about the difficulties that institutions faced in bringing about change, stemming principally from the way in which faculty are trained, socialized to their work, organized into disciplines and departments, and rewarded for doing research. Those institutions with the most entrenched and research-oriented faculty are those that have the most difficulty making changes. Change has been quickest and most substantial at the institutions in which the faculty have realized that their very livelihoods depend not on their national prestige or their mobility in the competitive marketplace, but on securing the economic viability of their own institutions.

We cannot help but recall that diversity and adaptability contribute to the survival potential of a species. Differentiation and experimentation are coming from the margins of the population—from the most vulnerable institutions. If they prove the validity of the ideas they are now exploring, we may see a higher education enterprise that revitalizes itself with new ideas about teaching and learning, about how to add value, and about how to make intelligent investments in the commitment and skill of faculty to provide undergraduate students with an extraordinary educational experience.

Part Three

Wise Moves

Chapter Seven

Analyzing the Institution's Condition

Each of the institutions we visited experienced stress in its own particular way. We were struck by how much the dimensions of stress varied from one institution to another. In some cases, declining state appropriations were clearly the major source of problems; in others, changes in population trends were more significant. Although economic recession played a substantial role in the fiscal health (or lack of it) among the site institutions, so, too, did management style and governmental policy at both the state and federal levels.

The main point, though, is that there is *no one cause*. More likely, institutions were challenged by a complex and interacting array of factors. Some were able to make highly informed assessments of their own situations. They could not always do much to control or change their circumstances in the short run, but they could at least make intelligent statements about their current condition and what they might be able to do in response.

Some institutions were distressingly short on good information, while others had all the information they needed. But such information served to help in diagnosing and planning only when it could be analyzed and communicated for the benefit of audiences inside and outside the institution.

So our next task is to propose ways in which institutions might analyze their own situations. We suggest that each of these factors be examined:

- The effects of economic, demographic, and political trends
- Trends in the institution's financial condition

- Stability, openness, and courage in management
- Vitality of educational programs
- "Interactivity"

Our goal in this chapter is to outline the important questions that we think CEOs and other leaders should be asking continuously. These questions provide a starting point for sensing and diagnosing the current state of a college or university. While the questions do not provide any real baseline for determining that a crisis exists or what specific actions an institution should take, they will help to locate the hot spots and leverage points in a stressed institution.

External Factors

Every institution we visited was vulnerable to the effects of the larger economic and demographic situation. In our view, institutions that seemed disconnected from or uninvolved with the political, social, business, and educational institutions (and leaders) of their communities and regions were the most vulnerable. These connections are vital if an institution is to be seen as a viable and contributing partner in economic growth and civic betterment. If a college or university does not (or is not perceived to) carry its responsibility in the broader world around it, it really cannot expect much support from others.

So it is important to start thinking about an institution's fiscal health by analyzing its external situation. But some of what happens cannot be controlled by anything that the college or university does. It is therefore also important to look at the big picture and to understand trends that will make a fundamental difference in how healthy or unhealthy an institution can expect to be if it changes nothing.

The Market

In the world of higher education, "the market" simply means "students." No institution could survive if it did not educate students.

Students demand (in the aggregate) a quality education that ensures upward mobility. Tuition dollars and state appropriations follow students. These few axioms represent the irreducible foundation of fiscal health at all of the institutions we studied. Other things impact fiscal health in marginal ways, but not the flow of students. It is a life-and-death factor.

The flow of students varies. In some states, such as North Dakota, the population of young people is projected to decline. In others, like California and Florida, it is growing rapidly. In still other states, such as New York and New Jersey, the composition of the potential student market is changing both economically and socially. The middle class is being squeezed out of its comparative affluence, and minority ethnic groups comprise an increasing share of the college-age population.

Since most institutions draw their students heavily from local, state, or regional populations, they have to understand precisely how trends are moving *at those levels*. An institution that has been successful at attracting a predominantly white, middle-class student body in a state with a changing ethnic mix might be in deeper trouble than is initially obvious if those white, middle-class students represent a declining share in the area it draws from most heavily. Or an institution with an attractive campus and a heavily residential student population of traditional college age might be in potential trouble if the population of its region is aging, growing poorer, and showing signs of increasing interest in part-time study or distance learning. Similarly, an institution with a long liberal arts tradition might find itself drawing from a population that is increasingly distressed economically and more and more interested in vocational or professional preparation.

In these cases—all of which are either synopses of conditions we found at specific institutions or slightly contrived variants—institutions may mislead themselves by assuming that as long as their enrollments do not actually decline, things can go on as before. This is dangerous and self-deceptive. Some of our site institutions had learned from earlier episodes in which they did not watch trends closely and had let the proverbial horse out of the barn before they responded.

It will cost an institution more in the long run if it waits for an economic crisis before reallocating and reinvesting program money into new or changing ventures. At the same time, it is politically more difficult to initiate change before an economic pinch hits; because people do not see problems or feel any immediate pain, they are not inclined to change. Someone—perhaps an institution's CEO—has to take the risk of saying that the outside world is changing and that the institution will have to change, too.

This is a risk that politically sensitive presidents and trustees do not like to take, especially if the basis of their assessment lies in relatively "soft" numbers or trends. But waiting until enrollment starts to drop, or until different kinds of students start to enroll, is likely to be even more explosive politically. That is because the financial and program effects of these trends bite hard into the daily lives of both faculty and students, who then begin to press for accountability ("Whose fault is it?") and for change ("Why haven't we done anything about it?").

We found some institutions to be very perceptive about their market situations. Some were also very responsive to the changing student markets, although not all had anticipated trends or engaged in very much internal talk about the meaning of those trends. But the trends cannot be escaped or leapfrogged, especially if the institution is in no position to relocate physically. A business corporation can close up its operation in, say, Ohio, and move to North Carolina. But a college cannot so easily close and sell its campus in Maine and buy or build another one in Florida (although population trends might make such a relocation the most sensible economic move some institutions could make).

The University of Texas at El Paso, the University of Maryland—Eastern Shore, and Bloomfield College provided especially interesting examples of institutions that had candidly assessed their markets. In all cases, the institutions were situated in and drew their students from predominantly minority population centers. They looked hard at the needs of their constituents and established purposeful programs to meet those needs, often focusing on professional preparation and on partnerships with community, business, and professional organizations in the region. They not only made a strong moral commitment to young people in their service areas, but they also met real market needs. This is a win-win formula.

Like these three institutions, most colleges and universities will have to continuously rethink the markets they are serving, especially in states where major changes can be anticipated. Good academic programs, even those with long records of productivity and national reputations, will not always continue to be successful in a market that changes substantially. And the market *will* change, because population demographics and economies are constantly moving, mixing in different ways, and altering the demand picture. An institution has to either seek a new market for old programs or adapt its programs to the shifting market in which it is inescapably situated.

The most important questions an institution needs to ask about its market include:

- Who is likely to want what kind of education, where, when, and at what price?
- How is this changing now, and how is it likely to change in the foreseeable future?
- Are these trends likely to generate more interest in and support for what a college or university now does well?
- Or are they likely to generate more support for different programs?
- What is the competition?

Competition

Colleges and universities compete for students. Some compete vigorously with well-known and well-understood rivals in heavily studied markets (for example, the elite private institutions in the Northeast). Others, such as a few in our group, do not have much competition and do not consciously think of themselves and others as competitors. But any institution that does not have as many applications as it would like from the kinds of students it wants obviously has competition.

We recognized three components to competition: quality, content, and price. *Quality* has to do with value. Price and other factors being roughly equal, a student considering two colleges may perceive more value at one institution and decide to maximize his or her returns by choosing that school. Quality is ephemeral, of course (especially in the minds of seventeen-year-old high school seniors): it may refer to better job prospects upon graduation, more National Academy of Sciences members on a faculty, comfortable and pleasant residence halls, a nationally ranked football team, or just friendlier admissions people.

Content refers to the actual program options available to students. A student interested in biomechanical engineering, for instance, is unlikely to attend a school with a full array of arts and music but no engineering school.

Price has become a terribly sensitive issue; it refers to the actual cash outlay a student must make to attend a college or university. Assorted programs of financial aid and the practice of discounting tuition with awards of all kinds has made "pricing" a college education more like haggling in a Middle Eastern bazaar. There is obviously a large gap in price between the public and private sectors, but within either sector a student might well find considerable variance in price, too.

Students presumably compare institutions on all three of these variables and appear to make one overall, simultaneous calculation about the mix of these factors when they choose a college. We have no way of knowing how they weigh each factor, but it probably depends on the range of institutions they are considering. For example, a student who receives a considerable price break (say, a merit scholarship) to one institution may nevertheless choose an alternate school with a higher price because the first institution's content or quality is not what he or she expected. Another student may be interested only in a highly similar group of institutions, perhaps all with strong engineering programs, and choose the one that offers the largest price break (a financial aid package, for example).

Here is where the competition comes in. Why and to whom does an institution lose its better applicants? A pattern may or may not exist, but if one does, it signals that something should be done. Is another institution moving in on a particular content area—the arts, for example? Or is a competitor targeting its price breaks to a certain type and quality of student? Are more students now going to institutions previously perceived as equal or lower in quality? How much is image and how much is substance?

An institution's position among competitors may be changing for many reasons. One is that the population and factors in the economy that affect student choice of college may be changing. What has worked for one kind of population may no longer work when the population changes. So by staying the course, an institution could be falling behind by default. Competitor institutions themselves may be changing and repositioning themselves: a new program here, a new residence hall there, more (or differently targeted) financial aid, a new viewbook, and other kinds of changes can all make a big difference in how an institution and its competitors are perceived.

The main lesson, clichéd as it may be, is that staying in place often means falling behind. Students have to be recruited one at a time. Some recruitment can be managed through public presentation of the institution and by image mongering. But eventually real questions about quality, price, and program content face every student who plans to invest heavily in his or her education. It is at this level that *real* marketing begins. Real marketing means that the institution offers real products for which there is substantial need at a fair value. Tradition, image, and visibility count for something, but students—the good students—find out rather quickly when their interests and their tuition dollars are not being taken seriously.

So it is extremely important for colleges and universities to analyze the flow of their applications and to look carefully at their "yield." Who really goes where and why? And how does the picture change from year to year?

Trenton State College accomplished its makeover into a high-quality, residential liberal arts college by doing a very careful analysis of the programs and environments at institutions it wanted to emulate. Trenton analyzed the competition and then built its program around specific goals for campus life, academic programs, and student quality. The leaders and staff (even the president) went personally to high school guidance counselors throughout New Jersey to ask that the best students get information about Trenton State. They brought students, parents, and counselors to the campus to see what was happening. And they stuck with their goals for the long term—even when it was politically tough to do so.

Trenton State is a good example of an institution that decided what its market would be, determined how it would situate itself in relation to the competition, and systematically built its student base—one student at a time. Trenton has done a good deal more than concentrate on image and presentation; it has made substantive changes at all levels of the institution, including an essentially reconstructed campus.

What Trenton State really offers *of value to students* is the bedrock of its marketing strategy. Students ultimately sell TSC to others, and their experience is the key. They feel they are getting good value, and they will spread the word. But if they were to feel they were not getting good value, they would spread *that* word. So giving value to students is the key—and tracking students and their experiences is an important part of the information base that institutions should have.

Public Policy

Public policy is second in importance only to the market in determining fiscal health. Public policy affected our site institutions both positively and negatively as the policy environment changed (sometimes erratically) to reflect economic and political trends.

Colleges and universities depend on state funding—it is virtually the only thing that keeps public institutions alive. Even for many private institutions, state support can provide the margin for survival. Yet it seems to us that colleges and universities have been slow to focus on accountability for public funds. The climate in state legislatures and governors' offices has changed dramatically in the past decade. Public officials have come under far more pressure to control spending, to reduce taxes, and to account to constituents for the "payoff" of public spending. That pressure has been shifted to state agencies, including colleges and universities, with the predictable effect of tighter and tighter preaudits and postaudits of public fund expenditures. Institutions that anticipate and respond to these pressures are better positioned politically than those that either do not foresee what is coming or lag in responding.

For the most part, individual institutions are at least theoretically insulated from the vagaries of political whim by governing or coordinating boards. These boards exist as buffers to smooth out the course of public policy. They help to inform lawmakers about current and future conditions and to work out plans with individual institutions to achieve the state's policy objectives. We found that they were only variably successful in performing this smoothing function. In a few cases, the state boards may actually have contributed to the problems of individual institutions we studied.

However, we also found some cases in which state boards had established conditions in which individual institutions could thrive.

Although the boards had to administer budget cuts or reallocations in most of the states we visited, they sometimes ameliorated those cuts by granting permission to campuses to be more entrepreneurial. Some of our site institutions had aggressively pursued these opportunities.

Southern Oregon State College, for example, was allowed to recruit students from California, to charge higher tuitions for those students, and to keep the proceeds. The college also looked for opportunities to establish programs in areas that, say, the University of Oregon was shedding (for example, tourism development). Texas-El Paso aggressively sought outside funding for its initiatives in support of minority students, and it ultimately won additional support from the system for these efforts. Trenton State negotiated an agreement with the state of New Jersey to cut enrollment and raise tuition, and the college enjoyed the support of at least one commissioner of higher education in pursuing this unusual plan to enhance quality. We also found that Maryland—Eastern Shore and Virginia Commonwealth University had both enjoyed the support of their respective state higher education agencies in pursuing special initiatives.

In all these cases, state agencies supported individual initiatives from the campuses. Though they had to overlook or change their own policies or traditional practices, the agencies seemed to understand that providing the freedom to experiment was a risk worth taking.

At least four important elements of a state's policy toward higher education must be monitored continuously: stability, balance of power, share of appropriations, and effects by sector.

Stability is a measure of political continuity. Frequent turnover of key officials is a sign of low stability. In Florida, for example, the legislative leadership changes every two years. By the time a new senate president or house speaker assumes office, he or she has already used up a good part of the office's potential power (Doherty, 1991). The best measure of power in Florida's legislative politics is an assessment of who is likely to achieve the speakership or senate presidency. In other states, legislative leaders accumulate power by remaining in chair positions or speakerships for many years.

Similarly, governorships in some states are impacted by term limits (such as in Virginia) or constitutional limitations on real power (such as in Florida). Turnover in term-limit states or constant deal making in states with weak governors may greatly affect how higher education fits into the real policy agenda at any given point in time.

The *balance of power* between political parties can greatly affect policy. Some states have conservative traditions, while others have liberal tendencies, especially with regard to how higher education is governed and funded. These traditions are unique to each state. Massachusetts, for example, has long been at least nominally liberal. Yet many of those we interviewed characterized the state's funding for public higher education as being somewhat disadvantaged by the loyalties of legislators to the major independent institutions and to those affiliated with the Catholic church.

In the time period we studied, the balance of power and ideologies of many states became increasingly fluid. This led to greater confusion about just what was expected of colleges and universities. Policy seemed fragmented and incoherent, with the institutions left very much on their own to guess at what they could do to meet the expectations of powerful politicians and interest groups about programs, funding, and management.

Unfortunately, the higher education community itself was not always effective in moving into the vacuum. Prone to disagreement, competition, and self-advancement, colleges and universities seemed often to be seeking individual competitive advantage, rather than working together to promote an informed consensus and rational differentiation of their respective missions. Instead of monitoring and shaping policy, individual actors from the various sectors of higher education sometimes sought to exploit policy makers' uncertainties for their own advantage. In other words, we think that the higher education community itself sometimes contributes to disruptions and disequilibrium in public policy—upsetting the sometimes delicate balance of political positions in order to gain a short-term edge.

Achieving a consensus on policy is easier in a state where one ideology or party dominates. But in the more fluid settings—states where parties and interests contest many issues and where there are no clear winners or losers—the higher education community has more to gain by careful assessment of the situation and by coming together in common interest. Balance sometimes has to be helped along and nurtured into place, especially when politicians are looking for handy topics to use in gaining visibility and power. Higher education loses as often as it gains in these situations, and temporary victories often contain the seeds of permanent losses. Therefore, we urge that the higher education community attend to the balance in state politics.

We are deeply concerned about the trend we saw in many states, namely the declining *share of appropriations* going to higher education. This decline (from, say, 12 to 15 percent of all state appropriations at the beginning of the 1990s to about 8 to 11 percent at mid-decade) signifies two things: state finances are more stressed than they were at the beginning of the decade, and higher education has become an issue of declining importance in at least some states. It has been displaced by issues of much more current political importance and by the continued shifting of federal obligations to the states.

In some states, declines in college enrollment account for some of the decreasing share of appropriations, but the decrease is too broadly spread among states for us to believe that it is the only cause. Certainly in states like Florida and California, where enrollment pressures are far beyond the capacity of the system, any decline in share of appropriations (as has occurred in these states) is cause for concern.

Concurrently, obligations for financing higher education are

being shifted over to tuition and fees—often without commensurate strengthening of public financial aid programs. Instead of making social investments in opportunities for higher education, states
are increasingly asking individual students to mortgage their futures
by investing their own private resources in tuition. This raises the
stakes in students' decisions about which college to attend and
which major to choose.

At the same time, though, states are *dis*investing in the capacity of those same colleges and universities to provide real value-
added returns on students' investments. So in a real sense, the issue
is not one of maintaining higher education's share of the state budget—it is what the balance ought to be between private and public investment in a college education.

Students and their families have demonstrated a certain amount
of resilience and persistence in absorbing this new financial burden
and investment risk, but they will reach a point at which they sense
diminishing value-added returns. At that point, colleges and universities will face the additive effects of diminishing state subsidies
and lower consumer demand.

Effects by sector are sometimes uneven. In most states we studied, we heard accounts of fierce rivalries and competition for funds
among research universities, comprehensive colleges, and community colleges, as well as between the public and private sectors.
Although public rhetoric may claim that higher education is "all
one system," we found considerable anecdotal evidence of competition for scarce funds.

Sorting out who is winning and who is losing is complicated by
a much fiercer territoriality than we had expected to find. Both public and private institutions have become aggressive in asserting their
individual claims to state legislatures. Monitoring and shaping the
politics of higher education funding is more crucial than ever. We
would argue, however, that more is needed than just sharp strategies in pursuit of an institution's own status and political support.
Seeking individual advantage may become a long-term liability in

the sense that each special appropriation not only draws limited funds away from the general pot available to all institutions of higher education, but it also establishes the principle that an institution's funding can be reallocated when another institution comes up with an attractive new idea.

In other words, playing by the principle of special interest and special appropriations may gain a temporary advantage, but it will signal other institutions to seek special advantage for themselves. As political fortunes wax and wane, an institution that gets a temporary special appropriation may generally expect to lose it when legislative or gubernatorial power shifts or when priorities change.

We have also seen that lobbying for special funding or advantaged positions in the distribution of regular funding often involves a certain amount of "negative campaigning"—playing up the shortcomings of rival bidders. This is at best a formula for temporary— and only temporary—advantage. At worst, it is a strong condemnation of higher education as a responsible steward of the public trust. If one educator disparages another's competence or good faith—even in the most indirect way—it lowers the level of trust in all of higher education. Obviously, if one sector or institution questions the merits of another, the floor is open to further debate on everyone's merits.

So we think it is important to work toward cooperative relations in seeking better support for higher education as a whole, and for understanding how the distribution of scarce resources should be managed. In our view, when any institution is disadvantaged in the distribution of funding, it is a loss for the higher education community as a whole. The goal ought to be an increase in the size of the pie for all of higher education, rather than fratricidal bickering over each institution's share.

For these reasons, we suggest carefully assessing the distribution of funding among sectors and institutions. But we also suggest careful assessments of the degree to which colleges and universities cooperate in advancing their collective interests—rather than competing with one another individually or by sector for what will almost inevitably be a merely temporary advantage. We recognize that this is easier said than done, but the current situation reminds us of the circumstances one finds in a lifeboat: salvation is generally more likely when the occupants cooperate toward a common end than if they begin fighting with one another.

Many of these same issues relate to federal funding for postsecondary education. We feel, however, that the institutions we visited had ceased to look to the federal arena for any coherent or truly helpful policy. The election returns of November 1994 appear to have left the policy directions of the federal government in an even more unclear state. We think that little constructive financial help can be expected from this quarter in the short term. The further withdrawal of the federal government from financing either student aid or research also appears very likely. Therefore, continued monitoring of the federal interest in and policy toward postsecondary education is a potentially important indicator of future financial conditions.

Financial Trends

In the institutions we visited, financial data and financial patterns varied considerably. We are not accountants, and we do not propose to establish any sort of standards for the definition of fiscal "crisis" or "stress." But we think that two specific practices can help an institution get through hard times: trend analysis and communicating to important audiences.

What trends should a CEO watch, and what signs mean trouble? We have tried to understand where the biggest problems lie and what indicators might help provide an early alert of impending trouble. We stress that indicators do not—and cannot—provide any sort of detailed analysis of financial condition. But they can signal cause for concern and can suggest when professional analysis or intervention might be warranted.

We saw four areas to watch closely; all seemed to signal—in one combination or another—a serious degree of stress in the fundamental financial health of the institutions we visited. We are overlooking such immediate indicators of crisis as cash flow and account balances. Any responsible business manager can see these sorts of immediate warning signs.

Instead, we are focusing on those variables that, when followed over time, suggest whether an institution is becoming stronger or weaker. In all cases, it is a good idea to peg the indicators to some kind of ratio—such as debt overhang per full-time-equivalent (FTE) student. Numbers by themselves may not carry as much meaning in isolation as they do when related to some kind of base and interpreted in context.

Inventorying Physical Plant Needs

We found truly alarming decay in the physical plant of some institutions, and at least a serious overhanging level of deferred maintenance at several others. (One institution estimated the value of its current inventory of deferred maintenance at more than $70 million.) A campus in disrepair is terribly unattractive to visitors and prospective students, as well as damaging to the morale of faculty and staff. So it costs the institution twice: once because it has, in effect, borrowed plant funds to balance its accounts, and second because its image is depressing.

Borrowing from plant funds in this way is perhaps more costly than borrowing from another source. By allowing buildings and infrastructure to fall into disrepair, an institution simply accepts the geometrically increasing cost to fix problems later, and also risks the accelerating decline of its capital stock. All kinds of hazards and risks increase as decay sets in, from slip- and-fall injuries to fire and loss to wind and weather damage. It is a frightfully shortsighted borrowing strategy, and the borrowing costs are virtually never included in any accounting for the institution's current financial condition.

This is precisely what makes deferred maintenance an addictive form of borrowing, though, because it so effectively hides the high costs associated with it.

Analyzing Trends in Debt Incurred by Students

Higher education is essentially funding itself by offloading debt onto students who pay tuition by taking out loans. Colleges and universities get current tuition payments, but students accumulate and pay off the debt in the future. Some institutions are able to accumulate scholarship funds and revolving loan funds at a level that helps control the amount of debt that students incur. However, there is widespread public concern about whether tuitions are too high and whether students receive adequate financial aid. (We are also concerned about the morality of burdening students with high levels of debt so early in their lives.)

Increasing levels of debt make it harder for students to continue in college and to select major fields that offer a less than adequate prospect for real financial returns on their investment. The problem is obviously much more serious for private institutions than for public institutions—at least as measured in dollar amounts. But many students attending public institutions have so few financial resources that any debt at all is sometimes a life-and-death matter—a choice between paying off loans or paying for food and rent.

Watching the trend line of student indebtedness can give an institution several clear signals. It can suggest which fields of study and what kinds of students are bearing the most serious debt burdens. It can also signal whether indebtedness is affecting students' ability to continue in school and/or attain their degrees in a reasonable length of time. Debt can push students out of residence halls and force them to cut back to part-time study or drop out of school altogether. One of our site institutions found that its students were transferring out in large numbers after the freshman or sophomore year because they could more easily afford tuition at nearby public institutions—colleges they could not get admitted to as freshmen but could qualify for after a year or two with a solid academic record.

Student indebtedness, then, may well be a proxy indicator for other patterns that directly impact the fiscal status of a college or university. On human, ethical, and policy grounds alone, any debt burden on students raises serious questions for a nonprofit institution. Specifically, it amounts to borrowing from clients to keep the business solvent. But on pragmatic grounds, it has the effect of making it harder to ensure a continuous flow of hard tuition funds from full-time students who can graduate in four years. In turn, securing more students to fill the tuition-income hole effectively increases the institution's cost of finding more students from whom to "borrow."

Following Trends in Private Fundraising

A third leg on which fiscal health depends—more heavily at some institutions than others—is private giving. Whether measured by current gifts and grants or in terms of capital funds, private wealth is an essential part of every institution's overall financial health. Trends vary, but one consistently important variable caught our attention: without constant attention and "maintenance," an institution's donor base will erode. Some of our site institutions candidly said that turnover of their development staffs had damaged relations with donors.

We think it is very important to monitor who gives, how much they give, and in what form they give. It is also important to know who has stopped giving and why, and to understand what donors are giving to or for—what their motives are. There is more to monitoring private giving than just watching the bottom line.

At some institutions, the amount of private giving is so small that a CEO should not be too concerned with details—unless there is a plan to increase the level of fundraising. At others, however, it is an absolutely fundamental part of the institution's ability to survive. At the smaller institutions, a substantial part of the stress they experience can be traced directly to a fall-off in private giving.

Unknowns are the most vexing part of this element in institutional finances. In a few of the cases we studied, major capital gifts more or less fell from the sky and enabled at least one private college to remain open; others had embarked on major capital fund drives. But the single factor most associated with increased levels of private giving was the attention paid to potential donors. In other words, "Ask and you will receive." It is a process that can be neither controlled nor reliably forecast. But effort does appear to pay off in expected and unexpected ways.

Institutions should watch the ratio of unrestricted current and capital gift accumulation to current fund expenditures, and should track this ratio consistently over time. We understand that institutions have various ways to measure these variables, and different ways of relating them to each other, and we would not pretend to make a technical recommendation. (For example, we do not necessarily mean that "accumulation" is the same as depositing gifts in a restricted endowment or quasi-endowment account, although that may be a very desirable practice in a conservatively managed institution.) But our point is simple. As more private funds are taken in relative to expenditures from current funds, institutions are arguably building a cushion against at least short-term financial problems. They are also building a base for reinvestment in program changes when such changes are needed.

Avoiding Capricious Interfund Transfers

The fourth and final indicator to watch is the use of interfund transfers to obscure real financial problems. Without going into all the technical details of fund accounting (and all of the flaws it holds as an indicator of an institution's current fiscal status), we know of one aspect on which there seems to be general agreement: covering fiscal problems with arbitrary interfund transfers is too easy.

We'll make our point with a simple example. An institution makes a transfer from "plant funds" to "current funds" when current expenditures exceed current income. This is really unrecorded borrowing. Plant funds probably (although by no means certainly) are set aside for replacement, maintenance, and repair. When an institution dips into these funds for current expenses, it is arguably borrowing from the (deteriorating) physical plant and failing to include either the deferred maintenance or nominal interest in its accounting.

It may well be that plant funds have become a place to salt away surplus current income in anticipation of hard times ahead, a practice we observed in at least one case we studied. Transfers may reflect heavy borrowing from endowment, heavy dependence on gift income (also a serious problem in a few of our cases), or other maneuvering to mask what is really a deficit in the operating budget.

We are not suggesting which accounting practices to use, nor would we substitute our judgment for that of a financial officer's. We are merely suggesting that CEOs continuously monitor these four warning signals about the general health of their institutions. The indicators we give are somewhat more subtle than the obvious income and expenditure data contained in regular financial statements. But we think that our suggestions have some value in predicting longer-term trends—and signaling potential trouble well before it shows up in current accounts.

Management Patterns

Management is the pivot point between programs and finance. If programs are in trouble, finance will follow. If finance is a problem, programs will follow. (See "Interactivity" below.) Management works out the balance between programs and funding. We found several indicators—all unique to academic management—that should be monitored as potential early warnings of trouble: turnover, isolation, style, process, and courage.

Turnover

Institutions that had experienced the most difficulty among those we visited were at the extremes on the continuum of "turnover." Some had presidents and staff who had been in place for extended periods of time, while others suffered from very rapid turnover and gross instability in such key functions as fundraising and admissions.

Either extreme is cause for some concern—but not necessarily for intervention. Take the case of a very long-serving president. The advantage, of course, is that there is a long and deep institutional memory at the top. Presidents who learn from experience, know how to adapt, and provide stability and continuity are extremely valuable to (and valued by) their institutions. But some presidents stay too long and become vested in certain practices and programs beyond the time when change and new ideas are needed.

There is obviously no critical time beyond which a president's tenure is good or bad. But we think that boards should become considerably more interested in performance reviews of their institutions and their presidents after about eight to ten years. This is an arbitrary period, to be sure, and we cannot defend it on any substantive grounds—or even on more than our own hunches. We just think that a certain self-interest builds up over long periods and that anyone can become too comfortable with the status quo. As we have learned, the status quo is a dangerous "status" in a changing environment.

But the more serious problem, of course, is churning in the administrative ranks. When people do not stay in their positions long enough to learn, grow, and produce, there are obvious problems. Perhaps they feel that the problems the job presents are so overwhelming that they leave to escape, or perhaps the human environment is so hostile that they take big risks to get out. Perhaps the person who hires people is making bad judgments.

One or two turnovers in a few years does not make a crisis, but three successive departures from any key management position in a three-year period should cause serious questions to be raised. Should rapid turnover be occurring in more than one management function, it is very likely that something is seriously wrong.

Isolation

Communication is the most fundamental tool of management. When channels are sealed off or interrupted, all kinds of problems begin to fester. We did not find this to be a current problem at the institutions we visited, but anecdotes confirmed that interrupted communication had occasionally been a factor in worsening an institution's stressed condition.

Two particularly hazardous communication gaps developed from time to time. In a few cases, communication with external (political) leaders had been or was becoming problematic. Obviously, this is a dangerous condition. It is personally dangerous for presidents of public or private institutions to be out of touch with legislative and executive leaders, but it is also dangerous for the institution as a whole.

Perhaps it is equally hazardous for leaders in the higher education community to be out of touch with one another. We observed one case in which a campus president and the CEO of the state higher education coordinating board seemed unable to communicate. Their strained relationship was threatening to spill over into policy and was potentially damaging to the institution.

The other main communication problem we found—to no one's surprise—was between faculty and administration. In a few cases, the relationship had deteriorated to the point of name-calling and finger-pointing. In one case, a vote of no confidence in the

CEO had been taken. While faculty clearly resented what they perceived as secretive and high-handed decision making, administrators were just as concerned about faculty who were misinformed, self-interested, and obstructive.

Where does the "blame" lie? We think that this question is unhelpful and suggest instead that both parties attempt to understand that communication must be continuous and effective. Especially in a crisis situation, it is extremely important to remain in close and open contact. While there will inevitably be conflict and unhappiness as budget cuts or reallocations are made, good communication at least ensures that decisions are made with the best available information and that all parties understand the bona fides of the other's position.

Therefore, we suggest monitoring the state of internal and external communication continuously—not because better communication will necessarily solve the basic problems of institutions, but because it will at least prevent extraneous conflict and wasted effort.

Sometimes the burden of communicating falls too heavily on CEOs alone. The responsibility for communication can sometimes be shared to good effect. In a few cases, we found that students, faculty, board members, and community supporters were the ones who most effectively communicated an institution's case to the legislature and other supporters.

The CEO also needs an administrative team that is adept at effective relations inside and outside the institution. In some cases, a CFO might be a negotiator extraordinaire in dealing with faculty, or a chief academic officer might be highly effective in the political arena. The particular assignments are not important, but the team requires good communicators to be working continuously with all the important stakeholders. The CEO's main interest is in monitoring continuity and effectiveness in the assorted lines of communication inside and outside the institution, and in acting to bridge important gaps where they may be widening.

Style

Management style is closely related to communication, but it is a good deal more than image and symbols. The CEOs we interviewed were actively working on their institutions' problems. They were attentive to the human and political dimensions of the situation, engaged deeply in the life of the institution and the community, and focused on the present and the future. They worked so hard at their jobs that we came away concerned about how they could sustain their level of effort over the long term.

In a few cases, we could see the potential for problems if a certain style of operation was intensified further. For example, some presidents were highly attentive to people and to the details of campus life. Their high visibility and continuous engagement could be misinterpreted by some as possessiveness or meddling. Too much "engagement" might also call so much attention to a CEO that he or she becomes associated with all the institution's problems, large and small—and thereby may assume far too much personal responsibility for solutions.

Sometimes highly engaged presidents may also have trouble delegating, and this in turn can result in more decisions passing upward for them to make. Needless to say, this causes overload and excessive concentration on a president's every move. Even if the president were right most of the time, no CEO can afford to take such complete responsibility.

However, no CEO can afford to allow an institution to drift or to accept passively every decision of a highly democratic process. Extreme disengagement is as hazardous to a CEO as overengagement.

There is no simple indicator of balance along these lines, but we would monitor the performance of an institution's leaders by looking for appropriate levels of activity and involvement. Obviously, if a crisis is at hand the leadership must be more engaged, decisive, and directive. But in better times they ought to be involving others and educating them in the substantive issues and governance processes of the institution's life, as well as training them for expanded responsibilities. In this way, the community might be stronger and more knowledgeable at critical times, and leaders might be less vulnerable as targets for discontent. They might also be able to build consensus more quickly when it is needed.

Process

Making decisions in a politicized setting is as much a matter of process as it is a matter of substance. How decisions are made can affect how people accept them inside and outside the institution; no matter how technically accurate or correct a decision might be, if it is made in an unacceptable way it is almost certainly doomed. Unfortunately, decision makers associated with too many such decisions may also be doomed.

Just as we looked for a balance between extremes in style, so it seems that a balance between extremes in process is also important. If a process is too closed and exclusive, "outsiders" seem to quickly feel alienated from both the process and its products. They almost inevitably begin to question and oppose any decision that does not seem to take into account their own interests and values. Except in the most pressing of circumstances, however, achieving a working consensus on hard decisions in open and participatory settings proved difficult at our site institutions.

No one process seems to work effectively in all settings. Institutions' cultures differ, and the severity and immediacy of the crises differ. In some cases, institutions simply have no time and very few options: presidents and boards have to act swiftly and responsibly. In real crises, few would begrudge the leaders the right and duty to make decisions for which they will be held accountable. However, when the need for action is less urgent and more speculative, it is a good opportunity to open up the process, generate ideas, foster cooperative decision making, and achieve consensus to the furthest extent possible.

We also think that a tight relationship should exist between *process* and the *scope* of decisions. When top management and boards take decisive unilateral action, and when participation is minimal, decisions ought to be as restrained and narrow as possible under the circumstances. But when time and resources permit a more open process, decisions should be made about matters of principle and strategy. If broad agreement can be reached on these issues, then administrators will have a clearer mandate to make timely tactical moves.

We found that the more communal and open attempts to formulate responses to fiscal crisis resulted in great difficulty—often even running aground—in getting down to specific decisions. But we also worried a good deal about whether CEOs and boards could gather enough information and set aside time for reflection and consultation during times of severe pressure. We suggest monitoring the decision-making process to see whether it is inclusive enough to gain broad acceptance for general strategy and whether leaders have enough support to move quickly and effectively during times of real stress.

Courage

When a fiscal crisis hits, all members of a college or university face upsetting realities and threats to their own careers and economic security. An institution whose constituents believe in its mission and are committed to its survival provide it with far more insurance than any other single factor.

It is perhaps slightly old-fashioned—even outdated—to talk about courage. But we must recognize that powerfully committed people have acted at considerable risk to themselves and their families to literally save some of the institutions we visited.

We have no real way to measure it, but just as a fighting spirit and a will to live are often credited for helping a critically ill person beat long odds, so too does commitment to the institution and the courage to persist help to bring a college or university through hard times. In our opinion, one closely related measure of this dedication is the extent to which people feel connected to and bonded with others at a college or university. At the sites we visited, it was quite common to find this "all for one and one for all" feeling among those at small private institutions. Faculty at large research universities, by contrast, often felt the most powerful connections and loyalties to their professions and disciplines instead of to their colleagues or others on campus. We almost felt that for these people, the main concern in the midst of crisis was how to move to an institution that would be better able to support their research interests.

These feelings—for that is what they are—can have a depressing effect when a college or university most needs to pull together and act courageously. If an institution has no sense of community and of mutual obligations, it will almost certainly have more difficulty getting through a financial crisis successfully.

Vitality of Educational Programs

Educational vitality and fiscal health seemed closely related at the institutions in our study. Colleges and universities in weaker condition had trouble attracting and holding good students, while institutions in better health attracted better students who had higher rates of timely graduation. These trends seemed to us to be good basic indicators of educational vitality and very appropriate proxy measures of current or future fiscal health. To be very practical, students who enter a college or university with high expectations of themselves, who are highly committed to the institution, who study full-time and live on campus, and who persist to graduation in four years are exactly what a healthy college or university wants and needs. (Community colleges, of course, are in a somewhat different position, both by reason of mission and because their students are far more diverse than those attending more traditional institutions.

But they, too, are strengthened when their students are purposeful, dedicated, and persistent.)

Current theory and research on college students seems to converge on certain key things an institution can do to promote effective undergraduate education (Chickering and Gamson, 1991). For the purposes of this chapter, we are primarily interested in which indicators might be watched on a regular basis. The indicators we mentioned in the last paragraph are a good start, but what about community colleges and urban institutions that have more part-time and commuting students?

We suggest that institutions take an inventory of the "seven principles" of effective undergraduate education (Chickering and Gamson, 1991). How many of these principles are part of students' actual experience? Where are they getting this experience? What is missing in the undergraduate experience? Other useful indicators might assess student progress toward degrees: how much time and how many credit hours do students accumulate before graduating, and what have they learned by the end of each year of study? The first index gives the institution some sense of whether its students are taking too few or too many courses. The second index charts what kind of learning students are doing and compares it either to the goals an institution has developed or to the needs of employers and graduate schools. Trends and relationships are perhaps as important as some arbitrary level of achievement: are students learning more of the right things as they go through the programs? Is each succeeding class learning more than its predecessor (or at least not doing worse)?

We also think it is very important to conduct an ongoing assessment of student satisfaction. By using focus groups, interviews, or surveys, a college or university can find out how students feel about various aspects of their experience. We think that the more satisfied students are with their academic experience, the more likely they are to persist and graduate. Obviously, it would be good to find that students are satisfied with other aspects of their college experience, too. But if they are highly satisfied with the "bread and cir-cuses" of student life, but dissatisfied with or indifferent to their aca-demic experience, something is fundamentally wrong.

If students' primary sources of satisfaction are immediate, then we have questions about the long-term value that is being added. Unless graduates become productive employees and intelligent cit-izens—and can become helpful supporters of the institution as alumni—then the institution's long-term health may be insecure. This is why it is important to assess whether students' academic experiences are perceived as positive and satisfying, especially in relation to the more transient and trivial and "fun" aspects of col-legiate living.

This book is not the place for a detailed discussion of the tech-nology and practice of assessment; a whole literature is now devel-oping around these subjects. We simply want to point out that student progress is a very important measure of an institution's edu-cational vitality, and therefore an indicator of its fiscal health.

"Interactivity"

We have gone to considerable lengths in this chapter to identify many different indicators of an institution's health—fiscal and oth-erwise. We have done so because we concluded that a wide array of causes acted jointly on all of the diverse institutions in our study.

Fiscal problems are but symptoms of several interacting causes that have more or less converged at a critical point. In other words, even though money may be short, the stronger and more resilient institutions are positioned in a way that differentiates their re-sponses from others'. So we think that monitoring an institution's overall health involves a great deal more than just watching its cash flow or account balances.

With this in mind, we have proposed four major vectors that colleges and universities can monitor as a way of keeping track of conditions and trends that *might* signal the onset of more serious problems and threats to survival. These vectors include environmental factors, financial patterns, management patterns, and educational issues. We think it is important to watch each vector in its relations to all the others—in other words, to develop a three-dimensional picture of what is happening to the institution.

Conclusion

The goal of this chapter is to develop indicators that colleges and universities can use to assess and diagnose their current condition. Fiscal stress at the institutions in our study turned out to be a symptom of a broader array of problems—all of which interacted with one another. The only way we could make sense of our data was to look at how these interactions worked to produce the underlying "disease."

We do not know how to identify some arbitrary critical point beyond which a serious fiscal crisis emerges. But we do think that watching several aspects of the institution's condition at the same time is a good way to get early signs that things are moving in the right or wrong direction, and indications of how fast they are moving. These indicators track:

- Trends in the external environment
- Financial condition
- Management effectiveness
- Educational vitality
- Interactions among these factors

Each college or university might want to develop its own critical indicators in these areas—indicators that are uniquely sensitive to the history, culture, and context of the institution itself.

Chapter Eight

Triage

Incremental change may not be enough for institutions in serious trouble. Either they are doing the wrong things to begin with, or they are so poorly managed they need revolutionary change, or they are confronted with conditions that demand fast thinking and quick acting. These institutions will have to make hard choices, and will have little time to engage in rational planning.

When colleges and universities engage in *triage*, they choose to be and do certain things and choose *not* to be and do other things. Given the long history of experimentation and expansiveness in American colleges and universities, triage is an unfamiliar and unsettling prospect. But it has to be done if scarce resources are to be used effectively.

Triage is a gut-wrenching and risky business. It requires sometimes brutal and always distasteful decisions. People get hurt when resources are reallocated and programs cut. But triage has to be practiced as honestly, quickly, and painlessly as possible at many colleges and universities if they are to survive in a time of fiscal uncertainty.

In this chapter, we will analogize the medical definition of triage to higher education's present circumstances and consider how triage might be applied in restoring fiscal health. We will also deal with the public side of triage—how to manage information during a crisis situation.

The Concept of Triage

In the medical world, triage involves deciding which patients will probably benefit most from the scarce resources available to treat

195

them, so that those resources may be rationed for the greatest good effect. Some patients will die (or at least not benefit) regardless of the treatment they receive. Others may benefit, and could—with ordinary care—recover eventually, although at the cost of time and personal expense. Somewhere in between, though, are the patients who may recover if—and only if—they receive the full benefit of available treatment and care. In other words, such costly interventions cannot be justified unless the payoff is clear; otherwise the resources may not be available to others who would clearly benefit.

Triage decisions obviously involve a good deal of subjective assessment. They are often made in emergencies when the demand for treatment far outstrips the available resources. Accordingly, the medical profession has developed norms and protocols for making triage decisions. Among the most recent is the guide to priorities published by the Society of Critical Care Medicine Ethics Committee. It has the following provisions (1994, p. 1200):

- Develop and make public a triage policy so that staff and patients will know what to expect should the demand for medical services ever exceed the supply.
- Give priority for intensive care unit (ICU) space to those who would benefit the most from intensive care and for whom nonintensive care would be insufficient.
- Do not use ICU resources for those with no hope of recovery.
- Consider your moral values, the wishes of patients, and the fiscal and psychological burdens of those affected.
- Assign the responsibility for triage decisions and set up dispute settlement mechanisms.

This statement suggests how colleges and universities can make decisions to invest or disinvest in programs and activities. But first, institutions might consider how to measure the severity of their condition.

How Do You Know if There Is a "Crisis"?

We believe that it is useful to think of "stress" as a cyclical phe-
nomenon. Most institutions—and certainly the ones we visited—
have gone through periods of greater or lesser financial health
during their histories. They have adjusted in more or less successful ways, depending on when they were able to recognize signs of
an approaching downturn.

We therefore think it is useful to *measure an institution's vital signs
continuously*. Combining several indicators at once may produce a
very useful diagnostic picture, especially if those indicators are com-
piled over a period of years. Take, for example, trend data on enrollment, tuition, and institutional student aid at one of our site
institutions. Enrollment was projected to decline, tuition was rising, and student financial aid was projected to hit 46 percent of
total tuition income. The CEO held briefings for campus constituencies in which he showed the zero-sum relationships among
these three variables and the distribution of salary. By doing this,
he was able to define the shape of a potential crisis—one that had
not yet hit but would do so if trend lines continued. Fortunately,
this particular private institution had operating reserves to protect
it, and it could afford time—perhaps three years—to consider and
implement action plans.

Another private institution was facing a far more serious problem. Enrollment was declining. All current gifts were being
deposited into current accounts. Half of the endowment had been
spent to meet current expenses. Short-term loans were being used
in the same way, and were obtained only by paying a top interest
rate. No consistent development plan was in place, and development and admissions staffs were turning over almost annually. The
new president analyzed these trends in 1989 and concluded that
the institution would be out of business in a year.

The problem is not always as obvious as it appeared to be for
these two private institutions. In another case, a small public college

had endured repeated threats of closure—often more perceived than real, but nevertheless alarming to faculty, staff, and community. These threats seemed to be coming from the legislature. Although they had not materialized, and although the community had mobilized to defend "its" college several times—even with bus trips to the state capitol—they were nevertheless alarming threats. This was confirmed by a state official during our visit, and was based essentially on projections for the capital repair and replacement. The entire campus was approaching obsolescence and needed extensive work, and in the state's current fiscal condition, it seemed unlikely that anything more than minimal work could be done. Thus, external threats to survival had reached a serious point, notwithstanding the fact that enrollment and current funds budgets were reasonably stable. The question was whether the state could afford to keep the campus open at all.

An institution's balance sheet need not be overwhelmed by red ink for a crisis to be imminent. By taking many different indicators and watching trends over time, institutions can draw a picture of where they are headed. A seemingly healthy institution may only appear that way because its plant is not being maintained. Or an institution that is running a surplus in its current accounts may be doing so by admitting lower-quality students. Conversely, an institution may be spending too much on financial aid to attract a shrinking cohort of students from the top 10 percent of their high school classes; while its indexes of student quality may remain strong, the institution may be on an unsustainable path by awarding more financial aid than it can afford in the long run.

So the only way to measure how close an institution is to health or to crisis is by accumulating good data and looking *continuously* at the trends. "Hard" and "soft" data are equally important in drawing a full picture. What people think, what they say, and how they react are not in and of themselves reliable data on current conditions, but observed along with more objective information, people's perceptions can be extremely helpful.

In some of our case studies, it was clear that faculty and staff perceived a crisis even when numbers alone did not indicate how close or how serious the problems were. People were able to sense that things were not going well, or at least that the future felt highly uncertain. In measuring an institution's health—as in measuring an individual's health—perhaps the first diagnostic question has to be "Where does it hurt?" This cannot be the only question (see Chapter Seven for our approach to analyzing the institution's condition), and we do not suggest that an institution base its assessment only on what faculty, staff, or students feel. But neither should their feelings be ignored: they often carry serious early warnings. Hearing students say over and over, "I can't ever see my adviser" or "I can't get the classes I need to graduate" should tell an institution something profound about its performance, about whether it has enough resources to do its job, and about whether those resources are being applied intelligently.

When Is a Good Time to Call Attention?

When is less important, we think, than *how*. If there is no particular line in the sand to delineate crisis from noncrisis situations, then there really is no one good time to "announce" that a crisis has arisen and that steps must be taken. Since the fiscal health of any college or university is really a dependent variable in a complex array of other variables that may be acting quite independently of one another (or perhaps in concert with one another), the best strategy we can suggest is to keep people informed about the key trends.

We have seen any number of cases in which presidents announce—via speech or letter to the community—that an unforeseen problem has arisen that will require people's cooperation and forbearance. Seldom, we think, has the problem really been so unforeseen. Careful monitoring—which most intelligent administrators already do continuously without having read this book—has almost always made it clear what is happening, although not always when a critical incident (an enrollment fall-off, a state budget rescission, a change in federal policy) will occur. By the time a general pronouncement is published, though, it is usually very late in the game.

We know from our own experience that it takes great fortitude for a CEO to tell the rank and file that things are suddenly and painfully worse. It reflects badly on the CEO's performance, for one thing. For another, it almost inevitably unleashes a vituperative public reaction. Then time is lost while explanations are constructed (and often reconstructed), committees formed, and further questions raised.

It seems far more constructive to think, as we said earlier, in terms of continuous assessment and interpretation. If information is widely shared, an institution should not find itself lurching into a crisis and catching constituencies blindsided by new data and a new definition of the situation. But sharing information alone will not *prevent* a crisis. What has to be done when real change is needed?

Confronting Reality

A college or university, like any other organization, has a role to play, a niche to occupy, a market to serve. Knowing itself and being good at its role is the beginning point for dealing with a crisis. Institutions that try to become something they are not—especially those that try to promote an unsubstantiated image—take huge risks.

The main risk is in the potential violation of the public's trust. Relatively speaking, college students and their parents invest as heavily in college education as they do in almost anything else, housing included. If they do not get real value for that investment, they will become a major problem for the institution *because they know they got a bad bargain and will resent it publicly.*

A second risk, however, is that of self-deception. We heard over and over again about unrealistic faculty aspirations and continual pressure to "be like Harvard." Although many may not know what Harvard is really like, the shorthand translation is that faculty want to do less undergraduate teaching and have more time for research. Notwithstanding the fact that national surveys of faculty do not confirm this assumption, it is obvious that the feeling is strong enough on many campuses to distort reality and affect campus values—including how rewards are distributed.

Most institutions survive by generating enrollment. Enrollment, in turn, generates tuition dollars and/or—by some more or less direct means—state appropriations. Research and other activities mostly do not pay for themselves with hard cash. Instead, in many institutions they serve as nonsalary subsidies to faculty. Attracting faculty requires that institutions provide working conditions that are competitive, and faculty expect to have the time and resources to do at least some research. It is not at all unreasonable for a college or university to compete for faculty in this way. But doing so can be costly.

A small number of faculty at a few institutions actually generate dollars to pay for their research and development activities. Our best estimate, drawing on unweighted responses to a survey of more than 25,000 faculty by the National Center for Education Statistics in 1992–93 (Zimbler, 1994), is that—at most—only 10 percent of *all* faculty have *ever* had grant funding for research. The actual number is likely to be more on the order of 5 to 6 percent. (The total percentage depends on which survey items are used as indicators, but the numbers are very small in either case.) So an institution that makes research, service, or other activities a substantial part of faculty assignments is asking its tuition-paying students and/or the taxpayers to subsidize it.

Tuition has been increasing at a rate that now concerns the higher education community—because at present levels in a soft economy, it threatens access. The same can be said for state appropriations, which are no longer dependably escalating with inflation; in fact, they have declined dramatically for some institutions.

In the meantime, data from our site institutions suggest that faculty have continued—at some but not all institutions—to press for more opportunity to do research at the expense of students. One CFO questioned the morality of this subsidy: "Faculty are taking their pay to do research, so we have to come up with money to pay [part-timers and teaching assistants] who will take up the slack and teach in their place." In other words, it can be argued that tuition and taxes are paying twice for someone to teach.

It is a rare president or chief academic officer who takes (or can afford to take) this issue to the faculty. But it is a fundamental problem in the financial health of many colleges and universities. It is not a question of whether faculty should do research—obviously they should, and it is an important part of their professional and intellectual development. Having the time and resources to do research is an important consideration to any faculty member in the job market, so colleges and universities really have little choice but to provide it.

Moreover, faculty research is analogous to pro bono or charity work by attorneys in a law firm or physicians working in a professional partnership. It is a social good that pays off in goodwill or in other indirect ways. So we believe that research is a legitimate activity and should be subsidized.

Further, as Johnstone (1993) has pointed out, most faculty are presently teaching at the practical limit of their capacity. When faculty divert their attentions to research, institutions may need to be concerned more about the quality of learning going on when faculty are overworked than about the quantity of learning.

But we are concerned about the honesty with which the effects on institutional economics are handled. We are even more concerned about the effects on the education of students. And here is where we return to our theme of triage: an institution facing a crisis must be utterly objective and brutally candid about where its money is going, what it is getting in return, and whether it is performing its mission.

Trends in financial data are important indicators, but so are other trends—for example, who is producing the credit hours that generate tuition? Do those credit hours reflect real learning? Are curricula, courses, and other learning experiences current, effective, and economically viable?

It is neither fair nor good management practice to base all decisions on narrow considerations like the "profitability" of individual departments or faculty. Some departments and some faculty are worth far more to an institution than the number of credit hours they produce. But it is both fair and good management practice to ask what is being subsidized heavily and why.

It is also reasonable to ask whether the institution is doing what it is supposed to be doing. Are its students learning? Are they being prepared for work or graduate school? Do they require remediation before undertaking college-level courses? Are they dropping out, or are they graduating on time? And what about the institution's conditions for learning and development? Does the institution encourage faculty and staff to use effective practices in the classroom and in students' extracurricular activities? Are measures in place to assess both process and results?

A financial balance sheet that shows problems is of great concern in an institution that is not sure of its answers to these questions. However, an institution that can answer these questions clearly and positively may have financial problems, but they will be far more manageable because the solutions can begin with a solid base of information and the ability to present a clear analysis of the problem.

Confronting reality, in our terms, means developing a clear understanding of *where the institution's resources are coming from, where they are going, and with what results*.

Actions Versus Images

The first principle of triage involves honest communication, understanding, and trust. It states that "staff and patients [should] know what to expect" (Society of Critical Care Medicine Ethics Committee, 1994, p. 1200). In a crisis, the bedrock on which all else is based is the ability of the actors to know what the institution stands for, what it can and will do, and what it cannot and will not do.

Institutions have problems because (a) they do not actually provide the kind of experience students need and want to pay for, and (b) they do not communicate effectively about what they really do. But institutions that are effectively adapting to crisis seem to focus on providing students with a "good" education and on communicating well with students as well as other constituencies.

We think that the current fiscal crisis is at least partially due to the erosion of trust of two important constituencies: students and public officials. Therefore, the first step in triage is to reestablish credibility by agreeing on what these two groups should be able to expect.

Students

Students are arguably the best public relations tool institutions can have. If students have a good experience, they voluntarily "market" the institution to others. If they have a bad experience, they may talk very publicly about their unhappiness. Therefore, whatever else an institution may do well, the experience its undergraduates have is ultimately going to affect its enrollment, its tuition receipts, and its state appropriations. One chief academic officer noted that the one most important thing she did was to "pay attention to student complaints"—understanding how important a source of information this was to building an effective program.

By "students," we mean prospective, current, and former students. Many of a college's or university's most important opportunities to educate come when a prospective student is exploring options, gathering information, applying, and deciding which institution to attend. At our site institutions, top administrators and others usually understood the impact of good relations with prospective students and with the high school counselors who advise them.

Trenton State College's strategy was perhaps more aggressive than most, but its commitment to providing a high-quality undergraduate experience made it essential to recruit statewide for the best students—rather than relying on their traditional base of local students. The president and other top administrators spent time during the early years of TSC's initiative "on the road"—meeting with guidance counselors and prospective students, making a personal commitment to top students that their experience at TSC would be of high quality. They were especially aggressive in hands-on, personalized recruiting of outstanding minority students, making these contacts one school, one student at a time.

One vice president said that this effort had been demanding of everyone from the president on down: "We opened a lot of restaurants on cold winter mornings" on road trips to visit with counselors around the state. Even so, this high-level personal effort did not pay off immediately. It took patience and persistence over a period of years: "Counselors needed to build trust; they said, 'okay, we'll send you one student—then we'll watch to see if you take good care.'"

At first, few counselors came to the annual campus meeting, but TSC's intensive and focused follow-through effort has obviously paid off, because the college now attracts a student body that is competitive with that of, for example, Rutgers University, New Jersey's flagship public university, and private liberal arts colleges.

The college had to follow up and meet the high expectations of incoming students, though, or it risked disillusioning them. The vice president for student affairs reflected the orientation of most of those with whom we talked: "TSC has built its reputation on word of mouth from satisfied customers."

Legislators

"Legislators" is our proxy term for the public. Trust is obviously important here, too. But trust between legislators and higher education has been in short supply in recent years. Judging by our interviews—and from our experience—legislators' attitudes toward higher education seem to gravitate to three propositions; none is necessarily true, but the beliefs can have a powerful hold on those who decide how the public's money will be spent:

- College and university leaders are haughty and condescending in dealing with legislators.
- College and university faculty do not return an honest effort for their pay.
- Colleges and universities do not care about undergraduate students.

Any one of these propositions, if true or if widely believed, would be damaging to the image and interests of an agency or corporation that depended on the public's trust. Unfortunately for many colleges and universities, public beliefs seem to have crystallized around all three beliefs.

Start, of course, with the assumption that legislators and the public are at least having great difficulty sorting out priorities for public funding. In many states, the current mood is a good deal more hostile toward government spending of all kinds. This puts legislators in an exquisitely difficult bind. They have federal programs and mandates downloaded onto their budgets without adequate funding to implement them. They cannot raise taxes without imperiling their political survival. And they have to demonize public spending of all kinds—even when the spending pays off—because the popular culture seems to demand that legislators play the role of "outsider."

Individual legislators, however, are highly supportive of the goals of higher education, and even of specific institutions. But they do not have much room to maneuver within the confines of a state budget that is stretched thinner every year trying to meet current needs. Even if they want to support higher education, these legislators cannot find the resources to do so. One external affairs officer noted that in her state, "the public is in a 'no new taxes, no new anything' mood."

In our view, however, this depressingly negative scenario simply begs for colleges and universities to fill the vacuum with substantive efforts to rebuild trust. It is not too difficult to imagine a set of relatively clear messages that might help the situation:

- Treat students and parents with respect.
- Give students a good experience and a good education.
- Be a good steward of public funds.
- Contribute to economic development.
- Do research that pays off and improves the lives and work of the people in the state or community.
- Get (and earn) good press coverage that reflects well on the institution (and, not coincidentally, on state government).
- Bring people together—at football games and other appropriate occasions—to celebrate good things, and be sure that some of the celebratory mood rubs off on people who support the institution.

Legislators and the public want colleges and universities to be successful and able to show how they are succeeding. Funding cuts are not really discretionary, nor are they really meant to punish higher education. One state coordinating board administrator pointed out, "Resource shortages are driving governors and legislatures into higher education's pockets." But without *seeing evidence of success and good stewardship*—and without being able to counteract myths about how poorly higher education is doing, legislators and governors find it harder and harder to trust and support the academic community.

Showing real success in things that matter to the public—rather than merely declaring such success in slick promotional campaigns about faculty publications and attendance at international meetings—is the most pressing matter for higher education's agenda. In the end, politics, in Thomas P. "Tip" O'Neill's widely quoted homily, is "all local." So political support undoubtedly depends on doing good for constituents, clients, and community.

This is one way in which colleges and universities misconceive their message and get cross-wired with political leaders. A key administrator on one public campus clearly saw the tension between seeking state support and trying to maintain an international presence:

> Can we be "America's best," as we have said publicly? The legislature doesn't resonate to this kind of rhetoric. . . . They want to know how best to allocate their scarce resources. [But] we are still being all things to all people. We didn't really tip our hand on what we can and will do and what we can't and won't do. There are problems when you do this. . . . There is political backlash, [which hurts when] there is lots of competition for scarce state dollars. The other state institutions get more per student than we get. They are more "democratic"—they don't have lots of foreign students, for example, and they produce the bulk of the state's teachers.

A system executive in another state focused on the same theme: "Ivory towers are no longer relevant [to state political leaders]. We have to be in the streets, getting pragmatic, making real changes. Places that don't produce high-level graduates with real skills should be shut. It is, on the whole, a refreshing period. We can use it as an opportunity to make real changes. If we don't, the legislature is going to say, 'If you are so good, go earn your keep in the marketplace!'"

Can colleges and universities satisfy students and earn the trust of legislators at the same time? One example from our study stands out as confirmation. Trenton State College found that it needed to take the radical step of imposing a tuition surcharge in the midst of a difficult state budget year. While the administration was ready with its arguments, it consulted with students about their views.

The students were so concerned with maintaining quality as they had come to know it at TSC that student government leaders testified on behalf of the surcharge—perhaps the ultimate test of an institution's effectiveness, and the ultimate proof that Trenton State had earned the right to the public's trust.

Trust is based on mutual honesty. Institutions that communicate with key constituencies may openly and candidly expect a greater measure of trust in return. As two prominent alumni at one institution noted: "People come forward when they know you have to adapt to tough times; you have to be up front with them about your situation." Although they were talking about fundraising campaigns, their advice probably applies equally well in dealing with other constituencies, including the legislature. In our view, the worst thing an institution can do is misrepresent its condition— whether through self-deceptive hyperbole ("best in America"), skewed data, or willful dishonesty. As one faculty leader put it, "Avoid lying, . . . Trust is so important."

We hasten to add that the institutions in our study all understood this principle well, but the popular press all too frequently reports cases in which colleges and universities engage in cover-ups, self-serving promotional excess, and actual lying. These stories do the academic community no good.

Doing Things That Count

The second main point in triage is to use resources in a way that produces real benefit: "Priority for ICU space should be given to those whom [intensive care] would benefit the most. . . . Do not use ICU resources for those with no hope of recovery" (Society of Critical Care Medicine Ethics Committee, 1994, p. 1201). Or, as the blunt political maxim of Mayor Richard Daley (the elder) of Chicago enjoins, "Don't back no losers!"

Colleges and universities have used public funds for the support of programs whose value is hard to demonstrate. Some programs, of course, have value that is poorly understood, hard to measure, and yet incalculably important. Much basic research falls into this category, but so do programs in the arts and human services. We would surely not wish to see higher education become so narrow in focus that it shed all programs that do not have immediate or obvious material payoffs.

Triage is difficult when the judgments are as complex as looking at returns on investment in the programs and activities of higher education. In fact, the varied group of institutions we visited simply would not be well served by one common set of criteria for deciding on what programs to keep and which ones to drop.

In discussing this theme with us, a prominent business leader active in alumni fundraising drew on his experience: "[You] start behaving more like business has to all the time. You take off your blinders periodically to see where you've been and what you might become. You try to start this before trouble hits you. It is a good idea to shed lines of business that can't support themselves. You have to concentrate on what you can do well and what supports you."

Pennsylvania State University's strategic planning exercise included an effort to focus on the school's special competence in particular areas of research: life sciences, environmental sciences, and materials science. Not only were these Penn State's areas of strength, but there was agreement that they were potentially the most important fields for growth in the future. Accordingly, in the process of "recycling" funds from other areas, these three fields had been targeted for special nourishment.

At Syracuse University the focus was different, but the principle was the same: develop a clear sense of mission and use it to guide the planning and budgeting process. Syracuse realized that its heavy dependence on tuition meant that it needed to focus on the undergraduate student experience. It focused on becoming more student-centered—which meant, among other things, holding the student affairs division harmless during budget reallocation. One dean described what this meant to his college: "We are refocusing on becoming a more student-centered institution. . . . There is going to have to be a shift in rewards to student-centered activities like advising, teaching, [and so on]." It was widely understood that becoming student-centered was the key to Syracuse's tuition base and budgetary priorities. Units that had yet to figure out that this value was driving all decisions found themselves penalized; others were quick to see the new rules and were being rewarded.

Other institutions also understood how important it was to identify their strengths and build on them. The University of Massachusetts at Boston, for example, stuck with its commitment to be an urban university and focused its efforts to develop doctoral programs on interdisciplinary approaches to urban problems and issues. The university might have taken a more traditional approach, but it would then have been in competition with an already highly developed group of graduate institutions in the Boston area. Instead, it carved out a particular niche and took a direction that would well serve its own future development, as well as the Boston community.

Bloomfield and Tusculum colleges both made clear commitments to sharper definitions of an undergraduate education. They both defined a set of particular outcomes and set up assessment programs that required collaboration among academic disciplines and between the academic and student affairs staffs. The University of Maryland-Eastern Shore and the University of Texas at El Paso both built their plans around the needs of their particular ethnic constituencies.

Cutting Back, Phasing Out, and Dropping Programs

Focusing on strength is the positive side of triage. But triage also requires that people or programs be set aside when they cannot benefit from the use of scarce resources.

Very little in the way of hard triage decisions had been made at the time of our site visits. Budgets had been squeezed across the board, administrative cuts made, maintenance deferred, tuition and fees raised, and fundraising pursued more aggressively. Salary increases had been held down, layoffs and furloughs implemented, early retirement options offered, and controls on current expenditures of all kinds exercised. But real program cuts had not generally been made. Reflecting a feeling we encountered on most campuses, a faculty leader said, "We've been getting 10 percented and 5 percented to death since [1989]. They've cut everywhere they can, and all the fat is gone."

Program closures were usually viewed as a last resort, and the potential for doing real damage is perhaps more than most institutions were willing to risk. In at least one case, a program cut was perceived on campus as counterproductive: the state board decided to shut down what had been a "signature" music program at Mayville State University. Not only had this been a part of Mayville's identity, but it had also been an important part of the isolated rural community's culture. Music majors played in the band at football games and provided entertainment at other events as well. The sense of loss was widespread on campus, among alumni, and in the surrounding community. It may or may not have been a rational economic, academic, or public policy decision, but it had clearly hurt the university's sense of itself and its place in the community.

Most institutions were very reluctant to go this far. There was a great deal of concern about accurately assessing the scope and depth of financial problems before making actual cuts. Even when seemingly catastrophic budget reversals are floated in news reports about state funding, the actual effects turn out often enough to be less than the worst-case projections. Although this kind of "learning" has perhaps engendered cynical disbelief and an unwillingness to entertain proposals for reasonable and prudent change on campuses, it may also have prevented actions that might have prematurely done needless damage.

An example of such scrambling to cut without sufficient forethought occurred in Oregon, a state that has been particularly hard-hit by recession. Too many campuses had decided at the same time to cut teacher education without knowing what the other institutions were planning to do. This kind of error can prove costly because it has to be reversed—and restarting a program is obviously more expensive than continuing one.

Furthermore, even the threat of a cut often produces public perceptions that are far ahead of (and more extreme than) any actual steps taken by the campus. Administrators at one campus in a small community expressed regret that there was so much press coverage of plans for program cuts. According to one:

> There was regret that [the cuts got] so much press coverage. The media situation is both a plus and a minus [here] in that there is a serious open-meeting requirement and practically everything gets discussed in public. The press covers faculty meetings and reads agendas for future meetings very carefully. [But] the press does not always understand that what is under discussion is not what is actually going to happen. There needs to be more understanding of how higher education does business in its collegial phases.

We saw other campuses grappling with this dilemma. On one level, it made economic and educational sense to consider program cuts; on another level, proposing cuts mobilized resistance and counterplays by those whose interests were affected.

Secrecy made the problem worse. Several committees that were charged with advising presidents or boards with recommended program cuts met privately to consider their recommendations. The campuses actually experienced heightened resistance from those who merely *imagined* that their programs might be affected.

Continuous Change

With this experience in mind, we suggest that the selection of program cuts be conducted with precision and with attention to the likely sources and intensity of resistance. It is also important to calculate risks and exposure, because layoffs or retrenchment open the institution to litigation and to greater economic damage than if it simply were to leave a weak program alone.

But this does not mean that institutions should just resign themselves to the status quo or give up on the idea of triage—to the contrary. All it means is that tighter, more timely, and more continuous decisions have to be made. When an intensive care unit does not have enough resources, people, or equipment to go around, one short-term way that it can make do is to monitor patients more closely so that those most in need get what they need when they need it. The analog in the business world—at least roughly speaking—is "just-in-time delivery," a process that keeps production moving at the most economical pace while supplies and parts are delivered as needed. In both the medical and business analogies, the supply and use of resources is calibrated to *current need* instead of to some arbitrary set of predictions, schedules, or classifications.

Continuous adaptation, continuous learning, and continuous quality improvement are interesting ideas that can complement strategic management and planning—and are largely based on the precept that continuous small adjustments to the current situation do as well to adjust the organization over the long run as attempting to predict and control the future.

The Human Dimension

The ethics of triage require decision makers to consider the fate of the people involved. Withholding or cutting off support will have predictable effects. In higher education, this means that students will not have opportunities, that faculty and staff will lose jobs, and that programs will wither and die. Real people are affected in real ways.

The Consensus Statement (Society of Critical Care Medicine Ethics Committee, 1994) emphasizes that responsibility for such decisions be identified, that dispute-settlement mechanisms be available, and that the impact of decisions be carefully weighed for their effects. People who will be affected need an opportunity to understand what is happening to them, why it is happening, and what the consequences will be. They also need the opportunity to have some control over the decision's impact on their lives. Giving them information, time, a way to negotiate and come to terms with the decision, and a sense of who is responsible and what led to the decision may all be helpful tactics.

In other words, if people are going to be hurt—as they almost inevitably will—institutions need to find ways to minimize the damage and maximize the control people have over how and when the damage will occur. Hard decisions do have to be made, so it may not be any less painful in the end, but it will certainly be more acceptable when care is exercised and respect is offered.

Conclusion

Colleges and universities with recent histories of almost unrestrained expansiveness, and whose internal culture tends to be one of consultative and democratic decision making, have had great difficulty in facing up to triage.

We have attempted to use the medical profession's ideas to propose realistic approaches to triage in colleges and universities. We suggest the following ideas as useful:

- Monitor vital signs continuously. Watch both hard and soft data for indicators of emerging problems.
- Keep people informed on the trends.
- Be honest about the institution's strengths and weaknesses.
- Be honest about the institution's finances—who is subsidizing what, and why?
- Be honest about what the institution is achieving and about what the outcomes really are.

- Build trust with students and the public through a clear statement of mutual expectations and responsibilities.

- Do things that count, and focus the use of scarce resources.

- Adjust continuously, and calibrate change to the information available and the level of damage a major change would cause.

- Take care to respect the human needs of people affected by adverse decisions.

- Accept the reality that hard decisions must be made and that the institution will change in sometimes painful ways.

We think that the triage model is useful because it suggests ways of maximizing the use of scarce resources while minimizing error and respecting the human needs of those affected.

Chapter Nine

Strategy and Realism

Promoting Enlightened Change

How can an institution in trouble—or about to be in trouble—get itself out of trouble? As a first principle, we believe that colleges and universities should adopt an approach to change and adaptation that is calibrated to the severity of their problems. The institutions we visited had tried many variants of strategizing and strategic planning. We boiled these different approaches down and found one overriding theme: Institutions have to define and seize control of planning their own futures.

Most institutions in our study faced the basic dilemma outlined by Schuster and others in *Strategic Governance* (1994). The authors studied how "joint big-decision committees" performed in making strategic changes during times of fiscal stress. They found that a balance had to be struck between making hard and timely decisions on one hand, and keeping the process as open and participatory as possible on the other.

But there is no one best way—no one formula—to solve these problems. The institutions we studied that seemed to be adjusting well were those that remained focused on the long term, were able to articulate a vision for their institution, developed good information and open communications, and engaged in continuous learning and adaptation.

Our goal for this chapter is to explore the basic tasks an institution has to accomplish in defining and controlling its future. Among the main issues we discuss are the following:

- Pressure for deep change
- Importance of a proactive stance
- Use of a vision
- Expectations about the president's role
- Information and communication
- Participation
- Cutting, shaping, and redesigning
- Continuous learning
- Entrepreneurship
- Enlightened strategic planning
- Accountability and responsibility
- Avoidance of pitfalls

Pressure for Deep Change

The people at almost every institution we visited sensed a need for deep change—change that would affect their missions and identities. Their institutions were being affected simultaneously by a flat or declining economy, by pressure to maintain and renew capital infrastructure, by an increasing reluctance of state governments to raise taxes, by political pressure to expand access, by pressure from the marketplace to control tuition increases, and by regulations that required increasing administrative expenses.

These pressures relentlessly squeezed existing resources while simultaneously demanding more spending. Most people we interviewed understood that "the only way to find new money is to cut from the old. All new program money is now going to have to come from internal reallocation."

These pressures made it unlikely that the site institutions could continue to make merely incremental changes. One vice president said, "We have to make strategic reallocations, not just incremental ones." A survey by the American Council on Education that was conducted at about the same time as our study confirmed that the vast majority of colleges and universities had begun "restructuring" themselves in response to fiscal constraints. Between one-third and one-half had "instituted multipronged restructuring strategies that include[d] tightening expenditure controls, seeking new revenue sources, reorganizing, and making selective decisions about academic programs" (El-Khawas, 1994, pp. 2–3).

Business as usual was not perceived as a viable alternative by any of our site institutions. Colleges and universities that chose to drift through this recent period of stress without initiating changes were courting failure. So the most important question these institutions faced was, "How do we change?"

Taking a Proactive Stance

Hard experience had taught many of those we interviewed the value of making a change before a crisis closed down options. Once the situation hardened and the dimensions of the crisis started to constrain decision makers, it became much tougher to begin planning. If ideas, directions, and plans are not in place before a crisis hits, then it is much harder to respond creatively and imaginatively.

Usually an institution is affected by financial crisis because it is overextended—or at least it has not been thoughtful about which of its activities are most important. Too many of our interviewees were able to say they regretted that their institutions had avoided hard decisions even after entering a period of stress. One said, "We have really only done reactive things so far; there have been too many crises. We can't get out of crisis mode."

Being in crisis mode often led institutions to put money first and ideas second. In other words, a financial crunch led to decisions about the distribution of money among existing activities, and not to decisions about whether the existing activities served the institution's mission. Funding decisions—particularly the internal politics of funding—began to drive strategy at some institutions, rather than vice versa. One administrator noted that his institution had fallen into the trap of "decremental protection of the status quo"—removing small and proportional amounts of money from everyone's budget while trying to keep some semblance of normal operation. He urged that we tell others facing a similar situation not to "let funding shape your goals."

A general theme that ran through our interviews converged on the idea that an institution is much better positioned to deal with crisis if it has a well-understood mission and strategy in place. Strategic planning was viewed in differing ways, depending on an institution's unique experience, but it was generally agreed that strategizing forced colleges and universities to make explicit which principles and values would guide decisions about change. But these principles and values can guide decisions only if they are clearly understood *before* a crisis arises; otherwise, it may be too late to do more than protect the status quo with thoughtless, across-the-board cuts.

Developing a Vision

It is difficult to think about the future in the middle of a period of stress. Yet a sense of what lies beyond the short-term horizon may be the most useful tool in coping and adapting. Our interviewees urged others to adopt longer time horizons and clear visions of what lay ahead—"ahead" meaning in years, not months or weeks. They felt that it was important to "have an outcome in mind" and to define the steps for getting there.

But getting immersed in process and reallocation without a vision to guide the outcome brought fears and insecurities to the surface. As a chief planning officer pointed out: "We were hanging on too much to the way it used to be; we have been scared to let go of the past." Others observed that decisions were too confined when they were based on "just coping with the exigencies." A number of our interviews repeated this theme: "Go out on a limb. Let go and be bold." The point was not that institutions should take big risks, but that they should construct a vision of the long-term future before getting into the process of coping with an immediate crisis.

Having a vision seems to directly affect the magnitude of decisions an institution can consider making. When it has no vision to legitimize its priorities, it may be stuck in the unproductive decremental protection mode: just taking nickels and dimes from all available sources without thought to the long-term impact.

One planning officer observed that having an overall vision allows an institution to make bigger decisions and to have a more substantial impact: "It gives license to make the sometimes appalling decisions that have to be made." Perhaps the choice of words is more dramatic than intended, but it illustrates the point nicely.

Whose Vision? The Presidential Burden

"Visions" do not emerge out of thin air. Yet without them, people do not seem to be as powerfully committed to the common interest. The vision that guides a college or university has to be constructed, and ownership of the vision has to be shared—not just among internal constituencies, but among friends, supporters, potential students, and leaders in the external world.

Vision is essentially a sense-making tool, a way of communicating the institution's intentions, of explaining its actions, and of giving meaning to the lives and work of those who commit to the institution. It gives shape to the strategy an institution adopts, and it justifies and rationalizes decisions as that strategy goes into operation.

Vision can come from many sources, but among internal and external constituencies we found a very powerful expectation that *the president* should bear a clear responsibility for seeing that the institution's vision was clear, that it was shared, and that it was communicated effectively. In some cases, presidents clearly preferred to delegate vision-forming tasks to others: committees or faculty senates or board of trustees' retreats were all mentioned as forums in which to hammer out vision statements. But the many constituencies of presidents at our site institutions nevertheless had high expectations for presidential leadership in vision development. The president must at least start the ball rolling and carry on until a satisfactory working consensus about both vision and strategy is in place.

Boards of trustees (and others, too, though to a lesser degree) expect presidents to lead. Members look to the president for signals, and they need to sense a consistency in message. After all, the trustees talk about the institution on the *outside* in terms of vision, and it is what they use to understand and evaluate decisions and performance on the *inside*. They look to the president to keep them *and everyone else with a stake in the institution* "on-message."

Board members are often drawn from the worlds of business and government, and they have learned to expect and demand a relatively tight and purposeful style of management—one that includes clear and useful vision statements as well as a purposeful and practical strategic plan. In several cases, we were able to see that trustees had been instrumental in pushing for visions and plans; in a few cases, they did more than push—they assumed leadership roles.

While presidents may or may not take personal responsibility for the vision statement or strategic plan, they are nevertheless directly involved in how it gets communicated. One president noted that having a clear vision for his college gave him the substance of the text he needed "to send out important messages to students and others." He also felt that the message positioned his college as a "trend setter" and effectively drew attention and support to it.

With this kind of message, he felt he could trust faculty and board members to speak on behalf of the institution at local and national meetings—because they could take pride in representing this kind of institution to the public and their peers. Unspoken, but clearly implied, was the realization that the more that faculty and board members (and others) talked about the institution in public, the more committed they would become in realizing the vision and following through with strategies designed to achieve it.

Presidents have to orchestrate the process of getting diverse constituents to converge on and share a vision. They also have to orchestrate the communication of that vision both internally and externally. But this still leaves unanswered the most important question: Where do good visions come from?

The burden here should not be the president's alone. In fact, there is considerable risk involved when a president single-handedly invents an idiosyncratic "vision." It may be unrealistic. It may be unattainable. It may be at odds with the real character of the institution. And it may backfire if it alienates too many powerful constituents. How does the president know what is reasonable, realistic, and acceptable?

Information is one key. Participation is the other.

Information and Participation

The most effective way to get a realistic vision in place—if the experience of our site institutions is a guide—is to generate good hard data about an institution's current condition and performance (see Chapter Seven). The most effective way to get people to share that vision is to have them participate in forming and implementing it.

The colleges and universities in our group had problems with both tasks. Some had undeveloped or underdeveloped institutional research functions. They simply could not gather and analyze good information in timely and useful ways, either for public information or as feedback to themselves. At one institution in particular, the relatively new CFO said: "We had to set up institutional research capacity to tie funding to what we were actually doing. We previously had no analytical capacity. [Then] we had to reconstruct our whole budget management strategy. We had to plan and to hold people accountable. Before, no one knew anything or was held accountable. The former CFO always 'made it okay' by transferring funds around, and there was no accountability or responsibility anywhere else in the operation." Other institutions confirmed that they, too, had sometimes engaged in an informal, seat-of-the-pants, hide-it-in-the-mattress approach to management.

Not only was information not shared freely, but—as this vignette makes clear—there was sometimes no information to share at all! When no one, not even the CEO, really knows what is happening and has no dependable way to find out, then the institution will not know where it is succeeding, where it is failing, or whether it can learn from experience. So we believe that the ability to gather good information and interpret it is really the starting point. Institutional research units can play much more than a "bean-counting" role. They can help to shape knowledge and understanding of the institution, assess progress toward goals and outcomes, and serve as leaders in rethinking and reshaping the institution.

Another difficulty in getting good information results from the insulation of faculty and students, both vertically and horizontally. Students and faculty often do not receive good current information about conditions and developments that may seem clear and obvious to top administrators. Without good information, faculty may not have adequate opportunities to see trends and understand the whole picture. They might be able to help more if they knew more.

Also, people often do not have any real knowledge of what is happening outside their narrow fields and their isolated departments. One of our site institutions was in the process of preparing for the visit of a regional accrediting association team and had established a large task force of more than 150 faculty to work on various parts of its self-study. Several of those we interviewed noted how important this opportunity had been. It pulled people together from across the campus in close working relations with one another—unusual in itself—and it required that they share information on a wide variety of issues.

Over and over again we heard about how valuable it had been

to "share information." The impact of openness of information was made very clear by a faculty leader at one institution: "Openness has been the key to change [here]. The budget committee under the previous [CEO] didn't know what was going on. Now we know the data, and we have been able to educate ourselves. We have had open forums, group discussions. There has been an effort to share the broad picture, the trade-offs involved in making key decisions, and opportunities to suggest options. . . . The move to open up information and share it is smart."

We think that it is at least as important that information also flow upward from individuals, departments, and colleges. People at the top need good data on what is going on throughout the college or university. They need to know how the big decisions affect daily operations. They also need to know what people are thinking and feeling and how they are reacting to change.

If good information is the first requirement in developing vision and in strategizing, participation is the second. Involving people in the process means that they add more perspectives, more information, and more intelligence about what will work and what will not. Involving people in the process will increase the sense of ownership and commitment to the vision and strategy.

These generalizations have the ring of truth, and they were largely confirmed throughout our site visits. One interviewee represented many in saying, "It is a good idea to start with a wide-open and participative process. . . . Make it a communal effort." Yet we also heard certain voices of caution. For example, one administrator said, "Set a vision at the top," providing for participation only during the planning and implementation phase. Another took a much harder view: "Too much faculty and student participation is a form of abdication" on the part of top administrators. Some feared that participation would mean filibusters against change: "Decisions can't be made by consensus; the faculty will talk it to death."

We saw evidence that supported both of these views. Participation helps; participation hurts. It is situational. On balance, we lean toward more participation. But we would stop well short of unconditional democratization. An institution facing a crisis needs to be led, and it needs to make and commit to decisions. It has to achieve a certain measure of internal discipline. The president and the board have to impose that discipline.

For this reason, we think it is very important to provide for clear charges and time lines to structure the work of consultative bodies. Some bodies may serve essentially as think tanks for developing visions; others may have to make clear operational decisions within a given time period. The two kinds of assignments should be carefully delineated and their functions kept separate.

In any event, it is clear that some balance has to be struck between participation and closure. The more immediate and more severe the crisis, though, the more pressure there will be for decisions and action. And the less understanding of the situation there is across the campus, the less acceptable the decisions will be to stakeholders. Most institutions would be well advised to anticipate these pressures and take a proactive stance: inform and consult as far in advance of a crisis as possible, so that the basic principles and the dimensions of the situation—as well as the ground rules for decisions—are widely understood.

Institutions with strong internal value systems—call it "culture," if you will—are better able to winnow their many options in crisis, because people will expect certain decisions to emerge. The values and major premises by which such decisions might be made are widely known, shared, and internalized, so that almost anyone in a position to decide would probably make roughly the same decision.

Cutting, Shaping, and Redesigning

Strategy is the operational plan for realizing a vision. It is the road map. Its central point is to keep effort focused on certain outcomes. When resources are plentiful, strategizing mainly involves figuring out what to support. When resources are tight, the choices are considerably less attractive. We saw three basic options (and their variants) being considered at most of the institutions we visited.

One option is to take big slices out of the institution. This strategy is based on cutting or cannibalizing some programs so that others may survive with enough funds to sustain their quality and effectiveness. This kind of triage is inevitably painful, because it requires a redefinition of the institution and a dislocation of people.

The second main option is to cut or "tax" all programs a certain amount—say 5 percent—to meet a shortfall. This is particularly irrational and heavy-handed, in our view. It really suggests that the institution has no vision and no plan, and it simply assumes that all programs are equal and treats them the same. This option also avoids hard decisions about weak or inefficient programs, and it risks missing targets of opportunity for new investment.

Some institutions have instituted a small "tax" of perhaps 1 to 3 percent to put in an "innovation fund" for seeding new ideas; we think this is a good idea. Most of the site institutions entered this crisis period, as far as we can tell, without a pot of available money for reinvesting and for promoting change. Perhaps some of them could have moved more quickly and purposefully if such funds had been available.

The third option, in contrast, starts with a premise we found at one institution: "We can't keep doing everything; we have to focus energy on what we are good at." There are two further branches in this path. One branch defines "good" in terms of mission. Some institutions (particularly Bloomfield and Tusculum colleges) essentially reformulated their major premises—their visions—on which they based everything else. They basically reconstructed the whole college on the basis of new principles.

The other branch of the third option—one that's more attractive to the more complex institutions—involves continuous adaptation and reshaping. Pennsylvania State University, for example, identified certain themes on which it felt it could build strengths and was selectively reallocating funds to programs that added to these strengths. It was anticipated that this process would make the university different in the long run, although precisely how different was as yet uncertain. The immediate changes were comparatively small, but the long-term cumulative effect of these changes—all driven by a vision that emphasized the strong points of the university—would be substantial.

This continuous reshaping has several virtues. The most important in our view is that it allows an institution to test its ideas on a relatively small scale while it also reevaluates the appropriateness and direction of its general strategy. In other words, it promotes continuous learning.

Continuous Learning

For most institutions most of the time, the situation will keep changing, so they must be ready to keep adapting. While they may have a strong consensus on a clear vision and strategy at one point in time, there is no guarantee that every change they make will work perfectly or that the strategy itself will continue to serve the institution well in the long run. The environment will be more turbulent and unpredictable at times, and more stable and predictable at others. Since there is little that anyone can do to control these events, the best way to manage is to keep learning from experience.

Henry Mintzberg's notion of "informal learning" published in the *Harvard Business Review* (1994) is very useful in helping us understand how continuous learning should work. Mintzberg suggests that organizations engage in a continuous effort to gather both "soft" and "hard" information, that this information be shared widely to stimulate creative thinking, that initiative be given to those "who are deeply involved in the specific issues" at the operational level (p. 108), and that continuous learning from experiments be fed back to others in the organization.

As we have noted several times, some colleges and universities have yet to develop the kinds of analytical capabilities they really need. But this newer concept of continuous learning introduces the idea of using soft data in addition to hard data. It places a high value on human experience, intuition, and judgment. Mintzberg refers to "the soft insights from [a manager's] personal experiences and the experiences of others throughout the organization" (p. 107) as a vital part of the mix of information flow that an intelligent organization gathers and uses. Note that he implies strongly how people *throughout the organization* should be sharing their insights and experiences.

So continuous learning involves constant interpretation of soft and hard data about the course of reshaping. Are new steps bringing the institution closer to achieving its vision? What might be needed to help the process along? Are there enough successes across the institution to support and validate the overall strategy? Or are things just not working as had been hoped or anticipated? What do people think and how do they feel about what is going on around them?

A quick sketch of the continuous learning process shows that it begins by developing a clear picture of where an institution is headed (vision) and how it plans to get there (strategy). The picture is then shared with the key constituencies inside and outside the institution, who often help sharpen the focus and provide feedback on how to make it work. As the plan unfolds and new ventures start up, there is a lot of formal and informal talk about how the plan is developing. This works best when constituencies trust each other enough to be honest about what is being done and what is not being done, about what is working and what is not working. The role of administration in this process is to listen, consult, facilitate, solicit feedback, to use information to stimulate rethinking (when rethinking seems to be needed), and—of course—to impose discipline in reaching decisions. Communications must be open both laterally and vertically in the organization, and good feedback from the external world should be sought continuously.

We found ourselves interested in one logical variant of this approach: entrepreneurship. It is an attractive—even seductive—option for institutions looking for a quick and visible success. But like all forms of gambling, entrepreneurship may rely too much on playing long odds.

Entrepreneurship

The president of one institution described its approach to crisis as one of "scrounging." The leaders looked around for opportunities—ideas and niches that they could use. They took advantage of changing circumstances as they went along. Another institution followed roughly the same approach: "Identify contingencies and hang loose. . . . Be nimble." For the most part, these institutions were being careful about indiscriminately investing in things that couldn't be justified within their overall missions.

"Entrepreneurship" means many different things. At the University of Texas at El Paso, for example, external grant funding had increased about three times in about as many years. Some of the grants were targeted to increase minority participation in sciences. Mayville State University had become a member of an economic development group promoting the Red River Trade Corridor and was working to bring new businesses to the area—creating its own opportunities by advancing the general economic health of the region. Penn State had taken a lead role in creating a research park adjacent to the campus. The park provided an incubator for start-up companies that would rely on expertise at the university, such as its materials research group.

Even relatively small ventures can help an institution in important ways. Tusculum College, for example, has established an official Andrew Johnson presidential library in a historic building on campus. The library and its exhibits were already attracting tourists and school groups to the campus before it was even completed.

But several of our site institutions informed us in some considerable detail of ventures that were badly conceived and had gone terribly wrong—in a few cases resulting in genuine threats to the institution's survival.

Up to a certain point, entrepreneurship is vital to any institution. It provides the new ideas, the new markets, and the new money. It is also somewhat risky, because it invites failure. But if modulated and directed by a sense of mission and strategy, entrepreneurship might be seen as a form of continuous learning—as a way to push the boundaries a bit, learn things, and perhaps stimulate change.

The most compelling argument for entrepreneurship, in our view, is that *it works*. James Brian Quinn (1989) studied strategy formation in ten major corporations and came to the conclusion that strategy was *emergent*—not dictated from the top down—and that it formed "incrementally and opportunistically" (p. 46). He points out that: "No organization—no matter how brilliant, rational, or imaginative—could possibly foresee the timing, the severity, or even the nature of all . . . events [precipitating a crisis]. Further, when those events did occur, there might be neither enough time, resources, [nor] information to undertake a full formal strategic analysis of all possible options and their consequences" (p. 47). Quinn contends that it is more practical and effective to remain nimble and aware of the way in which people respond to the developing situation—to concentrate on managing people's responses instead of trying to control an uncontrollable situation. He found that adaptation and change go more quickly when an organization uses its best ideas, people, and resources to find new opportunities and try better ways of doing business.

A second study takes us a bit closer to the idea of continuous learning. Stopford and Baden-Fuller (1994) examined stressed British corporations' efforts to recover. The authors found that the successful adapters essentially engaged in "cumulative incrementalism" and "inched forward . . . [making rapid] partial changes" (p. 533). These corporations avoided trying to engage in large-scale strategic change, choosing instead to "spread and minimize risks by initiating many different projects" (p. 523). This resulted in what the authors characterize as a condition of "concentric entrepreneurialism" (p. 524). By sorting out the more successful and less successful small experiments, the firms gradually returned to healthier states.

Just like the process of continuous learning we described above, entrepreneurship requires the free flow of creativity, serendipitous experimentation, and information among the various parts of an organization. This freewheeling, opportunistic approach may be uncomfortable to some, because it seems to ignore some of the traditional ideas and norms about control of information and decisions. It may also involve violating the basic values and competence of the institution—perhaps changing it in ways that are both upsetting and inappropriate.

Successful entrepreneurship actually takes a lot of attention to continuous experimentation and continuous learning. More people have to be more observant, and there has to be more talking, listening, and evaluating throughout the organization. Paradoxically, what looks like a loose, freewheeling gamble actually requires very tight management—analyzing opportunities, planning, deciding on what to invest, starting up, getting feedback, and redesigning. Pulling all of this together and fitting it under the institution's general strategy takes very close attention to details and requires a clear plan—with bail-out options. This is especially important when resources available for investment are tight.

Enlightened Strategic Planning

At this point we think that a difference emerges between intelligent, or "enlightened," organizations and those that simply blunder along without bothering to accumulate self- awareness. Continuous learning has to result in some kind of consensus on values and convergence on a plan of action. Otherwise, it is just wheel-spinning, mindless trial and error, and wasted motion—obviously not what we have in mind. One institution came out of a strategic planning exercise committed to taking more than thirty specific initiatives—a commitment that some viewed as overwhelming: "Make sure you get your purpose straight before you get into the process. We probably got into the process too soon. Don't turn a five-year process into a one-year blitz and try to do thirty-three things all at once. There is no guarantee that [all the] initiatives will make this a better place. We'll modify as we go along, but not all of [our] thirty-three initiatives are going to work." Efforts to change need focus, a sense of priorities, and some reasonably clear objectives. There is no magic number, but a few simply stated themes can help in most cases.

In our view, enlightened organizations are good at continuous learning because they have strong cultures and seem to enjoy well-developed communication skills (both internally and externally). They form strong internal value systems that serve to filter information from a wide variety of sources. They do not make "strategic" decisions in the old linear/rational way, but rather sense and flow in an almost invisible process of growth, change, and reimagining.

The key is that they know what the feedback means, because they have a shared framework of meaning through which they can filter information. At Trenton State, for example, there is a strong commitment to giving students a sense of community and of meeting high expectations. TSC staff look at everything from campus appearance to extracurricular activities to academic experiences in terms of one imperative: "Keep the students active and involved."

Or at an institution like Penn State, the competitive research culture clearly drives the way in which people judge events and decisions. One department chair told how he approached the inevitable funding crunch: "I came on in 1990 as department head and told the faculty there would be no new hard money. We would have to go out and get our own funding to support students and do research. We got our own, and . . . made ourselves competitive on the traditional benchmarks and were therefore allowed to hold faculty positions." Institutions such as Bloomfield College, the University of Maryland-Eastern Shore, and Texas-El Paso all focused on what would help their minority students "make it" in society. Each institution had worked hard to involve community leaders in the process of learning how to add value to the lives of its students.

Converging on solutions—not just adding more activity—is the ultimate goal of continuous learning. Getting to the point where people understand and agree on those solutions has to involve more than just gathering information; it must involve building shared values and understandings—cultures—that provide a way of filtering and interpreting experience. That is what we mean by "enlightenment."

Enlightened institutions perform differently in crisis. They do not have to rely so heavily on blunt, across-the-board cuts, because they have a better (and more broadly understood) sense of value. They also do not have to gamble blindly on new moves, because they know more certainly the kind of institution they are and want to become. Therefore they will be more purposeful and patient about experimenting and about entrepreneurial ventures.

But what makes an institution enlightened? We observed that some institutions were particularly attentive to how all of its pieces fit together, how operations in one part of it interacted with those of another, and how important it was to understand and track these relationships. Some institutions were also good at using this kind of information to build a sense of common experience. So we return to the problem of generating enough shared experience and shared information to produce this kind of learning.

Simultaneous Tracking

In Chapter Five we introduced the idea of *simultaneous tracking*, a conscious effort to attack a number of issues and problems at the same time. Simultaneous tracking, where we saw it happening, involved accumulating information from all of an institution's main activities, and making a purposeful and coordinated interpretation of that information to give people feedback on trends. Good simultaneous tracking sought out expertise and intelligence about what was going well and not so well. It fostered cumulative learning across the institution, so that experience could be used to achieve quicker and more effective approximations of good solutions.

If *separate* tracking by many different units is to become *simultaneous* tracking by the whole institution, someone has to synthesize what is going on and communicate what is being learned to the community as a whole. In the institutions we studied that used simultaneous tracking, people at all levels cooperated with each other, shared information, engaged in mutual feedback, and freely evaluated successes and failures. Although presidents and vice presidents had a great deal to do with establishing this spirit of openness, they neither controlled nor directed the process. They did, however, initiate it, coordinate it, learn from it, and engage themselves in it by doing a lot of listening, exchanging ideas, and giving permission to try things. They could even play provocateur without appearing heavy-handed and directive.

Cooperation in learning about successes and failures—simultaneous tracking—has a real practical value. It helps institutions converge on knowledge about what works and what doesn't. It also reinforces the cultural understandings that a college or university relies on to screen new ideas and practices. It builds resilience, because people gain confidence in their own efforts to contribute better ways to get results. Their efforts may fail in some cases, but they know where and how to get good feedback and ideas about what to try next.

We admit that this is a mildly idealistic picture, but we think these patterns of behavior are far more likely to build a strong, resilient, and successful organization than would the imposition of a single program for change by a president or board. Simultaneous tracking is more likely to draw people together, address real operational problems, and avoid the errors and unintended consequences that so often accompany top-down change.

But simultaneous tracking requires *leadership* of a particular kind. It requires a great deal of confidence in people and an ability to stimulate, monitor, and shape learning. It involves counterintuitive ways of producing change. Instead of thinking "vertically" about lines of command and accountability, for example, a leader of the simultaneous tracking process would think "horizontally" about whether good ideas and interesting experiments—and their results—are being shared. Instead of imposing solutions, a leader of this process would attempt to stimulate convergence around ideas that are consistent with the values of the institution and that seem to be valid or effective solutions to problems.

This kind of thinking accepts the principle of equifinality, or the idea that there are many possible ways to achieve a given result. No perfect solution to a crisis exists at any given point in time, *and* no permanent solution will satisfy the continually changing conditions in which a college or university may find itself situated. Therefore, institutions must continue to work toward what has been called "satisficing" solutions—those that work in a given situation but may fall short of some ideal of ultimate perfection (Birnbaum, 1988, p. 58). Satisficing solutions are advantageous because they are the best an institution can do at a given time and place—meaning that it takes advantage of opportunities with the available resources, knowledge, and people.

Individually, satisficing solutions are not the best, but collectively—if a lot of good decisions are made—an institution can accumulate considerable learning and enough success to shape its directions in intelligent ways. By whatever name, simultaneous tracking boils down to this: the assertive and continuous accumulation of reasonably good decisions, *and* the shared knowledge from the results of those decisions.

In short, we learned in this study that it is better to go ahead on many fronts at once, *seizing opportunities* that fit within an overall vision for the institution, and learning continuously and cumulatively from experiments and new initiatives. The returns may be small on each separate move, but the ultimate goal is convergence on the best ways to achieve the institution's mission. An intelligent, focused, and effective organization has to be built to do that.

An intelligent organization is one that begins by knowing its own values, by being selective about what it does, being purposeful in developing vision and strategy, and learning continuously through simultaneous tracking.

Simultaneous tracking is not the opposite of strategizing. In fact, we found that institutions with enough experience and confidence ultimately find their various constituents converging on an implicit or emergent strategy. In other words, eventually people find out what works, and this becomes a de facto strategy. Although it is the product of a temporary and malleable consensus, an emergent strategy helps the institution focus its scarce resources and stabilize its operations, reducing the need to experiment and explore alternatives.

Leadership

Leaders of an institution trying to successfully meet a crisis face unique pressures. They need patience, sensitivity, and communication skills far beyond what they might need in a hierarchical setting of command and control. But the biggest mistake that leaders can make in a crisis is to confuse patience with passivity. Passivity in the face of crisis can be fatal to the organization.

Searching for and experimenting with ideas, fostering teamwork, and promoting convergence require continuous and proactive attention to both process and substance. Presidents, vice presidents, deans, chairs, and faculty leaders all must be thoroughly engaged in and attentive to the framing of a vision, to the implementation of a strategy, to exploration of opportunities, to continuous learning, to simultaneous tracking, and to sharing information.

The work of leadership is to achieve an informed convergence and to reshape the use of resources around the directions in which the institution has *learned* to go.

Unfortunately, this view of leadership is not as romantic or glamorous as is some of the popular literature that glorifies visionaries, transformational leaders, strategists, and "Lone Rangers" galloping to the rescue. But we think that the pragmatic approach—continuous learning and simultaneous tracking—is far more likely to promote the long-term stability and health of the college or university. It is especially more effective when it gains the commitment of the many constituents whose buy-in is essential to any real change or redirection. It is also more realistic, because it builds on actual experimentation in the real environment that the college or university will have to live in over the long term. And it helps to validate and solidify an institution's commitment to and internal understanding of its mission and its core values.

Responsibility

Everyone with any claim to ownership or citizenship in a college or university shares in the responsibility to seek good solutions. We were concerned about the unrealistic and unreasonable burdens placed on presidents and big-decision committees at several institutions. The idea that centralized strategizing can produce some kind of quick fix puts too much pressure on too few people, and the result can be damaging to the institution's ability to find and experiment with a variety of solutions.

Whatever approach is chosen to address fiscal problems, it ought to encourage the sharing of responsibility among the stakeholders. Each unit and each person should take on their part of what is really a corporate and communal burden. The president can inform the community, initiate and stimulate the process, monitor progress, synthesize information, and work hard on convergence—as well as work out priorities for the allocation of resources. But presidents cannot (and should not) be held account-able if others do not assume responsibility for continuing experi-mentation and learning.

Pressure to respond under conditions of stress tends, unfortu-nately, to push decision making to the top. Several of our site insti-tutions were blindsided by midyear budget rescissions or other unanticipated events. Crises developed, and presidents had to move quickly and assertively. While they all understood the need to con-sult and to share information, they were in the unfortunate posi-tion of having to direct and control the strategy—sometimes with no advance warning at all. Several presidents discovered that push-ing hard to reach decisions had the main effect of generating resistance—without necessarily leading to intelligent or effective responses.

We urge that presidents calibrate the amount of personal responsibility they take and that they work toward building a sense of partnership and community responsibility among their many constituencies. But this has to occur before the situation becomes critical. If basic values and a general vision are not shared, or if there is disagreement under the surface, a crisis will almost certainly bring conflict to the front.

A cynical view that is common among faculty holds that the tenured professoriate can outsit any top administrator. Presidents, for example, serve relatively short terms of five or six years, but fac-ulty typically stay on through three or four presidential terms. If this is true, then faculty actually have a much greater stake in the long-term financial health of the institution than any president has! Given that their own interests are vitally affected, faculty probably have not assumed a commensurate share of responsibility at some institutions, remaining content to let top administrators tilt at fis-cal windmills and take the blame when things do not improve immediately.

It would be far healthier to find ways of spreading responsibil-ity around, especially to those with the greatest stake. Presidents will be held accountable, of course, and they will be criticized if they act too strongly or too mildly. But they will succeed only if their legacy is an institution committed to taking responsibility for its own future. That future is very much in the hands of the faculty, and they are too often insulated from this simple truth.

Potential Pitfalls

All of our site institutions were distracted as they worked out their individual ways of adapting and changing. Some of these distractions could be directly traced to the strategizing process itself. This was especially true when institutions were forced to react—having perhaps waited too long to frame their own vision and strategy. The problems we saw were very similar to those found by Schmidtlein (1990) and by Hearn, Clugston, and Heydinger (1993) in their studies of strategic planning in colleges and universities.

First, strategizing distracts people from the immediate situation. It requires that they divide their attention, putting aside their normal work to organize and conduct a new and unfamiliar task. That usually involves generating data and managing some kind of consensus-building process. All of this takes time and energy. Strategizing in the midst of crisis loads the organization with more work at just the time when it is becoming more stressed. It also forces decisions—whether right or wrong, good or bad—into an artificial envelope of time that's usually too short to allow serious analysis, careful thought, or realistic assessment of risks and opportunities. People feel compelled to make decisions for the sake of making decisions, which is a good way to produce bad decisions.

Solution: Separate the tasks of problem solving from the process of strategic planning. Strategy is important, but it will not solve immediate problems. Find a way to cross-pollinate so that problem solving is informed by strategic thinking, and so that strategy is responsive to real problems.

Second, strategizing also creates an illusion of control. If people dedicate themselves to constructing a strategy, they have to imagine that they can predict the future and can reorient themselves and others to a common vision of what the institution ought to be like in that future. Almost all of our site institutions faced very erratic and unpredictable environments, especially in the short run. Events in some cases simply outstripped the ability of any strategizing group to reach closure. They were continually chasing a fugitive reality, and they had to devote more resources to capturing that reality than we thought it was worth.

Even if a consensus about the situation could be developed, reality would continue to change, and the consensus would be outdated at whatever point it might have been reached. There is also no guarantee that a quick-start strategic planning process can generate information that is either valid enough or rich enough or timely enough to serve as a basis for making long-term commitments.

Solution: Seek continuous feedback; monitor the environment closely. The worst thing an institution can do is withdraw into itself and deal in fantasies about an ideal future. Although it is good to develop a vision, realism demands that it be related to the concrete world. Presidents and other key leaders should be in close touch with politics, business, the professions, and community interests to keep a sense of what will affect the institution and how it can fit in and make a contribution. As one president put it, "The role of leadership is to keep scanning."

A third pitfall can occur because trying to reach consensus on vision and putting long-term solutions in place is also a good way to bring latent conflict to the surface. People who feel confronted and threatened—as they will when immersed in the perceived threat of a fiscal crisis—are much quicker to defend their turf and their values than when they feel reasonably safe and secure. Sometimes they attack the process itself—a safer and more oblique way of defending themselves than directly confronting real issues. In a number of cases, no matter how well the decision-making process was conceived, it both produced and came under great strain when it was operating during a real or perceived crisis.

Most colleges and universities are too internally diverse and too loosely coupled in normal times to have fostered the kinds of skills needed in building consensus. Absent a consensus, there is still pressure to decide and act. The predictable result is conflict, because actions are perceived as unilateral and undemocratic.

Solution: Use the "challenge-and-support" approach. An institution in crisis is going to endure conflict because it has to make tough decisions. It has to change and it has to get things done in order to survive. But the pain of change can be mitigated if good conciliators are involved in the process. Bring in people who are sensitive to and supportive of the emotional realities of the situation. They can help process the inevitable anger and hostility that may erupt.

Conclusion

Our goal in this chapter was to describe how institutions might get out of trouble and construct a more secure future. In the course of our study, we came to believe that a pragmatic approach grounded in a balance between strategic planning and continuous learning from experimentation can work better than either of the two extreme alternatives: top-down management and random trial and error.

The main challenge of continuous learning, however, is to converge on values and on solutions that work. People who are asked to experiment have to trust that they will not be punished for failing. Leaders must focus on sharing information and engaging others in the process of searching for ideas and solutions—instead of falling back on familiar command and control patterns.

Leaders especially have to engage others' sense of responsibility to the long-term health of the enterprise, particularly the responsibility of faculty. We used the metaphor of continuous learning to describe an institution that adapts through horizontal sharing of information and cooperation, rather than solely on direction from the top.

Continuous learning means generating good information about everything that an institution is doing, sharing it widely, and concentrating on converging ideas. Stakeholders have to find out what works and then put their bets on those things—as long as they are consistent with the culture, values, and identity of the institution. In the end, though, the way out of crisis depends on all constituencies sharing the responsibility for finding, testing, and improving solutions to problems.

Chapter Ten

Resilience in Times of Fiscal Stress

How can institutions strengthen themselves in fundamental ways? How can they ride out the policy reversals and fiscal stresses of recent years and remain financially solvent and educationally effective?

The quality of resilience is central to the ability of institutions to thrive in good times and bad alike. In this chapter, we will describe the qualities of resilience we saw developing in our site institutions. The resilient institution is one that knows why it wants to educate students and has adopted effective ways to *add value*. It is also positioned to adapt and endure when the next crisis comes along. The defining characteristic in such an institution is that its students, faculty, and staff are all committed to achieving a common goal in effective and demonstrable ways.

Essentially, there are three components to resilience:

- Distinctiveness from other institutions
- Effectiveness in achieving a particular mission
- Quality—giving students the knowledge, skills, and values they need to be autonomous, achieving adult citizens

The resilient institution is successful in attracting, holding, and adding value to its students. It recognizes that its fiscal and educational health depend on succeeding at these basic tasks. We think that in the long run the resilient institution will beat the competition because students, their families, and society can trust it to deliver. Most important, it measures its success not in where it stands on the more traditional measures of input—such as endowment and physical plant—but in helping individual students learn adult responsibility, achieve academic success, and become contributing citizens of a democratic and multicultural community. While such measures as endowment and physical plant are not totally irrelevant, their mere presence is clearly not enough to make the right things happen educationally. We think that making the right things happen educationally is the essential property of a resilient college or university.

In this chapter, we will discuss what we found at site institutions that have developed the qualities of resilience. We will start with a brief description of two of our case-study institutions that were developing many of the qualities of resilience. That will lead us to a discussion of how institutions become resilient: having a distinctive mission comes first; accomplishing it effectively is the next step. How do institutions effectively attract, hold, educate, and graduate undergraduate students, the fiscal base on which all else depends? And finally, what kind of leadership is needed in resilient colleges and universities?

A Resilient Institution: Texas-El Paso

The University of Texas at El Paso was developing many of the qualities of resilience at the time of our site visit. We saw four important trends there:

- Acceptance of its particular setting and the opportunities that existed there
- Identification of its customer base and a dedication to understanding and serving those customers
- Identification of outcomes for all its programs, and a commitment to achieving them
- Aggressive pursuit of new resources beyond the regular state operating budget

Acceptance of Its Setting

Texas-El Paso, once a technical college with an emphasis on mining, has recognized and accepted its unique setting in the far southwestern corner of Texas, immediately adjacent to its border with Mexico. The university's principal base of potential students is the heavily Hispanic population of El Paso, and its actual enrollment has been increasingly Hispanic (67 percent of the undergraduate students at the time of our visit in 1994).

Although it is far from Texas's other large population centers (Dallas, Houston, Austin, and San Antonio), El Paso occupies a unique niche. Its population of about six hundred thousand is only one-third of the total metropolitan area when the 1.2 million people of Ciudad Juarez, Mexico, are added (the metropolitan area covers both sides of the border).

The potential of this metropolitan area for economic development and international trade had been greatly enhanced by the recent passage of the North American Free Trade Agreement (NAFTA). In turn, the university saw burgeoning needs for a more highly skilled work force, the emergence of new professions, and the need for bilingualism and biculturalism throughout the community.

Serving Customers

Texas-El Paso has committed itself to serve this unique population center by becoming a national role model for successful education for minorities. It identifies promising students during their junior year in high school and makes contact with them to emphasize that a college education is within their reach. It outlines the steps they must take to secure admission, and also works in partnership with the local schools to help them prepare students for college. While 80 percent of Texas-El Paso's undergraduates are first-generation college students, and a high percentage have deficiencies in math, the university offers them special help to ensure their success. Departments that commit to helping students overcome deficiencies and succeed are recognized and rewarded.

Focus on Outcomes

The president of Texas-El Paso was described by many as a visionary. She saw that although the institution did not have great power in the state system, it nevertheless could achieve a national reputation in its unique niche. She has concentrated on finding ways to meet her goals—often quite independently of tradition. Her main focus is to concentrate the institution's—and her own—attention on outcomes.

Texas-El Paso's plan builds on two strengths—its existing capacities in math, science, and engineering, and its access to a large population of minority students. Its programs emphasize preparation for business, engineering, and the health sciences.

Faculty hiring is a major piece of the overall strategy. New faculty hires in the two years preceding our visit had resulted in a 40 percent rate of tenure-track appointments going to women, and 32 percent to minorities. The campus is also building a strong office of institutional research, planning, and evaluation. It concentrates on gathering useful data and presenting it in forms that can be widely understood. This helps the president achieve broad participation in the planning process—a way of engaging the campus community in building a shared perspective and a consensus about outcomes.

Finding New Resources

Capitalizing on location, population, and the effort to develop clear, focused outcomes, the president has worked hard to raise external funds. She has taken advantage of programs designed to promote the advancement of minorities in critical fields like science, medicine, and engineering. At least one major grant on the order of

$5 million had been obtained from the National Science Foundation, with signs of more to come.

All of these initiatives dovetailed nicely to help Texas-El Paso play a special role in its own unique setting. Its president was ambitious about the institution, but in a focused and realistic way. She was well into the process of building a resilient university that knew its business well, understood its customers, and shaped its efforts to add value to its customers' lives in very meaningful ways.

Planning and Restructuring at Virginia Commonwealth University

Virginia Commonwealth University (VCU) is a public, urban research university located in Richmond, Virginia. VCU currently enrolls more than 21,000 students on two principal campuses, the downtown "academic campus" and the campus of the Medical College of Virginia. It serves a predominantly in-state clientele (95 percent of its students are Virginians), including a substantial proportion of minority students. VCU was established in 1968 by merging two smaller public colleges, the Richmond Professional Institute and the Medical College of Virginia. It is currently one of three major public research universities in Virginia, along with the University of Virginia and Virginia Polytechnic Institute and State University.

Facing budget cuts of as much as 21 percent, Virginia Commonwealth University (VCU) undertook a major program of fundamental and long-term restructuring. This process went beyond mere belt-tightening to eliminating and combining some units and programs. Its goal was to provide resources that would help it address new opportunities in fields that it could serve.

The Process

Restructuring at VCU came about as both self-study and planning processes resulted in development of a strategic plan. The plan was approved in September 1993 by the university's governing board. Both broad and deep in its scope, the plan was the result of three separate but parallel activities:

- Planning efforts to meet the state's requirement that each public university describe its action plans for restructuring in a time of fiscal stringency
- A comprehensive self-study and visiting team report from the Commission on Colleges of the Southern Association of Colleges and Schools
- Special studies conducted on individual units within the university

The plan was developed using twenty-two individual task forces, some of which, by plan, were existing university committees. Outside consultants were also employed to identify areas in which administrative costs could be cut by as much as 15 percent. The committees held hearings and open forums, and campus involvement was both intensive and extensive. Every standing administrative and governance group on the campus was given responsibilities for monitoring progress, reporting and communicating, and implementing details of the plan in its arena. Provision was made for the continued involvement of all members of the university community.

In a good example of simultaneous tracking, the responsibility for achieving progress on fifteen strategic directions was delegated to specific people (usually senior administrators). These directions included enrollment management, strengthening undergraduate education, strengthening graduate education, promoting targeted areas of excellence, facilitating research and creative activity, and achieving a ranking among the top fifty universities in the nation in external funding of research. Other targets included improvements in public service, use of information technology, strengthening of faculty skills and enhancement of their participation in decision making, improvement of administrative and support services, achievement of a high quality of student life, implementation of a program of staff and faculty development and rewards, and improvement of campus facilities.

Results

The results of VCU's plan are clearly visible across the university. Three selected examples include a new engineering school, improvements in undergraduate education, and the introduction of benchmarking.

The most exciting development was creation of the new school of engineering, largely set in motion by a pledge for start-up of $11 million from private sources. The state provided a large grant, which in turn stimulated Motorola Corporation to locate a manufacturing and technology center in the Richmond, Virginia, area. Motorola then became a partner with the new engineering school. Other Virginia colleges and universities are cooperating with the VCU plan for engineering, and VCU has established ties with the Virginia Biotechnology Research Park.

Second, the General Education Task Force has revised VCU's goals for undergraduate education and has developed a full set of outcome assessment mechanisms. Sixteen programs were initially identified for enhancement, and reallocated funds or other forms of support were made available to thirteen of them. Two baccalaureate programs and one master's program have been identified for elimination. An ongoing review of areas in which programs may duplicate other offerings is being conducted, and VCU has delegated certain remedial education tasks to the local community college.

VCU has committed itself to the use of benchmarking to monitor achievement of its plan. It is a participant in the National Association of College and University Business Officers' benchmarking project, and it uses both internal and external benchmarks.

Internal benchmarks are of two types: *numerical* and *qualitative*.

Numerical benchmarks include enrollment targets, savings from restructuring that can be applied to higher-priority functions, cost trends, measures of faculty work load, and time to degree for undergraduate and graduate students. Qualitative benchmarks include measures of student satisfaction and results of learning-outcome assessments.

External benchmarks include comparisons with other urban universities, and they range from rates of retention and graduation to measures of student diversity, space utilization, and research funding.

Resilience Through Planning

The VCU approach features both short- and long-term action plans, a spirit of seriousness, and built-in devices for follow-up so that agreements are reached, commitments made, and stakeholders involved. Early in the process, leaders at VCU understood that there would be hard choices and difficult decisions. In the words of a faculty member who played a major role in developing and implementing the plan, the choice facing the university was "drift [or apply] our collective foresight and intelligence." VCU chose the latter and turned what might have been a catastrophic reduction in state funding into an opportunity to create a more focused and responsive institution.

We think that the VCU model is a good example of how strategic planning can enhance an institution's resilience. It has helped VCU become more effective educationally while strengthening its fiscal condition. Several key lessons emerge from this case:

- Effective and courageous leadership by the president and others has resulted in a clear vision for the university and a clear plan for delegation of responsibility to achieve the plan's goals.

- Individual departments and units have been given responsibility to develop their own plans and to implement those plans—with appropriate accountability.

- A new Institutional Research and Evaluation unit has been established to generate information that the institution needs to monitor progress.

- Hard decisions have been made about program elimination and enhancement.

- A thorough examination of faculty roles and rewards is under way.

- A strong commitment has been made to partnerships with businesses and community organizations.

The VCU model is a clear example of how an institution can use a fiscal crisis to seize opportunities and change itself—becoming a more resilient university in the process.

How Resilient Institutions Develop

Each institution has to find a distinct niche that it can best serve at a given point in time. Concentrating resources, meeting real needs, and focusing on things that an institution can do well are all elements of distinctiveness. A college or university that chooses to be distinctive—special and different in certain ways—has a better chance to be known for its unique qualities and to serve its students in particular ways.

In his book, *The Distinctive College* (1970), Burton Clark examined several institutions that had established national reputations for providing "distinctive" educational programs. This idea has been explored more recently by Townsend, Newell, and Wiese (1992). The distinctive college holds a unifying set of values, fosters commitment to those values among faculty and students, and sets out to differentiate itself from other institutions on the basis of its beliefs about educational goals and the educational process.

We found that our site institutions were more or less assertively following this strategy of differentiating themselves. They had found several dimensions on which they could base a distinctive identity.

The first—and perhaps most important—dimension is to *build on existing strengths*. At Syracuse University we were told that "some parts of the university—for example, journalism and public administration—are well niched; others need better positioning." The "well-niched" schools drew capacity enrollments because they had strong national reputations. A faculty leader put it this way: "We shouldn't go for niches we can't fill. We should instead focus on what we do well."

A second way is to ask *from which competitors one should be different*. Syracuse was in the process of doing just this. Its overall strategy was to become an outstanding student-centered research university, something their competition had not yet tried: "Being student-centered is our edge over research universities, and being a research university is an edge over others. This is our niche."

A third way to differentiate is to concentrate on *recruiting particular kinds of students* to educate. In some cases, these choices were based on the needs of students who had traditionally been denied opportunities or were being overlooked by existing institutions. Texas-El Paso, for example, was successfully "capitalizing on the nature of the students and our location [and] focusing on niche programs related to the growing minority population." In addition to providing a real service to the people of its community, Texas-El Paso found this strategy to be attractive in fundraising, especially in relation to programs for minority advancement supported by the National Science Foundation, the Department of Defense, and NASA.

Bloomfield College also focused its distinctive mission on minority students in its immediate area. Not only was this consistent with the college's historical role (educating successive waves of new citizens in the metropolitan area), but it made financial sense, because New Jersey provided tuition assistance and direct institutional aid per capita for students from low-income families.

We hasten to point out that each of these institutions made a total commitment to serving the needs of minority students—they were not simply trolling for the subsidies available to minority groups. In each case, a top-to-bottom commitment was obvious, and programs had been redesigned or introduced with the specific goal of meeting the needs of the populations to whom the institution addressed itself.

Fourth, distinctiveness meant developing *unique approaches to the undergraduate experience*. An administrator at Mayville described how the university planned to differentiate itself: "We see that we need to be more proactive. We have to show that we have earned support, that we deserve it. We have to carve out our own niche instead of just 'keeping on.' Perhaps our niche is in new ways of delivering undergraduate instruction. For example, using performance-based assessment, using innovative and flexible teaching strategies. The idea is to give students a good experience."

A fifth way to be distinctive is to *meet the basic educational and service needs of the community or region*. Mayville was located in a rural area and served in many ways as a focal institution for programs that helped people meet various needs (it operated a Head Start program, served as a resource and professional development center for teachers, provided child care, and helped to incubate business consortia, among other things). Acknowledging this role, one person spoke for many others at Mayville: "We need to get focused on the major community needs and develop programs to address these."

The University of Maryland-Eastern Shore, also located in a rural area, had a similar sense of obligation to serve its community. It offered unique programs dealing with aquaculture, airways management, marine and environmental science, and hospitality administration, all of which responded to needs in the university's service area.

A sixth obvious way to differentiate an institution includes *offering programs in fields either that are growing or in which a need is not being met for a given population.* We saw examples of specialized programs in health care, business, and engineering technology that met needs in particular geographic regions—and that were based on partnerships with potential employers. One that impressed us was the carefully orchestrated plan of Virginia Commonwealth University to develop its new school of engineering.

"Niching" was going on in other ways, too. In Oregon, the state system was experimenting with differential tuition, meaning that certain programs on certain campuses could charge different tuitions. At institutions in other states, tuition was set (or discounted through financial aid) to help position the institution in relation to competitors. Trenton State College had invested heavily in a highly attractive residential campus and an active extracurricular life for its students. And Tusculum College employed a radically different calendar (one complete course per month).

None of these qualities taken alone would necessarily make an institution truly distinctive, but an institution could work on several dimensions at once to achieve a unique profile of appealing characteristics.

More than Image

Becoming distinctive involves going considerably deeper than image. The institutions we visited searched for particular needs to meet and adapted their own strengths to fit the needs they had identified. An administrator at the University of Massachusetts at Boston described the process this way: "We have to hustle to provide real service . . . and put our money where it does the most good." At a regional university, a vice president said much the same thing: "We have to identify real needs and decide what we can do together to meet those needs." Note that both institutions are focusing on meeting real needs—finding their particular role in the lives of real people whom they can serve.

Distinctiveness means very little if one simply imagines a unique service to perform for which there is no market. It also means very little if the niche is too narrow or ephemeral. In a few cases, we became concerned that an institution might have been pursuing a program for which there was a need, but capitalization of the program was all out of proportion to the potential return. Too few people would buy the program to justify what it would cost to start it up and keep it going. Likewise, some programs might generate a lot of interest, enrollment, and money in the short run, but might not be sustainable beyond a few years at the most.

In fact, Anderson (1977) showed that institutions electing to concentrate on distinctiveness may have suffered financially *in the short term*. But Green, Levine, and Associates (1985) found that at *successful* institutions they studied, "Resources followed programming, not the other way around" (p. 135). Put another way, if institutions concentrate on distinctiveness, support will follow as long as programs meet real needs. Indeed, the institutions in Anderson's study that concentrated on distinctiveness did emerge from crisis with better records of long-term survivability.

Partnerships

Partnerships were very helpful in strengthening some of the institutions we visited. Relationships with cities, hospitals, businesses, government agencies, and community organizations helped to focus programs, attract students, and promote goodwill. Partnerships do not always bring direct financial support, but they create conditions that often do. Students may be attracted to a professional program because they know that a potential employer is involved in some way. State legislators may feel good about a university that does beneficial things in its community. Businesses may feel they have a greater stake in a college that cooperates readily in the preparation of specialized workers.

Money may come with a partnership, but it may also be secondary. Tuition from students, appropriations from the legislature, and donations from community leaders may all be slightly stronger because of commitments and partnerships that draw people to the institution and convince them that their support yields a valuable return—either to individuals or to the community.

This spirit of cooperation with others came through clearly in some of our interviews. At UMass-Boston, for example, one interviewee felt strongly about looking outward: "We have to build partnerships with business, with nonprofits, and with other universities. We have to see this [crisis] as an opportunity and look for the good stuff to do." A faculty leader at Pennsylvania State University saw it as important to the long-term strategy of the institution: "We should be engaging in a continuous process of anticipating the future. We have to have a vision and our own set of values . . . and then cooperate and complement others' strengths for the greater good." This comment puts the idea of differentiating an institution in a whole different light. It suggests that institutions can both be different from others and work with others to complement those differences in ways that strengthen all who are involved.

Effectiveness

The health and viability of a college or university are based principally on effectiveness. Effectiveness means having a valid mission and the competence to pursue it. In the best of possible worlds, institutions would be free to pursue their own desires and impulses without accountability. But the need to maintain an income flow imposes discipline. In the real world, most institutions will find that income depends on their ability to attract and hold tuition-paying or appropriation-generating undergraduate students. And if undergraduates are the base of current fiscal health, their satisfaction with the educational experience and their subsequent willingness to repay in the form of political support, annual donations, and capital gifts are the basis of an institution's future fiscal health.

We believe that both research and experience show that institutions can *overspend* on almost everything they do, while *underinvesting* in the most important dimensions of undergraduate education. It helps to have slack resources—more money than is needed to meet immediate expenses—but money and what it can buy do not guarantee that the student experience will produce learning, growth, or development. Instead of maximizing income and maximizing spending, which is roughly how institutions have customarily defined quality, colleges and universities can "run smarter" by investing in the dimensions of the student experience that count.

Product quality in higher education refers to how the undergraduate experience is organized, how it engages students in learning and growth, and how it affects their performance as citizens, workers, parents, and consumers. If an institution does these things well, we think it stands a good chance of sustaining itself in the marketplace. If it is also intelligent about generating and maintaining capital (endowments or quasi-endowments), it stands a good chance of weathering changes in the marketplace that require it to *reinvest* from time to time in program development and change.

It therefore seems important to urge fiscally challenged institutions to focus on what produces the kind of learning they want to foster, and to invest in the type of education that produces that learning. For many institutions, producing a quality undergraduate experience will require making big changes in what students do, how they live, and what they learn both in and out of the classroom. Instead of concentrating spending on inputs (more books, plusher residence halls, bigger faculty offices, and so on), the institutions will have to reorganize and restructure the nature of the student experience.

Developing Educationally Effective Programs

Institutions can turn to a considerable body of experience and research to understand a few principles behind the keys to fiscal (and educational) health: attracting, holding, and adding value to students. We will focus here on the experience of our site institutions. To a very great extent, we found that initiatives being taken by these institutions ran parallel to lessons from current research. Readers with an interest in further exploring the derivation and application of principles of "good practice" should start by consulting Chickering and Gamson (1991).

Student-Centered Mission

Perhaps the most important starting point is in knowing the students. Personal contact by faculty and administrators with individual students before entry, during orientation, and throughout their degree program is one of the main leverage points in student development (Pascarella and Terenzini, 1991). Beyond this personal touch, institutions can learn a great deal about their students—their academic preparation, motives, aspirations, values, and interests— and help to make the educational experience more student-centered. During our site visit we learned that Bloomfield College was developing a sophisticated computerized assessment process that would help students and the institution track *each individual's progress* toward certain goals from the time of entry to graduation.

It may sound trite, but the principal goal of a college or university is to educate students. If by default or intent the goal changes— to, say, the advancement of theory—students will find out and will quickly come to understand where they fit into the overall mission of the institution. If the institution is not student-centered, it will have commensurately less impact on students' learning, growth, and development. However, considerable evidence shows that by organizing programs, services, and teaching to take students' needs, interests, and learning styles into account, an institution enhances the leverage it has over growth and development (Astin, 1993b; Pascarella and Terenzini, 1991).

We found that institutions that had endured serious threats to survival began their recovery with a real grass-roots commitment to *each* student they enrolled; providing close personal attention to each student was clearly the best way to foster real learning, high morale, and persistence to graduation. Trenton State's success in building a new identity can be traced in part to the president's extensive efforts to recruit the best students himself—one at a time when necessary.

Although it will be difficult for larger, more research-oriented, and nonresidential institutions to provide such personal attention to each student, certain practices may be reasonably close approximations. For unusually well prepared students—those with a strong academic background, self-confidence, and highly developed personal goals and values—it may be enough to give them opportunities to seek out personal attention and involvement in learning activities. But most students need much more than an "opportunity": they need an invitation and an expression of interest from adult figures who can serve as mentors. They also need the support of skilled teachers and advisers as they learn to learn.

Because faculty are not always prepared to devote this kind of attention to undergraduates, especially to students who are not inclined to initiate contact and get involved, we think that faculty need training, development, and incentives to become involved themselves.

Clear Goals

Some institutions state their goals for students very clearly, telling students in very explicit terms what they are supposed to know and be able to do when they graduate. They organize learning experiences around these goals both in and out of the classroom, and they provide plenty of opportunity for practice, reinforcement, and feedback. Bloomfield and Tusculum colleges both adopted out-come-based goals and tied student experiences directly to achievement of those goals. Students could assess their progress at any time and knew what they had to accomplish to graduate.

This is a far different approach than counting credit hours or setting up distribution requirements. It means, for example, that certain skills or content areas must be taught and reinforced across the curriculum. In the case of Tusculum, each of the elements of civic competence is taught in a number of courses. Students arrange their curriculum by taking courses that help them achieve the required amount of progress on each competence during each of four years. Focusing on learning outcomes is very different from simply asking students to select arbitrary courses or numbers of credits from a loosely arranged smorgasbord. It requires that students and faculty work closely on activities that promote very specific kinds of learning above and beyond the conventional content of the course.

It seems to us that students with a strong goal orientation and with many sources of stimulation and support that reinforce progress toward those goals are more likely to persist to achieve their degrees. They can measure themselves against some kind of standard and get support as they work toward a definable point of closure. This arrangement also gives the institution a fighting chance in dealing with student cultures (or other diversions) that distract students from purposeful learning and development.

High Expectations

These goals are ambitious enough to challenge students and promote real growth. Students are exposed to experiences and demands that force them to experiment with and master new skills and knowledge. In this way, the college experience becomes far more than a pro forma extension of high school. But the experiences have to be designed to promote learning. In general, the familiar formula of "challenge and support" seems to be the appropriate model.

Although college is a new and unfamiliar experience for most students, it may be so unstructured for many that they simply fall back on familiar (and thus far successful) repertoires of knowledge and skill. They can also submerge themselves in the anonymity of multiple-choice tests and large lecture halls. But the more resilient institutions design their programs so that every student must perform as an individual and meet high standards on clearly defined objectives. Trenton State organized its student life to engage as many students as possible in active efforts to lead and contribute to community improvement. Trenton students know that they are expected to challenge themselves and grow into leadership roles during their undergraduate years.

Performance-Based Assessment

We found interesting experiments being done with both continuous and outcome-based assessment of learning. By establishing clear goals and expectations, an institution can then define the kind of performance that will be required of students. Although performance can be measured by traditional means, richer and more useful kinds of assessment can either supplement or replace exams, papers, and lab reports.

The experiments we saw required students to develop portfolios, to demonstrate specific skills by performing in real or simulated situations that require those skills, and to demonstrate their achievement in more than one modality (such as a multiple-choice test) at more than one time. Assessment in some cases was continuous: students were required to show continuously higher levels of achievement during each of their four years in college.

The key to performance-based assessment is that each student is individually examined on—or demonstrates mastery of—a particular skill or area of knowledge. The student, often with considerable freedom to construct his or her own performance, actually shows how to do something or express an idea or test a hypothesis.

Performance-based assessment is a strong stimulus to student involvement. Pace (1982), Astin (1993b), and others have pointed out that students learn more and master it more completely when they are *involved* in their learning experience. Knowing that they will have to perform individually, sometimes before a faculty committee or even a large audience, is a powerful stimulus to creative planning, rehearsing, seeking feedback, and authentic presentation of a real skill.

Active Learning and Authentic Experience

We found that some outcome-based programs were experimenting with new ideas for learning through experience. For example, Tusculum was experimenting with courses that took students to historically or scientifically significant sites so that they could have "hands-on" experience with the subject. At other institutions, cooperative education was being tried; students worked at real jobs while alternating semesters in and out of school. And Syracuse was developing a program in which faculty would receive incentives to involve undergraduates in doing research.

Passive learning—sitting in class, listening to (or sleeping through) lectures, or reading textbooks—is generally understood to be one of the least effective routes to mastery. These new experiments promise to have interesting effects on levels of student interest, involvement, and achievement.

Active learning can also help *intensify* the student's experience. Learning at a high level requires effort and intensity. This is another element of "involvement." If a student is intensely involved, learning is quicker and deeper and more permanent.

Integrated Program Design

The kind of intense, engaging, and purposeful education that helps students learn and holds their attention and interest throughout the undergraduate experience does not happen at random. It has to be designed carefully, and it must be sustained through continuous care and attention.

Designing this kind of intensely involving education begins with the assumption that the whole student is at the heart of the learning experience. Conventional programs in higher education are typically organized around traditional units of subject matter or the faculty's current research interests. The newer approach turns traditional practice on its head and starts by deciding what kinds of learning experiences will help students achieve particular outcomes. Courses, faculty effort, and campus life all converge by design on those aspects of the student experience that support progress toward the outcomes an institution wants to achieve.

This means that experiences inside and outside the classroom will be complementary and mutually reinforcing. For example, one goal might be "to appreciate and understand other cultures." While students learn about other cultures through literature, history, and anthropology, they might also gain experience by visiting another country; attending films, talks, and exhibits; or even living with someone from a different cultural background.

To take it one step further, courses and activities might be coordinated so that certain themes are emphasized at common times. This would require a (perhaps uncommon) level of coordination and collaboration among faculty, who would teach about certain issues across the curriculum, and would do so in a way that builds on and develops certain common experiences.

We found that some of the institutions we visited had begun to bring student life and academic experiences much closer together. (Bloomfield was an especially interesting case.) The goal was to promote achievement of common goals by involving students in common activities.

Cooperative Learning/Collaborative Teaching

Some students learn better when they are encouraged to cooperate with other students or with faculty. Considerable research (for example, by Johnson and Johnson, 1993) now supports the effectiveness of cooperative learning. While students in some fields have been encouraged to compete with one another, they might actually learn more and gain self-confidence if they had opportunities to cooperate on learning activities.

Even if competitive success remains an important part of the learning culture, students still need to learn how to work in teams. For this reason, as well as for the potential gains in content knowledge for some students, cooperative learning is important. This idea leads directly to the logical next step: getting faculty to provide role models by collaborating with students and with other faculty. Some faculty we interviewed began promoting teamwork with their students by involving them in research. But more could be done if faculty were interested in and knowledgeable about the positive effects of cooperative learning.

Faculty Selection and Development

This kind of curriculum—one that promotes specific learning outcomes—also requires coordination. Faculty have to agree on outcomes (a laborious and wrenching process in a few of our cases) and they must rethink and redesign their courses. They also have to work closely together to coordinate students' experiences. This suggests a major change in the way faculty have traditionally worked. They will have to establish common ground in both content and method of instruction, instead of exercising individual freedom in what and how they teach.

Faculty at our site institutions were not always prepared to support these efforts. They were often being rewarded for research, publication, and other kinds of external visibility. In some cases, faculty felt that they devoted so much attention to these well-rewarded aspects of their careers that they simply didn't have time (or incentive) to develop the kinds of skills that would be valuable in teaching and advising undergraduate students. They recognized the need for those skills, and many would undoubtedly be attracted to opportunities (and incentives) to develop them.

Faculty selection and development are extremely important in building the resilient institution. We found in several cases that faculty searches were being conducted with special care to identify candidates who could accept and contribute to purposeful and collaborative undergraduate education. One institution even targeted veteran faculty from other institutions who were seeking new challenges in teaching and learning. At Virginia Commonwealth University, some of the funds being saved through program discontinuation and administrative restructuring were being dedicated to faculty development because, as the president said, "restructuring [will not] succeed if faculty do not relate their activities to the mission."

External grants had helped reshape and refocus the skills of faculty. In some cases, these grants helped faculty by giving them time and funding to rethink what it meant to teach their disciplines in a way that reinforced student progress toward given outcomes. In other cases, grants were supporting instructional-development projects conducted as ongoing experiments in existing courses. Faculty need this support, because they have been trained and rewarded to conduct education in one way and have to invest a great deal in learning about new and different ways to fit in and contribute.

We should add that in our study faculty were largely motivated to make the change and to be helpful in redesigning the curriculum. They were more fearful than recalcitrant in confronting their own lack of knowledge and experience in creating new ways to teach and in becoming focused on student development instead of knowledge transmission. Because the leadership for change must ultimately come from the faculty, we think that investing in (and providing incentives to) faculty learning and development will pay great dividends.

Chief academic officers, deans, and department chairs can play a strong role in promoting faculty interest and skill in instruction and student development. They can find ways of providing incentives; they can search for external funding, bring in consultants or arrange for faculty mentoring; and they can encourage, stimulate, and promote change. Small steps—especially if they really produce change—can have a very large symbolic value: they send a message about what is important and what people will be expected to do (and rewarded for doing).

Involvement

We think that institutions should require students to become much more active and more personally invested partners in their own education. Instead of assuming that a student learns more when more hard resources are spent on "inputs" (facilities, faculty salaries, library books, maintenance and upkeep, and so on), institutions should assume that students learn more when they have to work at producing the learning themselves. Bowen and Douglass (1971) long ago warned against creating environments in which students were encouraged to be passive and "overdependent" learners, arguing instead for more "self-reliance" (p. 93).

We would caution institutions about whether their patterns of spending on students is necessarily productive. While physical amenities and support services can make campus life more comfortable, they do not necessarily promote the kind of active learning and personal growth that research suggests ought to be the focus of effective undergraduate education.

(We were amused by a student's recent comment that "I don't know why they expect us to go to classes all the time. After all, we are in college, and college is supposed to be fun!" Obviously, the amenities and distractions of collegiate life can become too diverting! Too much bread and too many circuses may mean too little learning.)

Obviously, too, we could push our line of reasoning to somewhat radical conclusions. For example, Berea College and Warren Wilson College require that students do the basic jobs involved in maintaining the campuses. Students who must grow their own vegetables, clean their own toilets, and cut their own wood may well not have the time and energy to read, do laboratory experiments, and work for a community service agency. Yet the strongest evidence we have seen persistently supports the proposition that even such elemental work—especially when cooperatively organized— just might have a profound impact, at least on values, self-awareness, moral development, and other nonintellective outcomes considered important by most institutions.

We therefore urge fiscally challenged institutions to focus on what produces the kind of learning they want to foster, and to invest in the type of education that produces that learning. Taken to its logical extension, this line of thinking probably means making important shifts in emphasis for many institutions—shifts away from spending on inputs and toward reorganizing or restructuring the nature of the student experience. Institutions will also have to become more sophisticated about *assessing* the kind of learning that is taking place and about continuous modification of programs to achieve the outcomes they promise. (This has become a centerpiece of the standards now required by regional accrediting bodies, so it will essentially become mandatory.) Needless to say, each institution will find its own answer to this challenge.

New Students

"New" students—those from underserved populations, from minority groups, and from schools that have not prepared them academically or otherwise for college work—will comprise an increasing share of the undergraduate market in most parts of the country in the foreseeable future. So not only are institutions of higher education faced with redefining the undergraduate experience, they are also faced with doing so for a population with which they are largely unfamiliar.

Levine and Associates suggest that in the coming decades the more successful institutions will be those that embrace the "talent development" of these underserved and nontraditional populations (1989, pp. 171–180). We know that these students generally do not adapt well to traditionally organized learning, and that alternatives must be found. So at the very least, institutions that wish to respond to known trends in the prospective student population are well advised to explore new ways to generate powerful learning experiences—ways that need not be resource-intensive.

Resilience Depends on Quality

We believe that a high-quality education is one that produces authentic learning and growth in its students. It may or may not be an education that costs a large amount of money, but it is one that immerses the student in a rich and challenging experience. It is education that intends for certain kinds of learning to take place. And this education takes place in an institution that pays continuous attention to process and product—in other words, that follows the principles of "continuous quality improvement" (Chaffee and Sherr, 1992). This is a process that "includes only those steps that are required to produce the desired output" (p. 24). Quality is defined as doing those essential things as well as can be done, while carving away and shedding those things that are not essential.

The central idea is that outcomes—rather than inputs or processes—are the real test of quality. We think that this idea is superbly adaptable to colleges and universities facing difficult economic times. It serves to focus scarce resources on what makes for a high-quality undergraduate experience—not just on how to put more resources into undergraduate education.

Obviously, a financially richer institution has more to work with and a better chance to design and implement high-quality programs. But we saw institutions doing exciting things—producing students who were engaged in learning and who were experiencing personal and academic growth—without large endowments or state-of-the-art facilities or even large libraries. These institutions did not have much money, but they met our criteria for "resilience."

The resilient institution knows what it stands for, knows how and why it achieves its goals, focuses on doing these things particularly well, and believes in itself to the point that it can transcend immediate problems. Perhaps above all, it concentrates on adding value to the lives of the students it educates, thereby *earning the support it must have from society.*

The resilient institution does not merely manage its finances well, nor does it just create efficient operations and healthy reserves to serve it in hard times. Rather, it is committed to the valuable work of education and the betterment of young people's life chances.

Students who have had an exciting educational experience can become the most effective advocates of the institution. The students we talked with wanted to be challenged, wanted their college or university to stand out from others, wanted their undergraduate experience to feel like an integrated whole. They wanted, in short, to be different and better people as a result of their experience. Those who have had this kind of experience are enthusiastic about telling their friends, families, and communities about it. As students and alumni, they can be partners in creating and maintaining an institution's resilience—if they feel strongly about what they are getting from their experience. Resilient institutions draw out this commitment, and it is the commitment of its supporters that strengthens the institution and makes it resilient. We believe that money seeks out quality and that quality has to be developed in order to secure more money.

Both Waggaman (1991) and Keller (1983) suggest that colleges and universities are most productive when they develop clear missions and strategies. Effectiveness and quality depend more on *how and for what purposes colleges and universities spend the money they have* than on how much money they can raise.

We think that wealth can meaningfully be measured in human as well as financial terms. A healthy institution enjoys the loyalty of its alumni, the success of its graduates, the respect of its peers, the dedication and creativity of its faculty and staff, and the support of its community.

It is easier, of course, to look at fiscal health through the familiar lenses of cost accounting, management studies, and strategic planning. But previous research and what we have seen on the campuses we visited point to development of distinctive and effective educational programs as the best way to become resilient—strong enough to survive hard economic times.

In short, the higher education community might consider the alarming prospect that it is suffering from both a fiscal crisis and a crisis of commitment, human resource development, and public confidence. Massy and Wilger (1992), among others, provide a chilling summary of public opinion and professional criticism of higher education and its apparently self-absorbed sense of fiscal crisis.

It may be that "fiscal stringency" is simply the marketplace's way of telling us we aren't turning out a product that people are willing to buy at the price we want to charge. *What product are we supposed to be producing, and what is the best way to produce that product?* Are we prepared to redefine our programs in ways that will capture the imagination of faculty, students, and the public, all at the same time?

Managing and Leading a Resilient Institution

We found that leaders of the more resilient institutions were conscious of certain values and practiced certain behaviors. We do not want to imply that there is an "ideal" type of leadership that will—in itself—guarantee resilience, but we saw enough consistency to feel that we can point out these patterns. (Incidentally, "leaders" in this context refers to people who, by reason of position or sense of responsibility, step forward to help make and implement decisions.) We found these leaders among board members, alumni supporters,

faculty, students, and—of course—presidents and other administrators. In fact, leadership at the more resilient institutions seemed
more widely shared.

First, these leaders understand that "things will never be the
same again." They know it is impossible to hold on to the way the
institution was in the past. They look toward changing the status
quo and realize that in crisis there is also opportunity.

These leaders see opportunity in the real needs of real people.
This means they look outward and ask how the institution can
serve its constituents. They show an unusual skill at reading the
interests of the public and of policy makers and working with them
to create new programs and services.

But resilient institutions are also selective about what they do.
Their leaders are careful about building a particular identity, about
establishing a clear direction, and about enlightened planning to
get them to their intended objective. They delegate tasks to people
with the knowledge and skill to get the job done, and they insist on
disciplined follow-through. They appreciate the logic of simultaneous tracking—that progress may be uneven from unit to unit, but
as long as everyone is moving in the same direction, there is room
for individual creativity and initiative.

They also know how important it is to involve the entire campus community in bringing about change. This means that they
bring the most interested and most affected constituents into a
process that provides for open and balanced discussion of philosophy, values, and alternatives and is conducted candidly and honestly. The discussion is informed by good data gathered currently
and interpreted candidly. The leaders understand, however, that
strategies must be a good mix of vision and reality, allowing neither
to dominate in discussions.

Resilient institutions take a proactive stance in dealing with the
outside world. Their leaders defend and promote them and work to
overcome mindless or arbitrary constraints—especially those traditions, rules, and customs that dictate what the place and function

of the institution is "supposed to be." They understand that change requires forging a new identity and conducting continuous, energetic negotiation of that identity with state boards, legislative leaders and governors, and other important constituencies in the broader community.

Finally, leaders of resilient institutions appreciate how central a strong and successful undergraduate program is to their financial health. Whatever else they may do, they focus intently on making undergraduate education work—especially on ensuring that students feel good about its quality. Resilient institutions have an intensity about them that infuses campus life and concentrates on promoting a good experience for students. As one administrator said, "The core of the business is a really good undergraduate experience." At resilient institutions, that is what comes first; all else follows.

Faculty: The Key to the Future

Faculty (and the work they do) are the single most important resource colleges and universities have. But faculty are not always prepared or rewarded for designing and conducting effective undergraduate teaching and learning. More likely, graduate school has prepared them to do research and has generated expectations for them about how to build a successful career through research and publication. This value system has unfortunately put a diminished priority on attention to undergraduate education—and a diminished opportunity for rewards and upward mobility among faculty who invest their time and energy in it.

But resilient institutions need faculty who are committed to producing high-quality undergraduate education. Faculty with this kind of commitment—and with the teaching skills it requires—have to be prepared, selected, evaluated, rewarded, and tenured in different ways than is now standard.

We were encouraged by the degree to which this concept is broadly understood by leaders at all levels of higher education, especially organizations like the American Association for Higher Education through its Forum on Faculty Roles and Rewards. But we are also concerned about the lag in action and policy change underlying the need for new ways of structuring the faculty career.

Colleges and universities need faculty leadership, especially when they face major changes. We found that CEOs are often overextended and that the responsibilities for leadership in a resilient institution needed to be more effectively shared. (One vice president put it this way: "Everyone has to take more responsibility; it should not all be on the president's shoulders."

Faculty have the most responsibility for the long-term health of the institution. Their careers and economic security depend on it because their institutions' long-term financial health depends on its success in teaching undergraduates.

Faculty must lead responsibly if they are to lay any serious claim to a stake in their own futures and economic security. They are largely in control of the curriculum and they play a major—if not always controlling—role in hiring, promotion, tenure, and pay decisions. They have both the greatest stake in and the most direct authority over what really happens to students in the classroom.

Faculty also have to take some responsibility for the public's attitudes toward higher education. We have seen too many cases in which internal differences—typically between faculty and administration—become public disputes. Publicizing these conflicts has done considerable damage to the perception of higher education. Restoring the public's confidence will take self-control and a determination to resolve differences in forums where real solutions can be worked out.

If faculty want their institutions to be more competitive in the present and more resilient in facing future periods of fiscal stress, they have to commit to helping the institution achieve sound economic foundations. They have to concentrate—in virtually all institutions—on providing effective programs to tuition-paying (or appropriation-generating) undergraduate students. Just as partners in professional associations of lawyers or physicians must generate income for their group, so faculty must realize that money does not simply appear as a matter of right, nor does it go to those who decline to contribute to the institution's accepted mission.

We are not arguing that money should be the main determinant of all decisions about programs or people. But we do believe strongly that the more resilient institutions have achieved the internal discipline needed to generate resources and to use them in ways that advance the common good. While the market, public policy makers, and the institution's board ultimately and inevitably act to impose discipline, we would rather see faculty exercise leadership on behalf of good educational practice and on behalf of the sound fiscal condition of colleges and universities. It is certainly in their very basic interest to do so.

Conclusion

We think that institutions that focus on being distinctive, on defining and achieving a unique standard of excellence, and on helping their students learn, grow, and achieve—in other words, resilient institutions—have a better chance of attracting support and ensuring their own long-term financial health. Although the present heavy weather may be viewed as a purely fiscal crisis, we see it as a message to the academic community that its product—in its existing form—is not adding enough value to students or to society. The academic community has at least not convinced "buyers" that its product is a good value at the price being charged. If money follows value, as we think it does, then the key to resilience is to invest in providing students with the best possible educational experience.

Chapter Eleven

Unfinished Business

What are the next steps? During our study, we looked for signs that institutions were beginning to take their futures into their own hands—choosing to change on their own terms, but changing to meet higher expectations imposed by the public. Generally speaking, we found encouraging signs that they are reshaping missions, cutting or merging programs, redesigning the teaching and learning process, reallocating funds, and becoming more entrepreneurial.

Colleges and universities have enormously rich human resources and great resilience, and they still enjoy the commitment of friends within and outside of the enterprise. But they are also fragile institutions in some ways, and they are not always well equipped to respond quickly in times of crisis.

So we counsel persistence on the part of higher education's leaders, and patience on the part of our friends among the public and in business, government, and the professions. With reinforcement and support from inside and outside of the academy, colleges and universities will become more responsive to society's needs and more efficient in the use of scarce resources.

We are considerably encouraged by the wisdom, energy, and commitment of the people we interviewed and by the steps their institutions are taking as they work their way through a period of real challenge. But we come to the conclusion of this book still troubled by the challenges that remain to be met.

We believe that there is a great deal of *unfinished work* to be done on the road to change. We see five major tasks that colleges and universities need to accomplish if they are to construct a more secure and more productive future for themselves:

- Focusing identity on meeting society's needs
- Balancing decisiveness and democratic involvement
- Building support among friends of higher education
- Educating to improve students' lives
- Restoring trust by producing results

Reshaping and Focusing Identity

The role that higher education has played in society changes with almost every generation. It is now indisputably at the center of knowledge production, economic development, individual opportunity for advancement, efforts to create a just and fair society, and the preservation of important cultural traditions. More than any other institution—but increasingly in partnership with K–12 schools—higher education is the repository of society's hope for a better future, both for individuals and for the collective lives of all Americans.

Is higher education up to meeting these high expectations? Reluctantly, we found in our interviews that leaders themselves feel that they have not yet risen to the task. They are concerned that the public may be impatient with well-publicized excesses—too much arrogance from faculty who decline to teach, too much scandal from people in positions of responsibility and public trust, too much partisan ideology from purveyors of "political correctness," and too much laissez-faire attitude on campuses where students seem coddled rather than challenged.

Our interviewees also worry that the public is not convinced of higher education's good faith, because there is not enough evidence of its commitment to serving society or of caring, individual attention to undergraduate students. And they also say that the public needs more satisfying proof that its investment in higher education is being managed wisely.

In short, the time has come when others want to know what higher education is about, what its mission and sense of responsibility really are. We could clearly see a tug of war for the heart and soul of the academy going on. The disciplines and their stars tug in one direction—a direction that leads to new knowledge, economic development, and a society that is deep in self-understanding and rich in the expression of its values and culture. On the opposite end, the people—young, old, male, female, minority, majority—who put their hopes in a college education pull in the direction of something more pragmatic. Repeated surveys conducted over the last thirty years of college freshmen and their families show over and over that they want education that leads to jobs and self-improvement.

Obviously, as Martin Trow pointed out (1970, 1976), we need both the "elite" and the "popular" functions of higher education. We need higher education that broadens society's horizons and its fundamental capabilities to provide a secure and rewarding future for its people. We also need people who can serve their society well and make intelligent individual and social choices.

Individual institutions, unless they are very wealthy and secure, face the dilemma of deciding what balance they should establish between serving these competing goals. For this reason, we have argued that the system needs more differentiation among institutions. Each college or university can be stronger if it identifies its particular competence and offers that competence for a fair price.

Not to make an unfortunate analogy, but just as the automobile market is diversified, so the higher education "market" needs to diversify. At one end of a continuum, a wealthy and "elite" university may be able to concentrate on graduate education, research, and the frontiers of art, culture, and science. It may attract a worldwide clientele and a faculty with global backgrounds and interests. This sort of institution may not invest as heavily in undergraduate education, and it probably should not be expected to do so. Its value to society is based in something quite different.

However, many students and their families will value the good buy to be found at the community college, regional public college, or liberal arts college that offers undergraduates a high-quality experience to prepare them for useful and rewarding lives. These institutions should not be expected to invest as heavily in graduate education or research. Their basic mission is to shape their students' knowledge, skills, and values. As John Gardner said in *Excellence*, "There is a kind of excellence within reach of every institution" (1961, p. 85).

The unfinished work of higher education is to reshape the identity and mission of individual colleges and universities. As we have said repeatedly, no institution can afford to be imprecise about what it offers the public in return for tuition or tax money. Each should make an honest assessment of its own special competence and build its identity on what it can do well. Conversely, each institution should have the courage to focus—rather than expand—its ambitions.

Balancing Tensions in Decision Making

College and university administrators work under very intense cross-pressures and in an environment that is both erratic and unforgiving. Their financial resources are virtually always extended to the limit, so there is little room for truly discretionary spending. Change can be made at the margins, meaning that it is slow, incremental, and opportunistic—but not always strategic, purposeful, or bold. Administrators are simultaneously accountable to powerful constituencies—the legislature on one side, the tenured faculty on another, and assorted other claimants with diverse interests (such as state system offices, accrediting bodies, the federal government, students, and alumni).

Decisions are most likely to be working compromises among a

variety of interests. By chance, some decisions turn out to be better than others. But there is not always an underlying rationality (plan) to guide these decisions and evaluate them over time.

In flush times, the logic of compromise and distributive equity in the use of resources makes a certain kind of sense. Giving everyone at least a small piece of a steadily expanding fiscal pie may be good politics, but it is bad management. When hard times demand cuts and clear, forceful moves, leaders find themselves trapped in a "culture of fairness." One administrator described it this way: "Fairness is important. Little things have symbolic impact. You have to be careful about leaving the impression that one side or another is 'getting more.' [People expect] equity . . . because there is a lot of score-keeping going on."

But in a crisis someone eventually has to decide. If too deeply rooted, this pressure to distribute (or cut) resources as equally as possible weakens the authority of presidents and boards. It leads to expectations that hard decisions about what should receive more or less funding need not—or should not—be made except in the most extreme cases.

Faced with stress, colleges and universities tend to fall back on familiar and politically safe patterns of collegial decision making. Leaders who step forward to confront serious questions or explore hard alternatives—whether they are faculty leaders or presidents or deans—put themselves in a very exposed and politically dangerous position.

The danger, obviously, is that nothing will be decided, or that exquisitely "fair" decisions might fail to require enough change to make a real difference. Instead of imposing self-discipline and redirecting scarce resources toward more productive activities, an institution that does not make hard decisions may go on spending too much on the wrong things.

The effectiveness of any plan for redirection of scarce resources can and should be measured to the extent possible. Institutions that have established serious and quantifiable goals can and should ascertain how well the goals are being met in both the short term and the long term. Student retention, on-time progress toward degree completion, external fundraising, job placement of graduates, and increased diversity of faculty, staff, and student bodies are all examples of useful measures. They can be used as benchmarks for institutions to measure their progress against their own goals and against the performance of peer institutions.

The unfinished work is to balance decision-making power between the need for action and the need for consultation. Colleges and universities cannot respond effectively to serious threats if they are in a state of internal divisiveness and paralysis. They also cannot function effectively if faculty and staff (and the senates and unions that represent them) do not understand and support how the institution chooses to respond.

Boards of trustees can play a stronger role in helping presidents define the situation, calibrate decision making to the severity of the conditions, and reach closure. State coordinating or governing boards can also support change, but they must resist becoming too directive or intrusive. All stakeholders in healthy colleges and universities share the responsibility for getting these jobs done. In a healthy college or university, the stakeholders will also be able to trust each other to contribute to the overall strengthening of the institution.

Building Support Among Friends

Money is the focal point of the current period of stress, but we think it is helpful to think about this stress in broader terms than just as a shortage of money. For one thing, an obsessive concentration on money may divert attention from the more fundamental idea of "support."

Colleges and universities have enjoyed the support of a wide range of constituencies in the past. They have had extraordinary collective—if not individual—success in raising money for endowments, financial aid, buildings, and other good purposes—as well as remarkable political success in building a system that educates half of the population.

But there are signs of unease and alienation among these supporters. The declining share of state budgets being allocated to higher education is an alarming indicator of a fundamental shift in attitudes. Whatever the causes and effects of vacillating public support, it is clear to us—as it was to virtually everyone we interviewed—that colleges and universities are thoroughly dependent on the goodwill of the public and of their elected representatives in state and federal government. Quick fixes of the public relations sort do not appear to have much impact: our media-saturated society seems numb to game playing and shallow stunts. But we believe that society's long-term support will be drawn to colleges and universities (as well as to other institutions) that meet real needs, provide quality service, add value, and are candid and honest in talking about what they can and cannot do.

We think that higher education needs to connect more effectively and directly with its many publics. In other words, a college or university should give the public a clear statement about its mission and programs and should not be afraid to ask its constituents how well it is performing in return.

We have found that efforts to see one's own institution as others see it can have an important impact. Taking accrediting reports seriously, using consulting firms to take an objective look at both substance and image, and reaching out for feedback from core supporters all help build a sense of where an institution stands, how it looks, and whether people consider it an effective and efficient institution that is worth supporting. Image is surely not everything, but knowing what others think—and accepting information that disconfirms the status quo—is an important step toward change.

Colleges and universities have sometimes taken a perverse pride in their traditional position outside of society's main avenues of politics and commerce. They claim this "outsideness" as their natural position and as important to their function as societal critic. Indeed, we think that academic freedom requires a certain measure of distance from commerce, politics, and popular passions. But there is a critical point beyond which no amount of public relations can salvage an institution that has become too self-absorbed, unrealistic, arrogant, or uncaring. Colleges and universities can serve while criticizing, but service is of paramount value.

The unfinished work is to broaden and deepen support for higher education. Colleges and universities need all the friends they can get. The best way to get friends and keep them is by working hard to provide quality and value. This means reaching out to clients, identifying real needs, and providing real added value to people who place their trust in the institution. It also means getting others' views on what kind of job higher education is doing. Those views—discomforting as they may be—must come from the outside and must be taken seriously.

Educate to Improve Students' Lives

What do parents and students get when they invest $20,000 or $50,000 or $100,000 in a college education? What do voters get when they decide to back bonds for a new community college campus? What do taxpayers get when their money goes into research time for faculty? How do they know they got what they paid for? And is the result worth the price? How many colleges and universities try to answer these questions? How many provide any kind of public assessment of their own performance?

If this gauntlet of questions seems unreasonable, the reader might then ask what should be expected when investing that amount of money in a house or a mutual fund or a work of art. One would want to know a great deal about the value of the purchase, as well as about the honesty of the seller in representing the condition of the property.

Colleges and universities provide information about themselves to prospective students, and in some cases even spend a good deal of money recruiting them. But students generally enter college without much information about what they are expected to learn, how they are expected to learn it, what assessments will be conducted, and how they can get help if and when they need it. Nor, diploma and handshake aside, will they typically get much information about what they have really achieved at the end of the experience.

As tuitions rise, though, and as financial aid becomes harder to get (we assume), the consumer will feel entitled to ask some very hard questions. We found that the consumer is already beginning to drive a hard bargain, learning how to get tuition discounts and searching for "extras." With technology providing alternatives and with students demanding options and choices, colleges and universities may find themselves having a harder time marketing their offerings against increasingly tough competition. Or they may have a harder time holding down price if they cannot position themselves effectively against their competitors.

In the consumer's mind, "added value" means that the transaction is considered a favorable one. Higher and higher prices make it increasingly difficult to convince the customer that the transaction was a good deal, unless the value added is very clear, real, tangible, and—above all—durable. At the prices now being charged, most students and their families will not invest willingly if they feel that the return is too speculative.

What can be done to convince students and their families that their investment in college will bring a good return, a lifetime return? More to the point, what can an institution do to offer good value to students? We think that colleges and universities who do add value and show students the evidence will be in a very advantageous position in an increasingly competitive market.

The unfinished work is to add value and measure outcomes. Really educating undergraduate students in a coherent, purposeful, authentic, and durable way is the heart of the higher education business. The public will pay a fair price for—and demand in return—education that improves students' lives in measurable ways. The public will increasingly want assurance that students are getting good value for their money, and higher education will have to convince the public that they are getting that good value.

Doing the Right Things

As we concluded this project, we came to the realization that fiscal health is merely one indicator of the general vitality of the higher education enterprise. It is an important indicator, but it is not an end in itself. The more fundamental goal is to get our values clarified and our product (and its price) right, and to be sure the public understands and supports our work.

Higher education may have become a bit too self-centered and self-congratulatory through its long period of expansion and emergence as a major institution in social and economic advancement. These attitudes are probably not very appropriate as society begins to look to institutions of higher education for different things. Those of us who operate these institutions have tended to emphasize how rich and elite we are (we may say "excellent," but the public reads it as "rich and elite"), how much we pay our faculty and presidents, and how many books and articles we produce.

We have not been telling the public very effectively about how we make a difference to the young black man who is a gifted mathematician, or to the returning Hispanic woman who has two kids and an ambition to run her own business, or to the white middle-class kid who has a new car and a trust fund but has never held a job, or to the employer who is looking for people ready to go to work without a great deal of additional training. What do these people want and need from us? Who should pay and what kind of attention should we give them? How can we help? What do we have to give back? And how much is it worth to them? How much is it worth to the people of the state? To its businesses?

These kinds of questions have to be answered clearly, honestly, and concretely. As money for higher education has become harder to find, the marketplace has become less and less responsive to abstract pleas for "continued" funding—which is too easily interpreted as a claim to entitlement. The marketplace increasingly demands performance, quality, and competitiveness.

The unfinished work is for educators to make an ethical and moral commitment to care and to teach. It is the professional duty of faculty and the administrators who serve the public to show that they care, that they teach, and that the students who trust them grow, learn, and develop.

If this trust is fulfilled, if students really learn, and if what they learn is valued by others, then higher education will have earned the support it needs. But colleges and universities must earn that support by performing a real service—and the better they serve, the more readily they will be supported. That is the key to fiscal health. There is no magic formula, no clever management technique, and no fundraising ritual that works better. Add value, tell the public what kind of value it can expect, and they will come.

Conclusion

The problems and challenges that higher education faces are serious, and they will take a long time to solve. But they are really the individual problems of each institution—now well over three thousand of them. In the United States, there is no one grand design we can offer, but if our study accomplishes nothing else, we hope that it convinces public officials, trustees, administrators, faculty, and friends of higher education of two things. First, higher education is not especially well adapted to dealing with the dislocation it is now experiencing. We hope that by describing some of the problems in intimate detail we will have promoted a wider understanding among stakeholders of the present crisis and the ways in which institutions are responding. We hope that this will lead to patience and understanding, as well as to badly needed commitment and support, as colleges and universities become increasingly effective at redefining their purposes, reshaping their programs, and strengthening their commitments to serving society well.

Second, higher education needs all the friends it can get. It needs to work through its current period of stress with as many partners in the process of change as will volunteer to help. Faculty in particular are among the prime beneficiaries of fiscally healthy colleges and universities. Historically, faculty and professional and support staff have borne the brunt of fiscal problems—largely through economic deprivation—during earlier periods of stress and dislocation. But the present crisis comes after a long period of comparative prosperity and economic well-being for faculty. It is certainly painful for them to find their independence and economic power threatened.

Our final watchwords are *purposeful change*. All of the institutions we visited either had made or were facing major changes in their missions and identities, their ways of educating, and their decision-making cultures. Those institutions that find the courage to work together and make tough, intelligent decisions will be prepared for what can only be more challenges in the future. Colleges and universities emerging from the present hard times will not be the same again. But they will be more resilient in the face of the challenges to come. Those challenges will always be painful in the short run, but resilient institutions will seize them as opportunities to become better and more responsive institutions in the long run.

References

Anderson, R. E. *Strategic Policy Changes at Private Colleges: Educational and Fiscal Implications*. New York: Teachers College Press, 1977.

Anderson, R. E. "A Financial and Environmental Analysis of Strategic Policy Changes at Small Private Colleges." *Journal of Higher Education*, 1978, *49*(1), 30–46.

Anderson, R. E., and Meyerson, J. W. (eds.). *Productivity and Higher Education: Improving the Effectiveness of Faculty, Facilities, and Financial Resources*. Princeton, N.J.: Peterson's Guides, 1992.

Ashar, H., and Shapiro, J. Z. "Are Retrenchment Decisions Rational? The Role of Information in Times of Budgetary Stress." *Journal of Higher Education*, 1990, *61*(2), 121–141.

Astin, A. W. *The American Freshman: National Norms for Fall 1989*. Los Angeles: Higher Education Research Institute, University of California, 1989.

Astin, A. W. *The American Freshman: National Norms for Fall 1990*. Los Angeles: Higher Education Research Institute, University of California, 1990.

Astin, A. W. *The American Freshman: National Norms for Fall 1991*. Los Angeles: Higher Education Research Institute, University of California, 1991.

Astin, A. W. *The American Freshman: National Norms for Fall 1992*. Los Angeles: Higher Education Research Institute, University of California, 1992.

Astin, A. W. *The American Freshman: National Norms for Fall 1993*. Los Angeles: Higher Education Research Institute, University of California, 1993a.

Astin, A. W. *What Matters in College: Four Critical Years Revisited*. San Francisco: Jossey-Bass, 1993b.

Birnbaum, R. *How Colleges Work: The Cybernetics of Academic Organization and Leadership*. San Francisco: Jossey-Bass, 1988.

Bok, D. "Reclaiming the Public Trust." *Change*, 1992, *24*(4), 12–19.

Bowen, H. R., and Douglass, G. K. *Efficiency in Liberal Education*. New York: McGraw-Hill, 1971.

Bowen, H. R. *The Costs of Higher Education*. San Francisco: Jossey-Bass, 1980.

Bowen, W., and Sosa, J. *Prospects for Faculty in the Arts and Sciences*. Princeton, N.J.: Princeton University Press, 1989.

Boyer, E. L. *Scholarship Reconsidered: Priorities of the Professoriate*. Princeton, N.J.: The Carnegie Foundation for the Advancement of Teaching, 1989.

Bradburd, R. M., and Mann, D. P. "Wealth in Higher Education Institutions." *Journal of Higher Education*, 1993, 64(4), 472–493.

Breneman, D. W. *Liberal Arts Colleges: Thriving, Surviving, or Endangered?* Washington, D.C.: The Brookings Institution, 1994.

Breneman, D. W. *A State of Emergency? Higher Education in California.* San Jose: The California Higher Education Policy Center, 1995.

Breu, T. M., and Raab, R. L. "Efficiency and Perceived Quality of the Nation's 'Top 25' National Universities and National Liberal Arts Colleges: An Application of Data Envelopment Analysis to Higher Education." *Socio-Economic Planning Sciences*, 1994, 28(1), 33–45.

Brinkman, P. T. "Factors That Influence Costs in Higher Education." In C. S. Hollins (ed.), *Containing Costs and Improving Productivity in Higher Education.* New Directions for Institutional Research, no. 75. San Francisco: Jossey-Bass, 1992.

Cameron, K. S. "Organizational Adaptation and Higher Education." *Journal of Higher Education*, 1984, 55(2), 122–144.

Carnegie Council on Policy Studies in Higher Education. *Three Thousand Futures: The Next Twenty Years for Higher Education.* San Francisco: Jossey-Bass, 1980.

Carnegie Foundation for the Advancement of Teaching. *1989 National Survey of Faculty: Technical Report and Detailed Tabulations.* Princeton, N.J.: Carnegie Foundation for the Advancement of Teaching, 1989.

Chaffee, E. E. "Successful Strategic Management in Small Private Colleges." *Journal of Higher Education*, 1984, 55(2), 212–241.

Chaffee, E. E., and Sherr, L. A. *Quality: Transforming Postsecondary Education.* ASHE-ERIC Higher Education Report, no. 3. Washington, D.C.: George Washington University, School of Education and Human Development, 1992 (ED 350 972).

Cheit, E. F. *The New Depression in Higher Education: A Study of Financial Conditions at 41 Colleges and Universities.* New York: McGraw-Hill, 1971.

Chickering, A. W., and Gamson, Z. F. *Applying the Seven Principles for Good Practice in Undergraduate Education.* New Directions for Teaching and Learning, no. 47. San Francisco: Jossey-Bass, 1991.

Clark, B. R. *The Distinctive College: Reed, Antioch, and Swarthmore.* Chicago: Aldine, 1970.

Clark, B. R. (ed.). *The Academic Profession: National, Disciplinary, and Institutional Settings.* Berkeley: University of California Press, 1987.

Clotfelter, C. T., Ehrenberg, R. G., Getz, M., and Siegfried, J. J. *Economic Challenges in Higher Education.* Chicago: The University of Chicago Press, 1991.

Cohen, M. D., and March, J. G. *Leadership and Ambiguity: The American College President.* New York: McGraw-Hill, 1974.

Colgan, C. S., and Slavet, J. S. (eds.). *The Fiscal Crisis in the States: Lessons from the Northeast.* Portland: Edmund S. Muskie Institute of Public Affairs, University of Southern Maine, 1993.

Committee for Economic Development. *The Management and Financing of Colleges.* New York: Committee for Economic Development, 1973.

Doherty, P. C. *Development and Impact of Legislative Involvement on Selected Aspects of State University System Operations, 1954–1990.* Ph.D. dissertation, Florida State University, 1991.

Dunn, J. A., Jr. "Retrench or Else: Public and Private Institutional Responses." In Carol S. Hollins (ed.), *Containing Costs and Improving Productivity in Higher Education.* New Directions for Institutional Research, no. 75. San Francisco: Jossey-Bass, 1992.

Eckl, C. L., Hutchinson, A. M., and Snell, R. K. *State Budget and Tax Actions 1992: A Preliminary Report.* Denver: National Conference of State Legislatures, 1992.

El-Khawas, E. "Restructuring Initiatives in Public Higher Education: Institutional Response to Financial Constraints." *Research Briefs,* 1994, 5(8), 2–3 (ED 377 753).

Evangelauf, J. "Enrollment Projections Revised Upward in New Government Analysis." *Chronicle of Higher Education,* 1992, 38(20), A1, A36.

"Fact File: Projections of College Enrollment, Degrees, and High School Graduates, 1993 to 2004." *Chronicle of Higher Education,* 1994, 40(20), A34.

Fairweather, J. "Faculty Reward Structures: Toward Institutional and Professional Homogenization." *Research in Higher Education,* 1993, 34(5), 603–623.

Finkelstein, M. J., Farrar, D., and Pfnister, A. O. "The Adaptation of Liberal Arts Colleges to the 1970s: An Analysis of Critical Events." *Journal of Higher Education,* 1984, 55(2), 242–268.

Finkelstein, M. J., and Pfnister, A. O. "From the Firing Line: Adaptation from the Administrator's Perspective." *Journal of Higher Education,* 1984, 55(2), 297–312.

Fox, M. F. "Research, Teaching, and Publication Productivity: Mutuality Versus Competition in Academia." *Sociology of Education,* 1992, 65(4), 293–305.

Frances, C. (ed.). *Successful Responses to Financial Difficulty.* New Directions for Higher Education, no. 38. San Francisco: Jossey-Bass, 1982.

Gardner, J. W. *Excellence: Can We Be Equal and Excellent, Too?* New York: HarperCollins, 1961.

Geiger, R. L. "The College Curriculum and the Marketplace." *Change,* 1980, 12(8), 16–23, 53–54.

Gilmore, J. L., and To, D. "Evaluating Academic Productivity and Quality." In C. S. Hollins (ed.), *Containing Costs and Improving Productivity in Higher Education.* New Directions for Institutional Research, no. 75. San Francisco: Jossey-Bass, 1992.

Gold, S. D., and Ritchie, S. "Fiscal Crisis in New England: How the States Responded, 1989 to 1992." In C. S. Colgan and J. S. Slavet (eds.), *The Fiscal Crisis in the States: Lessons from the Northeast*. Portland: Edmund S. Muskie Institute of Public Affairs, University of Southern Maine, 1993.

Green, J. S., Levine, A., and Associates. *Opportunity in Adversity: How Colleges Can Succeed in Hard Times*. San Francisco: Jossey-Bass, 1985.

Grubb, W. N. "Correcting Conventional Wisdom: Community College Impact on Students' Jobs and Salaries." *Community, Junior, and Technical College Journal*, 1992, 62(6), 10–14.

Hearn, J. C., Clugston, R. M., and Heydinger, R. B. "Five Years of Strategic Environmental Assessment Efforts at a Research University: A Case Study of an Organizational Innovation." *Innovative Higher Education*, 1993, 18(1), 7–36.

Hearn, J. C., and Heydinger, R. B. "Scanning the University's External Environment: Objectives, Constraints, and Possibilities." *Journal of Higher Education*, 1985, 56(4), 419–445.

Higher Education Directory 1995. Falls Church, Va.: Higher Education Publications, 1995.

Hodgkinson, H. L. *Institutions in Transition: A Profile of Change in Higher Education*. New York: McGraw-Hill, 1971.

Jaschik, S. "One Percent Decline in State Support for Colleges Thought to Be First Ever." *Chronicle of Higher Education*. 1992, 39(9), A21, 26–28.

Jellema, W. W. *From Red to Black: The Financial Status of Private Colleges and Universities*. San Francisco: Jossey-Bass, 1973.

Jencks, C., and Riesman, D. *The Academic Revolution*. Garden City, N.Y.: Doubleday, 1968.

Johnson, D. W., and Johnson, R. T. "Creative and Critical Thinking Through Academic Controversy." *American Behavioral Scientist*, 1993, 37(1), 40–53.

Johnstone, D. B. *Learning Productivity: A New Imperative for American Higher Education*. Studies in Public Higher Education, no. 3. Albany: State University of New York, 1993.

Jonsen, R. W. "Small Colleges Cope with the Eighties: Sharp Eye on the Horizon, Strong Hand on the Tiller." *Journal of Higher Education*, 1984, 55(2), 171–183.

Keller, G. *Academic Strategy*. Baltimore: Johns Hopkins University Press, 1983.

Kerr, C. *The Uses of the University*. New York: HarperCollins, 1966.

Kerr, C. "What We Might Learn from the Climacteric." *Daedalus*, 1975, 104(1), 1–7.

Lattuca, L. R., and Stark, J. S. "Will Disciplinary Perspectives Impede Curricular Reform?" *Journal of Higher Education*, 1994, 65(4), 401–426.

Layzell, D. T., Lovell, C. D., and Gill, J. I. "Developing Faculty as Assets for States and Institutions." Presented at the Annual Meeting of the Association for the Study of Higher Education, Tucson, Ariz., November 12, 1994.

Lenth, C. "The Context and Policy Requisites of National Postsecondary Assessment." *Journal of General Education*, 1993, *42*(1), 9–32.

Levin, H. M. "Raising Productivity in Higher Education." *Journal of Higher Education*, 1991, *62*(3) 241–262.

Levine, A. L., and Associates. *Shaping Higher Education's Future: Demographic Realities and Opportunities, 1990–2000*. San Francisco: Jossey-Bass, 1989.

Lozier, G. G., and Dooris, M. J. *Faculty Retirement Projections Beyond 1994: Effects of Policy on Individual Choice*. Boulder, Colo.: Western Interstate Commissions on Higher Education, 1991 (ED 370 495).

McKeown, M. P., and Layzell, D. T. "State Funding Formulas for Higher Education: Trends and Issues." *Journal of Education Finance*, 1994, *19*(3), 319–346.

Massy, W. F., and Wilger, A. K. "Productivity in Postsecondary Education: A New Approach." *Educational Evaluation and Policy Analysis*, 1992, *14*(4), 361–376.

Massy, W. F., Wilger, A. K., and Colbeck, C. "Overcoming 'Hollowed' Collegiality." *Change*, 1994, *26*(4), 10–20.

Meeth, L. R. *Quality Education for Less Money*. San Francisco: Jossey-Bass, 1974.

Mercer, J. "States Turn to Community Colleges as Route to Bachelor's Degree as Four-Year Campuses Face Tight Budgets and Overcrowding." *Chronicle of Higher Education*, 1992, *38*(35), A1, A28.

Mingle, J. R. "Faculty Work and the Costs/Quality/Access Collision." *AAHE Bulletin*, 1993, *45*(7), 3–6, 13.

Mintzberg, H. "The Strategy Concept II: Another Look at Why Organizations Need Strategies." *California Management Review*, 1987, *30*(1), 25–33.

Mintzberg, H. "The Pitfalls of Strategic Planning." *California Management Review*, 1993, *36*(1), 32–48.

Mintzberg, H. "The Fall and Rise of Strategic Planning." *Harvard Business Review*, 1994, (1), 107–114.

Mintzberg, H. *The Rise and Fall of Strategic Planning*. New York: Free Press, 1994.

Mooney, C. J. "Critics Within and Without Academe Assail Professors at Research Universities." *Chronicle of Higher Education*, 1992, *39*(10), A17–A19.

Mortimer, K. P., and Tierney, M. L. *The Three "R's" of the Eighties: Reduction, Reallocation, and Retrenchment*. AAHE-ERIC Higher Education Research Report, no. 4. Washington, D.C.: American Association for Higher Education, 1979 (ED 172 642).

Pace, C. R. "Achievement and the Quality of Student Effort." Presented at a meeting of the National Commission on Excellence in Education, Washington, D.C., May 25, 1982.

Pascarella, E. T., and Terenzini, P. T. *How College Affects Students*. San Francisco: Jossey-Bass, 1991.

Penney, S. H., and MacCormack, J. F. "Managing on the Edge: Massachusetts After the Miracle." *Journal of Higher Education Management*, 1992, 7(2), 23–52.

Quinn, J. B. "Strategic Change: 'Logical Incrementalism.'" *Sloan Management Review*, 1989, 30(4), 45–60.

Riesman, D., and Stadtman, V. A. (eds.). *Academic Transformation: Seventeen Institutions Under Pressure*. New York: McGraw-Hill, 1973.

Rudolph, F. *The American College and University*. New York: Knopf, 1962.

Rudolph, F. *Curriculum: A History of the American Undergraduate Course of Study Since 1636*. San Francisco: Jossey-Bass, 1977.

St. John, E. P. "A Framework for Reexamining State Resource-Management Strategies in Higher Education." *Journal of Higher Education*, 1991, 62(3), 263–287.

Schmidtlein, F. A. "Planning for Quality: Perils and Possibilities." Presented at the Annual Forum of the European Association for Institutional Research, Lyon, France, September 9–12, 1990.

Schroeder, C. C. "New Students—New Learning Styles." *Change*, 1993, 25(4), 21–26.

Schuster, J. H., Smith, D. G., Corak, K. A., and Yamada, M. M. *Strategic Governance: How to Make Big Decisions Better*. Phoenix, Ariz.: The American Council on Education/Oryx Press, 1994.

Society of Critical Care Medicine Ethics Committee. "Consensus Statement on the Triage of Critically Ill Patients." *Journal of the American Medical Association*, 1994, 271(15), 1200–1204.

Stadtman, V. A. *Academic Adaptations: Higher Education Prepares for the 1980s and 1990s*. San Francisco: Jossey-Bass, 1980.

Stark, J. S., and Lowther, M. A. "Exploring Common Ground in Liberal and Professional Education." In *Integrating Liberal Learning and Professional Education*. New Directions for Teaching and Learning, no. 40. San Francisco: Jossey-Bass, 1989.

Stopford, J. M., and Baden-Fuller, C.W.F. "Creating Corporate Entrepreneurship." *Strategic Management Journal*, 1994, 15(7), 521–536.

Sykes, C. J. *Profscam: Professors and the Demise of Higher Education*. Washington, D.C.: Regnery Gateway, 1988.

Tinto, V. "Learning Communities: Building Supportive Learning Environments in Urban Settings." Presented at the annual meeting of the Association for the Study of Higher Education, Tucson, Ariz., November 12, 1994.

Townsend, B. K., Newell, L. J., and Wiese, M. D. *Creating Distinctiveness: Lessons from Uncommon Colleges and Universities*. ASHE-ERIC Higher Education Report, no. 6. Washington, D.C.: George Washington University, School of Education and Human Development, 1992 (ED 356 702).

Trow, M. "Reflections on the Transition from Mass to Universal Higher Education." *Daedalus*, 1970, 99(1), 1–42.

Trow, M. "'Elite Higher Education': An Endangered Species?" *Minerva*, 1976, 14(3), 355–376.

Trow, M. "Class, Race, and Higher Education in America." *American Behavioral Scientist*, 1992, 35(4–5), 585–605.

Volkwein, J. F., and Carbone, D. A. "The Impact of Departmental Research and Teaching Climates on Undergraduate Growth and Satisfaction." *Journal of Higher Education*, 1994, 65(2), 147–167.

Waggaman, J. S. *Strategies and Consequences: Managing the Costs in Higher Education*. ASHE-ERIC Higher Education Report, no. 8. Washington, D.C.: George Washington University, School of Education and Human Development, 1991 (ED 347 921).

Weick, K. "Educational Organizations as Loosely Coupled Systems." *Administrative Science Quarterly*, 1976, 21(1), 1–19.

Wilson, R. A. (ed.). *Responses to Fiscal Stress in Higher Education*. Tucson: Center for the Study of Higher Education, University of Arizona, 1982.

Winston, G. C. "The Necessary Revolution in Financial Accounting." *Planning for Higher Education*, 1992, 20(4), 1–16.

Winston, G. C. "New Dangers in Old Traditions: The Reporting of Economic Performance in Colleges and Universities." *Change*, 1993, 25(1), 18–23.

Winston, G. C. "The Decline in Undergraduate Teaching: Moral Failure or Market Pressure?" *Change*, 1994, 26(5), 8–15.

Woolf, A. G. "The Economics, and Economic Analysis, of Boom and Bust." In C. S. Colgan and J. S. Slavet (eds.), *The Fiscal Crisis in the States: Lessons from the Northeast*. Portland: Edmund S. Muskie Institute of Public Affairs, University of Southern Maine, 1993.

Zimbler, L. J. *Faculty Instructional Staff: Who Are They and What Do They Do?* Washington, D.C.: National Center for Education Statistics, 1994.

Index